Texas Instruments

Real-World Math with the CBL 2™ and LabPro

Activities for TI-83 Plus, TI-83, and TI-73

Chris Brueningsen
Bill Bower
Linda Antinone
Elisa Kerner

Revised by
John Gastineau
Will Cortez

Important notice regarding book materials

Texas Instruments Incorporated
7800 Banner Drive, M/S 3918
Dallas, TX 75251

Attention: Manager, Business Services

IMPORTANT

We invite your comments and suggestions about this book. Call us at **1-800-TI-CARES** or send e-mail to **ti-cares@ti.com**. You can also call or send e-mail to request information about other current and future publications from Texas Instruments.

Visit the TI World Wide Web home page. The web address is: **education.ti.com**

Contents

Preface vi

About the Authors vii

Calculators Used with Real-World Math viii

Data Collection Devices Used with Real-World Math viii

Getting Started with Real-World Math viii

Files on the CD ix

Function Types Studied in the Activities x

Sensors Used in the Activities xi

Activity 1: **Walk the Line: Straight Line Distance Graphs** 1
Topic: Linear function

Activity 2: **Making Cents of Math: Linear Relationship Between Weight and Quantity** 9
Topics: Linear function, slope, independent/dependent variables

Activity 3: **Pool Plunge: Linear Relationship Between Water Depth and Pressure** 19
Topics: Linear function, slope, independent/dependent variables

Activity 4: **Funnel Volumes: Volume and Weight** 29
Topic: Linear function

Activity 5: **Keep It Bottled Up: Linear Rates of Pressure Increase** 39
Topic: Linear function

Activity 6: **Graph It in Pieces: Piecewise-defined Functions** 49
Topics: Piecewise functions, linear functions, point-slope form of line

Activity 7: **Mix It Up: Mixing Liquids of Different Temperatures** 61
Topics: Proportional reasoning

Activity 8: **Spring Thing: Newton's Second Law** 69
Topic: Proportional relationship

Activity 9: **Stretch It to the Limit: The Linear Force Relation for a Rubber Band** 81
Topic: Proportionality

Activity 10: **What Goes Up: Position and Time for a Cart on a Ramp**..91
Topic: Quadratic function, intercept form

Activity 11: **That's the Way the Ball Bounces: Height and Time for a Bouncing Ball**..........................103
Topic: Quadratic function, vertex form

Activity 12: **Walk This Way: Definition of Rate**...........................115
Topic: Area under a curve

Activity 13: **Velocity Test: Interpreting Velocity Graphs**............123
Topic: Rates and graphical interpretation

Activity 14: **From Here to There: Applications of the Distance Formula**......................................133
Topic: Distance formula and Pythagorean Theorem

Activity 15: **Under Pressure: The Inverse Relationship between Pressure and Volume**.................................145
Topic: Inverse function

Activity 16: **Light at a Distance: Distance and Light Intensity**...157
Topic: Inverse square model

Activity 17: **Chill Out: How Hot Objects Cool**............................165
Topics: Exponential function

Activity 18: **Charging Up, Charging Down: Exponential Models**...175
Topics: Exponential function

Activity 19: **Bounce Back: The Exponential Pattern of Rebound Heights**..185
Topics: Exponential function

Activity 20: **Sour Chemistry: The Exponential pH Change**.........199
Topics: Exponential function, reverse form

Activity 21: **Stepping to the Greatest Integer: The Greatest Integer Function**..........................209
Topics: int(x) function

Activity 22: **Swinging Ellipses: Plotting an Ellipse**.....................219
Topics: Ellipse equation, phase plots

Activity 23: **Crawling Around: Parametric Plots**.........................227
Topics: Parametric plots, sine function

Activity 24: **Lights Out: Periodic Phenomena**............................237
Topics: Period, frequency

Activity 25: **Tic, Toc: Pendulum Motion**......................................247
Topics: Sine and cosine functions

Activity 26: **Stay Tuned: Sound Waveform Models**.....................255
Topics: Sine and cosine functions

Activity 27: **Up and Down: Damped Harmonic Motion**..............265
Topics: Sine and cosine functions, exponential functions

Activity 28: How Tall? Describing Data with Statistical Plots.... 279
       Topic: Statistical box plots

**Activity 29: And Now, the Weather: Describing Data
with Statistics.. 289**
       Topics: Statistical concepts: Minimum, maximum, mean

**Activity 30: Meet You at the Intersection: Solving
a System of Linear Equations 301**
       Topic: Systems of linear equations

**Activity 31: Titration Curves: An Application
of the Logistic Function... 313**
       Topic: Logistic functions

Appendix A: Sensors for Real-World Math................................... 323

Appendix B: Equipment and Supplies 327

Appendix C: DATAMATE Reference.. 329

Appendix D: Firmware Updates for CBL 2 and LabPro 339

Preface

This workbook provides students with an interesting way to explore math and science concepts. It is a revision of the earlier Texas Instruments publication *Real-World Math with the CBL™ System: Activities for the TI-83 and TI-83 Plus*. The activities are written to use Texas Instruments graphing calculators in conjunction with the Texas Instruments CBL 2™ and the Vernier LabPro® data collection devices. The device is used to collect data from a variety of sensors, such as motion, force, sound, light, and temperature. The data collection software called DATAMATE is run on the calculator. This versatile, easy-to-use program sets up the data collection and then retrieves the data from the data collection device. Powerful analysis features built into the graphing calculator help students build mathematical models.

You will find a wide range of activities in this book. Whether you teach introductory or advanced mathematics, you should find a large number of activities that match the objectives of your course. Background information, set-up diagrams, and general instructions with clear calculator keystrokes are given for each activity. Space is provided for students to record data and complete easy-to-follow exercises. Extensions and further applications are included in most activities to allow for advanced, independent investigations. Following each student activity, there is an extensive Teacher Information section with sample results, answers to questions, directions for preparing equipment, and other helpful hints regarding the planning and implementation of a particular activity.

Activities in this book can be used unchanged or they can be modified using the Microsoft® Word files provided on the CD. Students will respond differently to the design of the activities, depending on teaching styles of their teachers, math background, previous experience using calculators, and the scope and level of the mathematics course.

It is important for you to read the front matter and appendices. They include valuable information that can help make you more comfortable with your initial use of this equipment.

Many people helped create the third edition of this book. Thanks to the staff at Texas Instruments who supervised the production of the book. Thanks to Rick Sorensen of Vernier Software & Technology who helped revise and edit the activities. Special thanks go to Will Cortez for his valuable contributions, extensive editing, and testing.

— *John Gastineau*

About the Authors

CHRIS BRUENINGSEN is Director of Studies and Mathematics Chairman at Brunswick School in Greenwich, Connecticut. In 1996, he received the Presidential Award for Excellence in Mathematics Teaching and was a Member of the NCTM Task Force on Integrated Mathematics. He teaches math and science to middle and high school students and has co-authored several Texas Instruments technology workbooks. He has also written a number of articles for math and science journals and speaks frequently at educational conferences.

BILL BOWER is a teacher and Chairman of the Mathematics Department at The Kiski School in Saltsburg, Pennsylvania. Throughout his 18-year career he has taught all levels of high-school math. In recent years, graphing calculator technology has become an integral part of his teaching. He is a co-author of *Math and Science in Motion: Activities for Middle School.*

LINDA ANTINONE is the Secondary Mathematics Coordinator for the Fort Worth Independent School District in Fort Worth, Texas. She received Ohio's Presidential Award for Excellence in Mathematics Teaching in 1993 and was named Fort Worth's Secondary Teacher of the Year in 1995. She has taught both mathematics and science to students in grades 7 – 12 and has served as a T^3 (Teachers Teaching with Technology) instructor since 1993. Linda co-authored *Modeling Motion: High School Math Activities with the CBR,* and two publications for the American Association of Physics Teachers on the use of graphing calculators and CBL.

ELISA KERNER teaches math and is Head of the Mathematics Department at Convent of the Sacred Heart school in Greenwich, Connecticut. She has taught at all levels from 6th grade math through Calculus, including Physical Science. Elisa has been a T^3 instructor since 1995 and is a co-author of *Math and Science in Motion* and *Discovering Math on the TI-92.*

JOHN GASTINEAU earned a Ph.D. in Physics in 1986 from the University of Wisconsin, Madison, doing experimental work in atomic collisions. As a university-level physics instructor for ten years, his primary teaching interest has been the introductory physics course. He uses microcomputer-based lab tools and simulations extensively in his lecture-lean teaching, and has given invited talks on their use at both national and international physics and science education meetings.

John is the Staff Scientist for Vernier Software & Technology. He is an author of *Physics with Calculators, Physics with Computers,* and *Nuclear Radiation for Computers and Calculators,* published by Vernier Software & Technology, as well as *College Physics for the CBL and TI-86,* published by Texas Instruments. An avid whitewater kayaker and mountain biker, he is also a member of the National Ski Patrol (but is only seen on a snowboard these days).

WILLIAM CORTEZ majored in mathematics at Portland State University in Portland, Oregon. In 2001 he received his Bachelor of Science Degree in Mathematics. While attending college, he was a teacher assistant for a calculus class and a private tutor. He was also employed part time at Vernier Software & Technology. In 2002 he completed Portland State University's Graduate Teacher Education Program. He is currently teaching mathematics at Sunset High School in Beaverton, Oregon. His favorite past time is soccer, which he plays and coaches.

Calculators Used with Real-World Math

The thirty-one activities in this book are available in versions for these calculators:

♦ TI-73

♦ TI-83

♦ TI-83 Plus

♦ TI-83 Plus Silver Edition

♦ TI-86

♦ TI-89

♦ TI-92

♦ TI-92 Plus

The TI-81, TI-82 and TI-85 calculators **cannot** be used with this book.

Data Collection Devices Used with Real-World Math

These activities are designed for the DATAMATE software, which is written for the Texas Instruments CBL 2™ and Vernier LabPro® data collection devices. This software runs on the TI-73, TI-83, TI-83 Plus, TI-83 Plus Silver Edition, TI-86, TI-89, TI-92, and TI-92 Plus. The procedure for starting the software is slightly different for each calculator. For instructions, see Appendix C.

The original TI CBL™ System cannot be used with DATAMATE, and so cannot be used with this book. Users of the original CBL System should obtain a copy of the earlier edition of this book, *Real-World Math with the CBL System*.

Getting Started with Real-World Math

To perform the activities in this book, you need a TI Graphing Calculator, a data collection device (either a TI CBL 2™ or a Vernier LabPro®), and some sensors.

The sensors needed for these activities include the Motion Detector, Force Sensor, Gas Pressure Sensor, Temperature Probe, Light Sensor, Voltage Probe, pH sensor, and Microphone. All of these are available from Vernier Software & Technology, http://www.vernier.com. You can find more information on these sensors in Appendix A of this book. For specific sensors used for each activity, see page xii.

Additional equipment, such as balls or springs, is required for some activities. You can find detailed information on the necessary equipment on the materials list for each lab, and in the teacher information for many labs.

Files on the CD

The CD inside the back cover of this book contains Microsoft® Word files and sample data for the TI-73, TI-83, TI-83 Plus, TI-83 Plus Silver Edition, TI-86, TI-89, TI-92, and TI-92 Plus. Word Files for the TI-73, TI-83, TI-83 Plus, and TI-83 Plus Silver Edition are identical to the printed version of this book. Word files for the TI-86, TI-89, TI-92, and TI-92 Plus include instructions specifically for those calculators. Users of these calculators can print these versions for classroom use.

The Word files provide a way for you to edit the activities to match your situation, your equipment, or your style of teaching. They contain all figures, text, and tables in the same format as the printed book.

Files can be opened directly from the CD or copied onto your hard drive first. These files are in Microsoft® Word 97 - 2000 format. If you are using an older version of Word, you may need to install file conversion tools available from Microsoft. (Go to **www.Microsoft.com** and search for **converters and viewers**.)

Sample data files are also provided for each activity for each type of calculator. The sample data is not required to perform the activities. Most teachers will use these files only for evaluating an activity. Use TI™ Connect or TI-GRAPH LINK™ software to transfer the data to your calculator. For instructions for using the sample data files, see Appendix C.

You will find these folders on the CD:

📁 **TI-73**

📁 **TI-83**

📁 **TI-83 Plus** (also applicable for TI-83 Plus Silver Edition)

📁 **TI-86**

📁 **TI-89**

📁 **TI-92**

📁 **TI-92 Plus**

Each folder contains Word files and sample data for each of the 31 student activities in this book.

Sensors Used in the Activities

	pH sensor	Temperature sensor	Dual-Range Force sensor	Voltage sensor	Motion detector or CBR	Light sensor	Gas Pressure sensor	Microphone
Activity 1: Walk the Line					X			
Activity 2: Making Cents of Math			X					
Activity 3: Pool Plunge							X	
Activity 4: Funnel Volumes			X					
Activity 5: Keep It Bottled Up							X	
Activity 6: Graph It in Pieces					X			
Activity 7: Mix It Up		X						
Activity 8: Spring Thing			X		X			
Activity 9: Stretch It to the Limit			X		X			
Activity 10: What Goes Up					X			
Activity 11: That's the Way the Ball Bounces					X			
Activity 12: Walk This Way					X			
Activity 13: Velocity Test					X			
Activity 14: From Here to There					X			
Activity 15: Under Pressure							X	
Activity 16: Light at a Distance						X		
Activity 17: Chill Out		X						
Activity 18: Charging Up, Charging Down				X				
Activity 19: Bounce Back					X			
Activity 20: Sour Chemistry	X							

Sensors Used in the Activities (continued)

	pH sensor	Temperature sensor	Dual-Range Force sensor	Voltage sensor	Motion detector or CBR	Light sensor	Gas Pressure sensor	Microphone
Activity 21: Stepping to the Greatest Integer					X			
Activity 22: Swinging Ellipses					X			
Activity 23: Crawling Around					X			
Activity 24: Lights Out						X		
Activity 25: Tic, Toc					X			
Activity 26: Stay Tuned								X
Activity 27: Up and Down					X			
Activity 28: How Tall?					X			
Activity 29: And Now, the Weather		X						
Activity 30: Meet You at the Intersection					X			
Activity 31: Titration Curves	X							

E X P L O R A T I O N S

Activity 1

Walk the Line: Straight Line Distance Graphs

Objective

♦ Record distance versus time data for a person walking at a uniform rate.

♦ Analyze the data to extract slope and intercept information.

♦ Interpret the slope and intercept information for physical meaning.

Materials

♦ TI-83 Plus, TI-83, or TI-73

♦ CBL 2™ or LabPro® data collection device

♦ DATAMATE software

♦ TI CBR™ or Vernier Motion Detector

When one quantity changes at a constant rate with respect to another, we say they are *linearly related*. Mathematically, we describe this relationship by defining a linear equation. In real-world applications, some quantities are linearly related and can be represented by using a straight-line graph.

In this activity, you will create straight-line, or constant-speed, distance versus time plots using a motion detector, and then develop linear equations to describe these plots mathematically.

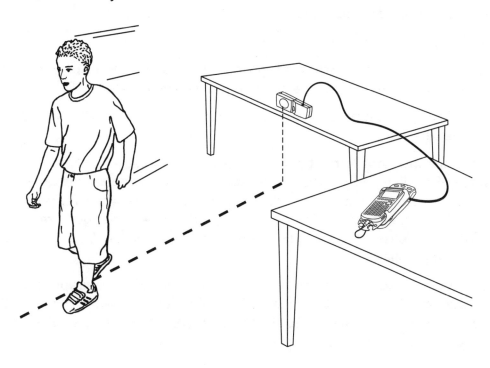

Procedure

1. Position the motion detector on a table or chair so that the disc is pointing horizontally out into an open area where you can walk. There should be no chairs or tables nearby.

2. Plug the motion detector into the DIG/SONIC port of the CBL 2™ or the DIG/SONIC 1 port of the LabPro®. Use the unit-to-unit cable to connect the TI graphing calculator to the data collection device. Press in the cable ends firmly.

3. Turn on the calculator and start the DATAMATE software. Press CLEAR to reset the software.

4. Stand about a meter from the motion detector. When you are ready to collect data, select **START** from the main screen. Walk away from the motion detector at a slow and steady pace. You will have five seconds to collect data.

5. The graph selection screen will appear. Press ENTER to display the distance versus time graph.

6. Examine the graph. It should show a nearly linearly increasing function with no spikes or flat regions. If you need to repeat data collection, press ENTER and select **MAIN SCREEN**. Return to Step **4**.

7. Once you are satisfied with the graph, press ENTER, select **MAIN SCREEN**, and select **QUIT** to leave DATAMATE. Follow any instructions to return to the calculator's home screen.

Analysis

1. Redisplay the graph outside of DATAMATE.

   a. Press ZOOM.

   b. Press ▼ until **ZoomStat** is highlighted. Press ENTER to display a graph with the x and y ranges set to fill the screen with data.

   c. Press TRACE to determine the coordinates of a point on the graph using the cursor keys.

2. The slope-intercept form of a linear equation is $y = mx + b$, where m is the slope of the line and b is the y-intercept value. The independent variable is x, which represents time, and y is the dependent variable which represents distance in this activity. Trace across the graph to the left edge to read the y-intercept. Record this value as b in the Data Table on the *Data Collection and Analysis* sheet.

3. One way to determine the slope of the distance versus time graph is to guess a value and then check it by viewing a graph of the line with your data. To do this, enter an equation into the calculator, and then enter a value for the y-intercept and store it as variable **B**.

a. Press [Y=].

b. Press [CLEAR] to remove any existing equation.

c. Enter the equation **M∗X + B** in the **Y1** field.
    (On the TI-73, go to the alphabetic entry screen by pressing [2nd] [TEXT].)

d. Press [2nd] [QUIT] to return to the home screen.

e. Enter your value for the *y*-intercept. Press [STO▶] **B** [ENTER] to store the value in the variable **B**.

4. Now set a value for the slope *m*, and then look at the resulting graph. To obtain a good fit, you will need to try several values for the slope. Use the steps below to store different values to the variable **M**. Start with **M** = 1. Experiment until you find one that provides a good fit for the data.

    a. Enter a value for the slope *m*. Press [STO▶] **M** [ENTER] to store the value in the variable **M**.

    b. Press [GRAPH] to see the data with the model graph superimposed.

    c. Press [2nd] [QUIT] to return to the home screen.

5. Record the optimized value for the slope in the Data Table on the *Data Collection and Analysis* sheet. Use the values of the slope and intercept to write the equation of the line that best fits the distance versus time data.

6. Another way to determine the slope of a line to fit your data is to use two well-separated data points. Use the cursor keys to move along the data points. Choose two points (x_1, y_1) and (x_2, y_2) that are not close to each other and record them in the Data Table on the *Data Collection and Analysis* sheet.

7. Use the points in the table to compute the slope, *m*, of the distance versus time graph.

$$m = \frac{y_2 - y_1}{x_2 - x_1} =$$

⇒ Calculate the slope and answer Question 1 on the *Data Collection and Analysis* page.

8. You can also use the calculator to automatically determine an optimized slope and intercept.

▶_____**TI-73**_____

a. Press [2nd] [STAT] and use the cursor keys to highlight **CALC**.

b. Press the number adjacent to **LinReg(ax+b)** to copy the command to the home screen.

c. After the **LinReg(ax+b)** command, press [2nd] [STAT] and select **L1** by pressing the number next to **L1** . Then press [,]. Repeat the procedure to select **L6**.

d. After selecting **L6**, press [,] then press [2nd] [VARS].

e. Use the cursor keys to select **Y-Vars** and press [ENTER] .

f. Press [ENTER] to select **Y1** and copy it to the expression.

On the home screen, you will now see the entry **LinReg(ax+b) L1, L6, Y1**. This command will perform a linear regression using the x-values in **L1** and the y-values in **L6**. The resulting regression line will be stored in equation variable **Y1**.

g. Press [ENTER] to perform the linear regression. Use the parameters a and b to write the equation of the calculator's best-fit line, and record it in the Data Table.

h. Press [GRAPH] to see the graph.

⇒ Answer Questions 2-5 on the *Data Collection and Analysis* sheet.

▷ **TI-83 and TI-83 Plus**
_____

a. Press [STAT] and use the cursor keys to highlight **CALC**.

b. Press the number adjacent to **LinReg(ax+b)** to copy the command to the home screen.

c. Press [2nd] [L1] [,] [2nd] [L6] [,] to enter the lists containing your data.

d. Press [VARS] and use the cursor keys to highlight **Y-VARS**.

e. Select **Function** by pressing [ENTER].

f. Press [ENTER] to copy **Y1** to the expression.

On the home screen, you will now see the entry **LinReg(ax+b) L1, L6, Y1**. This command will perform a linear regression using the x-values in **L1** and the y-values in **L6**. The resulting regression line will be stored in equation variable **Y1**.

g. Press [ENTER] to perform the linear regression. Use the parameters a and b to write the equation of the calculator's best-fit line, and record it in the Data Table.

h. Press [GRAPH] to see the graph.

⇒ Answer Questions 2-5 on the *Data Collection and Analysis* sheet.

Data Collection and Analysis

Name _____

Date _____

Activity 1: Walk the Line

Data Table

y-intercept b	
optimized slope m	
optimized line equation	
x_1, y_1	
x_2, y_2	
regression line equation	

Questions

1. How does this value compare to the slope you found by trial and error?

2. How do the values of the slope and intercept as determined by the calculator compare to your earlier values? Would you expect them to be exactly the same?

3. Slope is defined as change in y-values divided by change in x-values. Complete the following statement about slope for the linear data set you collected.

    In this activity, slope represents a change in _____

    divided by a change in _____

4. Based on this statement, what are the units of measurement for slope in this activity?

5. The y-intercept can be interpreted as the starting position or the starting distance from the motion detector. What does the slope represent physically? **Hint:** Consider the units of measurement for the slope you described in the previous question.

Teacher Notes
Walk the Line: Straight Line Distance Graphs

1. Place the motion detector at waist level for the walker. The walker should not be closer than 0.5 meter to the detector when data collection begins. Clear the area of other materials such as desks or chairs.

2. The walker must maintain a constant rate while walking directly away from the motion detector.

3. Either a TI CBR™ or a Vernier Motion Detector can be used. The CBR must be connected to a data collection device and not directly to the calculator.

4. Some motion detectors will not be automatically identified by DATAMATE. If you are using such a detector, you must manually set up DATAMATE for the detector:

   a. Select **SETUP** from the main screen.

   b. Press ⬛▼ until the cursor is next to DIG (CBL 2™) or DIG1 (LabPro®).

   c. Press ENTER to access the SELECT SENSOR menu.

   d. Select **MOTION(M)**.

   e. Select **OK** to return to the main screen.

Sample Results

Actual data will vary.

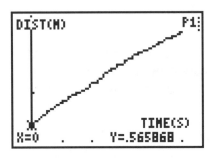

Raw data in DATAMATE

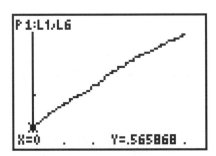

Data re-graphed
with trace to y-intercept

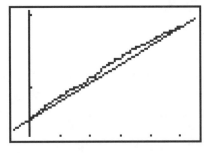

Optimized model fit

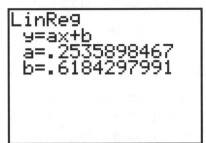

Calculator regression result

Data Table

Sample data; actual data may vary.

y-intercept *b*	0.565 m
optimized slope *m*	0.25 m/s
optimized line equation	$y = 0.565 + 0.25*x$
x_1, y_1	0, 0.565
x_2, y_2	1.6, 1.01
regression line equation	$y = 0.62 + 0.25*x$

Answers to Questions

1. The slope determined by the two-point calculation is nearly the same as the one found by trial and error.

2. The slope and intercept determined by the calculator are similar to those obtained by trial and error. They are not exactly the same, but you would not expect them to be the same. The trial and error line used only one point to determine the *y*-intercept, while the calculator used all the points.

3. Slope represents a change in distance from the motion detector divided by a change in time.

4. The slope has units of meters per second, or m/s.

5. The slope represents the velocity of the walker.

EXPLORATIONS

Activity 2

Making Cents of Math: Linear Relationship between Weight and Quantity

The slope of a line describes its steepness. The numerical value of the slope can represent a number of other important mathematical concepts. Given any two points on a line, (x_1, y_1) and (x_2, y_2), the slope of that line can be computed using the formula:

$$m = \frac{y_2 - y_1}{x_2 - x_1}$$

where m represents the slope of the line, x_1 and x_2 represent the *independent variable* coordinates, and y_1 and y_2 represent the *dependent variable* coordinates.

In this activity you will use a force sensor to collect a linear set of data points. Specifically, you will measure the weight of 8, 16, 24... pennies. You will then analyze this data and interpret the meaning of the slope as it relates to the independent and dependent variables. A model will help you predict future measurements and interpret past results.

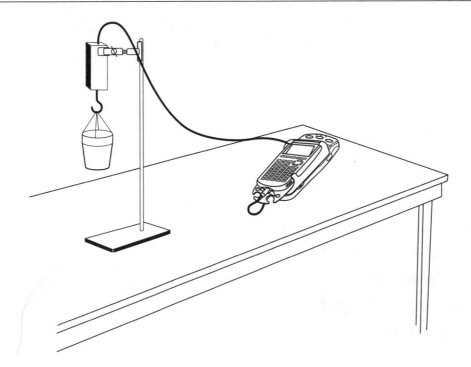

Procedure

During this activity the force sensor will be used to determine the weight of the pennies placed in the cup. The sensor must be positioned as shown in the setup diagram and should remain level at all times.

1. Use a pencil to poke small holes on opposite sides of the coffee cup near the top rim. Thread a piece of string through the holes, and then tie the ends of the string together to hang the cup.

2. Suspend the cup from the hook on the end of the force sensor.

3. Separate your pennies into four stacks of eight pennies each. As you do this, confirm that all pennies are dated after 1982.

4. Prepare the force sensor and the cup for data collection.

    a. Connect the force sensor into CH 1 of the CBL 2™ or LabPro® data collection device.

    b. If you are using a Vernier Dual-Range Force Sensor, set the range switch to 10 N.

    c. Use the unit-to-unit cable to connect the TI graphing calculator to the data collection device. Firmly press in the cable ends.

5. Turn on the calculator and start the DATAMATE software. Press CLEAR to reset the software.

6. Set up the calculator and data collection device for a force sensor.

   a. Select **SETUP** from the main screen.

   b. If the calculator displays a force sensor in CH 1, proceed directly to Step 7. If it does not, continue with this step to set up the sensor manually.

   c. Press ENTER to select **CH 1**.

   d. Select **FORCE** from the SELECT SENSOR menu.

   e. Select the correct force sensor (**DUAL R FORCE 10(N)** or **STUDENT FORCE(N)**) from the FORCE menu.

7. Set up the data-collection mode.

   a. To select **MODE**, press ▲ once and press ENTER.

   b. Select **EVENTS WITH ENTRY** from the SELECT MODE menu.

8. In this experiment you only want to measure the weight of the pennies, and not of the cup and string. To account for the weight of the cup and string, you need to zero the force sensor.

   a. The empty cup should now be hanging from the force sensor.

   b. Select **ZERO** from the SETUP screen.

   c. Select **CH1-FORCE(N)** from the SELECT CHANNEL screen.

   d. Wait until the cup stops swinging so that the reading is stable. Press ENTER to zero the force sensor. This will set the current weight reading to zero, and so ignore the weight of the cup.

9. You are now ready to collect weight versus number of penny data.

   a. Select **START** to begin data collection.

   b. Press ENTER to record the weight of zero pennies.

   c. Type in **0** for the number of pennies now in the cup. Press ENTER to store this weight-number data pair.

   d. Place eight pennies in the cup, and allow the cup to stop swinging.

   e. Press ENTER to record the weight of eight pennies.

   f. Type in **8**, which is the number of pennies in the cup. Press ENTER to store this weight-number data pair.

   g. Continue with this procedure using 16, 24 and 32 pennies. In each step enter the total number of pennies in the cup.

   h. Press STO▶ when you have finished collecting data.

10. The calculator screen shows a graph of weight versus number of pennies. The graph should appear linear. If you want to repeat data collection, press ENTER, and return to Step 9.

11. If you are satisfied with the data, press ENTER to return to the main screen of DATAMATE. Select **QUIT** to leave DATAMATE. Follow any instructions on the calculator screen to return to the home screen.

Analysis

1. Before you can work with the data on the calculator, you need to redisplay the graph outside of DATAMATE.

   a. Press ZOOM.

   b. Press ▼ until **ZoomStat** is highlighted. Press ENTER to display a graph with the x and y ranges set to fill the screen with data.

   c. Press TRACE to determine the coordinates of a point on the graph using the cursor keys.

2. Round the values of your points to the nearest 0.01 Newton and record them in the Data Table on the *Data Collection and Analysis* sheet.

3. The slope of a line can be determined from two points on the line. Using the two points, the slope is defined as the ratio of the change in a pair of y-values to the change in their corresponding x-values.

⇒ Answer Questions 1 through 6 on the *Data Collection and Analysis* sheet.

4. Next, plot the line whose equation you just determined. You can plot the line on the same graph as the data.

   a. Press Y=.

   b. Press CLEAR to remove any existing equation.

   c. Enter the equation for the line you determined into the **Y1** field. For example, if your line is $y=4x+3$, enter 4∗x+3.

   d. Press GRAPH to see the data with the model equation superimposed.

⇒ Answer Question 7 on the *Data Collection and Analysis* sheet.

5. Instead of using a model from only two points, you can use the calculator to do a linear regression, a type of least-squares regression, on all the data points.

   ▶   TI-73

   a. Press 2nd [STAT] and use the cursor keys to highlight **CALC**.

   b. Press the number adjacent to **LinReg(ax+b)** to copy the command to the home screen.

c. After the **LinReg(ax+b)** command, press 2nd [STAT] and select **L1** by pressing the number next to **L1** . Then press , . Repeat the procedure to select **L2**.

d. After selecting **L2**, press , then press 2nd [VARS].

e. Use the cursor keys to select **Y-Vars** and press ENTER .

f. Press ENTER to select **Y1** and copy it to the expression.

On the home screen, you will now see the entry **LinReg(ax+b) L1, L2, Y1**. This command will perform a linear regression using the x-values in **L1** and the y-values in **L2**. The resulting regression line will be stored in equation variable **Y1**.

g. Press ENTER to perform the linear regression. Use the parameters a and b to write the equation of the calculator's best-fit line, and record it as the regression equation in the Data Table on the *Data Collection and Analysis* sheet.

h. Press GRAPH to see the graph.

⇒ Answer Questions 8-10 on the *Data Collection and Analysis* sheet.

TI-83 and TI-83 Plus

a. Press STAT and use the cursor keys to highlight **CALC**.

b. Press the number adjacent to **LinReg(ax+b)** to copy the command to the home screen.

c. Press 2nd [L1] , 2nd [L2] , to enter the lists containing the data.

d. Press VARS and use the cursor keys to highlight **Y-VARS**.

e. Select **Function** by pressing ENTER .

f. Press ENTER to copy **Y1** to the expression.

On the home screen, you will now see the entry **LinReg(ax+b) L1, L2, Y1**. This command will perform a linear regression using the x-values in **L1** and the y-values in **L2**. The resulting regression line will be stored in equation variable **Y1**.

g. Press ENTER to perform the linear regression. Use the parameters a and b to write the equation of the calculator's best-fit line, and record it as the regression equation in the Data Table on the *Data Collection and Analysis* sheet.

h. Press GRAPH to see the graph.

⇒ Answer Questions 8-10 on the *Data Collection and Analysis* sheet.

Extension

The data you collected in this activity depends on the fact that your pennies were all dated after 1982. Repeat this activity with a group of pennies dated before 1982. Use the modeling procedure described in this activity to find the average weight of a pre-1982 penny. Look in a coin book and determine why the model for pre-1982 pennies differs from the model for post 1982 pennies. How do your values for the weights of pre-1982 and post-1982 pennies compare with their official weights?

Data Collection and Analysis

Name _____

Date _____

Activity 2: Making Cents of Math

Data Table

Number of Pennies	Weight in Newtons
0	
8	
16	
24	
32	
Model equation	
Regression equation	

Questions

1. Find the slope of the line passing through any two points in your table and record it below:

   $m = $ _____

2. What do the x-values in this problem represent?

3. What do the y-values represent?

4. If slope can be described as change in y over change in x, then from Questions 2 and 3 above, slope represents the change in the _____ divided by the change in the _____.

5. Simplifying the answer to the previous question, the value for slope in this data set represents the _____ per _____.

6. The slope-intercept form of a line is $y=mx+b$, where m represents the slope and b is the y-intercept. The y-intercept is the y value when $x = 0$. Determine this value from the table and record it below:

    y-intercept: $b =$ _____

    Use the values for m and b found above to write the equation of the line through your data. Record the equation in the Data Table above as the model equation.

7. Is your line a good fit for the data? _____

8. Are the values of a and b in the linear regression equation consistent with your results from Step 4? _____

9. How would using quarters instead of pennies affect the slope of the graph?

10. What would the slope of a graph made with quarters represent?

Applications

Use your regression equation from the activity to answer the following questions.

1. Courtney has been saving her pennies for a rainy day. She has lived in the desert all of her life. By the time the rainy day arrives, she has saved $4,763.89! What is the total weight of her pennies?

    _____ Newtons

2. While cleaning out the attic Kelly finds an antique milk can that contains a large number of pennies. He weighs the can of pennies and finds that it weighs 450 Newtons. He then empties the can and weighs it. He finds that the can weighs 100 N without the pennies. Use your model to find how much money Kelly has found.

    $_____

Teacher Notes
Making Cents of Math: Linear Relationship between Weight and Quantity

1. Be sure that the force sensor is positioned as shown in the setup diagram and that nothing is in contact with the hook except for the penny cup string.

2. Pennies minted between 1959 and 1981 are composed of 95% copper and 5% zinc with an average weight of 0.030 N, or a mass of 3.11 g. Pennies minted from 1983 on are composed of 99.2% zinc and 0.8% copper with an average weight of 0.0245 N. That's why it is important to sort the pennies by date before conducting the experiment.

3. Each time pennies are added to the bucket, students should wait until it stops swinging before pressing ENTER to collect the weight data. Be sure that nothing is touching the penny bucket while readings are being taken.

Sample Results

Actual data will vary.

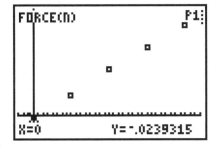

Raw data in DATAMATE

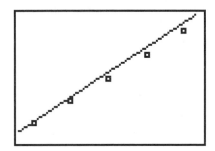

Data with model line

Data Table

Sample data; actual data may vary.

Number of Pennies	Weight in Newtons
0	-0.01
8	0.17
16	0.36
24	0.56
32	0.77
Model equation	$y = -0.01 + 0.026\,x$
Regression equation	$y = -0.02 + 0.024\,x$

Answers to Questions

1. Answers will vary but should be close to 0.025.

2. The x values correspond to the number of pennies.

3. The y values correspond to the weight of the pennies.

4. The slope represents the change in the weight of the pennies in Newtons divided by the change in the number of pennies.

5. The value for slope in this data set represents the weight in Newtons per penny.

6. The y-intercept is ⁻0.01 N, as read from the table.

7. The model is a good fit for the data, but not all the points are similarly close to the model line.

8. The calculator's regression line is very close to all the points, and is similar to the model developed using only two points for the slope.

9. Since quarters weigh more, the slope of the graph would be larger.

10. The slope would represent the weight in Newtons per quarter, or the weight of a quarter.

Activity 3

Pool Plunge: Linear Relationship Between Water Depth and Pressure

If you dive to the bottom of a swimming pool you will feel an increasing pressure on your eardrums as you descend. The deeper you dive, the more water there is above you to push down on your body and your eardrums, so the more pressure you experience. There is a simple mathematical relationship between your depth in the pool and the pressure you feel.

In this activity you will lower a section of tubing into a water-filled pipe and collect pressure readings at different depths with the use of a pressure sensor. You will then find a model for your data and use this model to understand the relationship between depth and pressure.

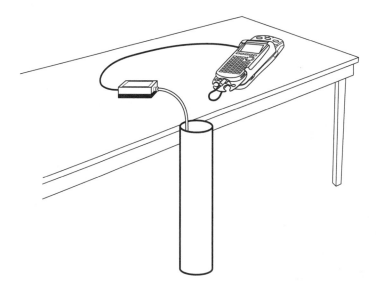

Procedure

1. Make a small hole in one end of the plastic aquarium tubing. Attach a paperclip to the tubing through the hole. This clip will be used as a hanger for the sinker weight.

2. Attach the sinker weight to the paper clip. Attach the other end of the plastic tubing to the pressure sensor.

    ◆ Newer Vernier Gas Pressure Sensors have a white stem protruding from the end of the sensor box. Attach the tube directly to the white stem with a gentle half-turn.

    ◆ Older Vernier Pressure Sensors have a 3-way valve at the end of a plastic tube leading from the sensor box. Before attaching the tube, align the blue handle with the stem of the 3-way valve that will *not* have the tube connected to it, as shown in the figure at the right, closing this stem. Then attach the tube directly to the remaining open stem of the 3-way valve.

3. With the clear pipe oriented vertically, cap down, secure the pipe safely to a stationary object. Fill the pipe with water, leaving a few cm at the top unfilled to allow for the tubing volume.

4. Set up DATAMATE and the data collection device for data collection.

    a. Connect the gas pressure sensor or pressure sensor to CH 1 of the CBL 2™ or LabPro® data collection device.

    b. Use the unit-to-unit cable to connect the TI graphing calculator to the data collection device. Firmly press in the cable ends.

5. Turn on the calculator and start the DATAMATE software. Press (CLEAR) to reset the software.

6. Set up the calculator and data collection device for a gas pressure sensor or pressure sensor with units of kPa.

   a. Select **SETUP** from the main screen.

   b. If the calculator displays a pressure sensor in CH 1 with units of KPA, proceed directly to the Step 7.

   c. Press ENTER to select CH 1.

   d. Select **PRESSURE** from the SELECT SENSOR menu.

   e. Select the correct pressure sensor (**GAS PRESSURE SENSOR, PRESSURE SENSOR,** or **BIOLOGY GAS PRESSURE**) from the PRESSURE menu.

   f. Select the calibration listing for units of (**KPA**) to return to the setup screen.

7. Set up the data collection mode.

   a. To select **MODE**, press ▲ once in the setup screen and press ENTER.

   b. Select **EVENTS WITH ENTRY** from the SELECT MODE menu.

   c. Select **OK** to return to the main screen.

8. You are now ready to collect pressure and depth data.

   a. Select **START** to begin data collection.

   b. With the weighted end of the tubing out of the water, wait until the pressure value stabilizes, then press ENTER.

   c. Enter **0** on the calculator for the depth. Press ENTER to store this and all other numeric values.

   d. Hold the meter stick so that the zero mark is even with the top of the water in the clear pipe, with the scale increasing downward. Lower the weighted end of the tubing into the pipe until the air-water line in the tubing is 10 cm below the water surface in the clear pipe. Adjust the meter stick and tube as needed so that there is a 10-cm air column in the tubing below the water surface. Hold the tube in this position until the pressure value displayed on the calculator screen stabilizes.

   e. Press ENTER and type in **0.1**, the depth in meters.

   f. To collect another data point, lower the tube so that the air-water interface is 20 cm deep. When the pressure reading stabilizes, press ENTER and enter **0.2** as the depth in meters

   g. Continue in **10-cm** increments with **0.7 m** as the last point.

   h. Press STO▶ when you have finished collecting data. A graph will be displayed.

9. The pressure versus depth plot should be nearly linear. If you are not satisfied with the data, press ENTER to return to the main screen and start again.

10. If you are satisfied with the data, make a rough sketch of the pressure versus depth data. Press ENTER to return to the main screen, and select **QUIT** to leave DATAMATE. Follow any instructions on the screen to return to the calculator home screen.

Analysis

1. Before you can work with the data on the calculator, you need to redisplay the graph outside of DATAMATE.

   a. Press ZOOM.

   b. Press ▼ until **ZoomStat** is highlighted. Press ENTER to display a graph with the x and y ranges set to fill the screen with data.

   c. Press TRACE to determine the coordinates of a point on the graph using the cursor keys.

2. Use the cursor keys to move along the data points. Choose any two points (x_1, y_1) and (x_2, y_2) along the data plot and round the pressure values to the nearest kPa. Record these data points in the Data Table on the *Data Collection and Analysis* sheet.

⇒ Answer Questions 1-3 on the *Data Collection and Analysis* sheet.

3. Next, plot the line whose equation you just determined in Question 3. You can plot the line on the same graph as your data.

   a. Press Y=.

   b. Press CLEAR to remove any existing equation.

   c. Enter the equation for the line you determined in the **Y1** field. (On the TI-73, go to the alphabetic entry screen by pressing 2nd [TEXT].)

   d. Press GRAPH to see your data with the model graph superimposed.

⇒ Answer Question 4 on the *Data Collection and Analysis* sheet.

4. You can use the calculator to do a linear least-squares fit to the data. Instead of using only two points to determine the slope, the calculator can be used to automatically determine the slope and intercept for the line that bests fits the data.

   ▶ **TI-73**

   a. Press 2nd [STAT] and use the cursor keys to highlight **CALC**.

   b. Press the number adjacent to **LinReg(ax+b)** to copy the command to the home screen.

c. After the **LinReg(ax+b)** command, press ⌊2nd⌋ [STAT] and select **L1** by pressing the number next to **L1** . Then press ⌊ , ⌋. Repeat the procedure to select **L2**.

d. After selecting **L2**, press ⌊ , ⌋ then press ⌊2nd⌋ [VARS].

e. Use the cursor keys to select **Y-Vars** and press ⌊ENTER⌋ .

f. Press ⌊ENTER⌋ to select **Y1** and copy it to the expression.

On the home screen, you will now see the entry **LinReg(ax+b) L1, L2, Y1**. This command will perform a linear regression with **L1** as the x-values and **L2** as the y-values. The resulting regression line will be stored in equation variable **Y1**.

g. Press ⌊ENTER⌋ to perform the linear regression.

⇒ Use the parameters a and b that appear on the calculator screen to write the equation fit by the calculator, and record it in Question 5 on the *Data Collection and Analysis* sheet.

h. Press ⌊GRAPH⌋ to see the graph.

⇒ Answer Question 6 on the *Data Collection and Analysis* sheet.

▶ TI-83 and TI-83 Plus

a. Press ⌊STAT⌋ and use the cursor keys to highlight **CALC**.

b. Press the number adjacent to **LinReg(ax+b)** to copy the command to the home screen.

c. Press ⌊2nd⌋ [L1] ⌊ , ⌋ ⌊2nd⌋ [L2] ⌊ , ⌋ to enter the lists containing the data.

d. Press ⌊VARS⌋ and use the cursor keys to highlight **Y-VARS**.

e. Select **Function** by pressing ⌊ENTER⌋.

f. Press ⌊ENTER⌋ to copy **Y1** to the expression.

On the home screen, you now see the entry **LinReg(ax+b) L1, L2, Y1**. This command will perform a linear regression using the x-values in **L1** and the y-values in **L2**. The resulting regression line will be stored in equation variable **Y1**.

g. Press ⌊ENTER⌋ to perform the linear regression.

⇒ Use the parameters a and b to write the equation fit by the calculator, and record it in Question 5 on the *Data Collection and Analysis* sheet.

h. Press ⌊GRAPH⌋ to see the graph.

⇒ Answer Question 6 on the *Data Collection and Analysis* sheet.

Data Collection and Analysis

Name _____

Date _____

Activity 3: Pool Plunge

Data Table

x: Depth (m)	y: Pressure (kPa)

Questions

1. Use the points in the table above to compute the slope, m, of the pressure-versus-depth line and record it here.

$$m = \frac{y_2 - y_1}{x_2 - x_1}$$

2. You can model the data with a linear equation of the form $y = mx + b$, where b represents the y-intercept (that is, the zero-depth pressure reading). Use the cursor keys to move the cursor to $x = 0$ and record the y-intercept value below.

$$b = \underline{\hspace{2cm}}$$

3. Use the values of m and b you determined to write a linear equation that models your data, and record it here.

4. Is your line a good fit for the data? Does the line pass directly through any points?

5. Use the parameters a and b that appear on your calculator screen to write the equation fit by the calculator. Record it below.

6. Is the line suggested by the regression consistent with your results from Question 2? Why might they be different?

Applications

Use the regression equation developed in this activity to solve the following problems.

1. Recall that the first pressure reading in this activity was out of the water. This pressure is known to be 1 atmosphere (atm). How many kPa (kilo Pascals) are equal to 1 atm?

    _____ kPa

2. Your cousin Susie is always bragging about her exploits. When you tell her that you touched the bottom of your 4-m deep pool she quickly responds that her pool is two-and-a-half times that deep, and she always touches the bottom. Use your model to find the pressure at the bottom of Susie's pool and record your answer in the space below.

    _____ kPa

3. Beginning divers are advised not swim in deep waters where the pressure exceeds about 275 kPa. Use your model to determine how deep a novice diver can safely swim.

    _____ m

4. The Mariana Trench contains some of the deepest waters ever measured on earth. One location, called the Challenger Deep, was found to be 11,033 m. Use your model to predict the pressure at this depth, and record your answer in the space below.

    _____ kPa

    At this depth, what is the pressure in atmospheres?

    _____ atm

5. The wreck of the Titanic rests on the floor of the Atlantic Ocean nearly 4 km beneath the surface of the water. What is the pressure on the remains of the hull at this depth? **Hint:** 1 km is 1000 m.

    _____ atm

Teacher Notes
Pool Plunge: Linear Relationship Between Water Depth and Pressure

1. Note that the unit for pressure measurement is the kPa, or kilopascal. Water pressure increases by about 9.8 kPa for every depth increase of 1 meter, and the pressure at the surface of the water is about 100 kPa. Accordingly, the pressure-versus-depth equation should be close to $p = 100 + 9.8d$. You may wish to have your students compare their findings with this typical result.

2. Instead of using a clear tube to contain the water, a PVC pipe or a swimming pool can be used. However, it is then difficult to measure the actual height of the air column in the tubing. Since water is forced into the tubing end, you cannot simply measure the length of submerged tubing and still obtain the expected slope. If you do measure only the tubing length, you'll get a linear relationship but the slope will be reduced by about 20% due to water intrusion.

3. Pressure sensors come with a short piece of tubing with two luer locks attached. Remove one luer lock from the tubing for use with the long tubing used in this activity.

4. We used a clear tube called a Tube Lamp Guard, designed to fit over a fluorescent lamp. A 1-¼ inch PVC cap will fit snugly over the open end. Lamp Guards are available at home improvement stores or lighting shops. Other clear tubes can also be used.

5. The Vernier Biology Gas Pressure Sensor can also be used for this activity.

Sample Results

Actual data will vary.

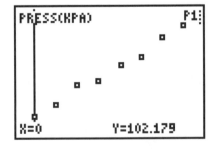

Raw data in DATAMATE

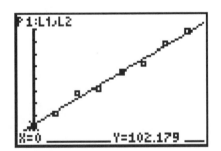

Data with regression line

Data Table

Sample data; actual data may vary.

x: **Depth (m)**	y: **Pressure (kPa)**
0.0	102
0.7	109

Answers to Questions

1. Slope is 11 kPa/m.

2. The y intercept is 102 kPa.

3. The model expression is $y = 100 + 11\,x$.

4. The fit is fair; the line passes through the two points used to find the slope.

5. Fitted line is $y = 10.5\,x + 102$.

6. The least-squares fit is slightly different from the model fit; the least-squares fit is closer to the points on average. The fit is different because the least-squares fit used all the points to determine the slope and intercept, while the model equation used only two or three (the two used for slope calculation and the intercept).

Applications

The following applications were calculated using the relation $p = 100 + 9.8d$. Values will differ for other models.

1. Recognizing the atmospheric pressure varies with weather and altitude, for the data presented here, one atmosphere is about 100 kPa.

2. At 2.5 * 4 m, or 10 meters depth, the pressure is 198 kPa, or about two atmospheres.

3. 18 m

4. 1.08×10^5 kPa, or 1080 atmospheres!

5. 390 atm

Activity 4

Funnel Volumes: Volume and Weight

Objective

♦ Record weight versus time data for a draining funnel.

♦ Describe the data using concepts of intercept and slope of a linear function.

Materials

♦ TI-83 Plus, TI-83, or TI-73

♦ CBL 2™ or LabPro® data collection device

♦ DATAMATE software

♦ Vernier Dual-Range Force Sensor or Student Force Sensor

♦ Funnel

♦ String

♦ Bucket

♦ Water

Water drains from an open funnel. How is the volume of water changing with time? At what rate is the water level decreasing? How long will it take for the funnel to drain completely? These are a few questions that can be investigated by collecting weight data for a draining funnel, and then developing a mathematical model to describe the data.

In this activity, you will use a force sensor to measure the weight of a water-filled funnel as it drains. The weight versus time data can be graphed and analyzed using the calculator's statistical features.

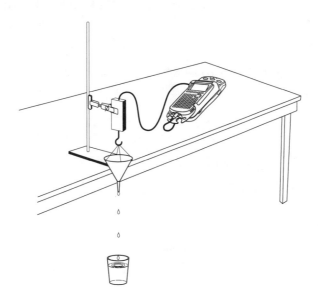

Procedure

1. Make two small holes on opposite sides of the funnel near the top rim. Thread a piece of string through the holes, and then tie the ends of the string together to create a handle as shown in the drawing.

2. Place a cup or bucket on the floor to catch water as it drains from the funnel.

3. Block the funnel hole with your finger and fill the funnel completely with water. How long will it take for the funnel to drain? Remove your finger from the funnel hole and estimate the time required for the funnel to empty. Make a note of the time in seconds; you will use this value later.

4. Prepare the force sensor for data collection.

    a. Connect the force sensor to CH 1 of the CBL 2™ or LabPro® data collection device.

    b. If you are using a Vernier Dual-Range Force Sensor, set the range switch to 10 N.

    c. Use the unit-to-unit cable to connect the TI graphing calculator to the data collection device. Firmly press in the cable ends.

5. Turn on the calculator and start the DATAMATE software. Press (CLEAR) to reset the software.

6. Set up DATAMATE for the force sensor.

    a. Select **SETUP** from the main screen. If CH 1 shows a force sensor in units of N, skip to the Step 7.

    b. Press (ENTER) to select CH 1.

    c. Select **FORCE** from the SELECT SENSOR menu.

    d. Select the correct force sensor (**DUAL R FORCE 10(N)** or **STUDENT FORCE(N)**) from the FORCE menu.

7. In this activity you only want to measure the weight of the water in the funnel. To do this, you need to reset the force scale so that the force sensor reads zero when supporting the weight of the empty funnel and string.

    a. Hold the sensor so that the funnel can hang downward from the hook. Place the bucket under the funnel. Allow the funnel to stop swinging.

    b. Select **ZERO** from the setup screen.

    c. Select **CH1:FORCE** from the select channel screen.

    d. Press (ENTER) to zero the force sensor.

8. If the drain time is less than three seconds, skip to Step 9. If the estimated time to drain the funnel is more than three seconds, adjust the data collection time.

a. Select **SETUP** from the main screen.

b. Press ⬜▲⬜ to select mode and press ⬅ENTER⬅.

c. Select **TIME GRAPH** from the mode screen.

d. Select **CHANGE TIME SETTINGS** from TIME GRAPH SETTINGS.

e. Enter **0.1** as the time between samples in seconds if your funnel's emptying time is less than ten seconds. Use **0.2** if it is more than ten seconds.

f. Enter **100** as the number of samples.

g. Select **OK** twice to return to the main screen.

9. You are now ready to collect weight versus time data.

a. Block the funnel hole with a finger, and fill the funnel completely with water.

b. Select **START** to begin data collection.

c. When you hear the data collection device beep, remove your finger from the funnel and allow it to empty. Take care to not touch the funnel while it is emptying, and make sure that it does not swing.

d. After data collection is complete you will see a graph of the weight of the water in the funnel versus time.

10. Your graph should be a uniformly decreasing function, with a horizontal section at the end. If you need to repeat data collection, press ⬅ENTER⬅ to return to the main screen, and return to Step 9.

11. Since data collection probably did not exactly coincide with the emptying of the funnel, you need to remove the data taken before you released the water and after the funnel was empty.

a. Press ⬅ENTER⬅ to return to the main screen.

b. Select **GRAPH** from the main screen. You will see the graph again.

c. Press ⬅ENTER⬅ to see the graph options screen.

d. Select **SELECT REGION** from the graph options screen.

e. Use the ⬜►⬜ key to move the cursor to the left edge of the smoothly decreasing portion of the graph. (You may not need to move the cursor at all if data collection started after the water started to flow.) Press ⬅ENTER⬅ to mark this position.

f. Use the ⬜►⬜ key to move the cursor to the right edge of the smoothly decreasing portion of the graph. Press ⬅ENTER⬅ to mark this position.

g. The calculator will remove data outside the region you just marked. A new graph will be displayed showing only the linearly decreasing weight of the water remaining in the funnel as a function of time.

12. For further analysis, leave DATAMATE by pressing ENTER, selecting **MAIN SCREEN**, and then selecting **QUIT**. Follow any instructions to return to the home screen of your calculator.

Analysis

1. Redisplay the graph and prepare to trace values from it.

    a. Press ZOOM.

    b. Press ▼ until **ZoomStat** is highlighted. Press ENTER to display a graph with the x and y ranges set to fill the screen with data.

    c. Press TRACE to determine the coordinates of a point on the graph using the cursor keys.

2. Trace across the graph to choose two well-separated points on the graph. Round the x and y coordinates to 0.01, and record the values in the Data Table on the *Data Collection and Analysis* sheet.

3. Use the two points to find the slope of the weight versus time graph. Record the slope, with units, in the Data Table.

⇒ Answer Question 1 on the *Data Collection and Analysis* sheet.

4. You still need to find the y-intercept of this segment, but you cannot just trace to the y axis because the line segment does not necessarily go that far. However, using the definition of slope we can write the point slope form of a line, or $y - y_1 = m(x - x_1)$. Here y and x are variables, m the slope, and x_1 and y_1 are the values of a point on the line. Record the y-intercept in the Data Table.

⇒ Answer Question 2 on the *Data Collection and Analysis* sheet.

5. Next, plot the line whose equation you just determined. You can plot the line on the same graph as your data.

    a. Press Y=.

    b. Press CLEAR to remove any existing equation.

    c. Enter the equation for the line you determined in the **Y₁** field. For example, if your expression is $y = 4x + 3$, enter 4*x+3.

    d. Press GRAPH to see your data with the model graph superimposed.

⇒ Answer Question 3 on the *Data Collection and Analysis* sheet.

6. Determine the x intercept for the linear equation you have found. Record the value, including units, in the Data Table.

⇒ Answer Question 4 on the *Data Collection and Analysis* sheet.

7. You can use the calculator to do a linear least-squares fit to the data. Instead of using only two points to determine the slope, the calculator can automatically determine the slope and intercept for the line that bests fits your data.

TI-73

a. Press 2nd [STAT] and use the cursor keys to highlight **CALC**.

b. Press the number adjacent to **LinReg(ax+b)** to copy the command to the home screen.

c. After the **LinReg(ax+b)** command, press 2nd [STAT] and select **L1** by pressing the number next to **L1** . Then press ,. Repeat the procedure to select **L2**.

d. After selecting **L2**, press , then press 2nd [VARS].

e. Use the cursor keys to select **Y-Vars** and press ENTER .

f. Press ENTER to select **Y1** and copy it to the expression.

On the home screen, you will now see the entry **LinReg(ax+b) L1, L2, Y1**. This command will perform a linear regression with **L1** as the x-values and **L2** as the y-values. The resulting regression line will be stored in equation variable **Y1**.

g. Press ENTER to perform the linear regression.

⇒ Answer Question 5 on the *Data Collection and Analysis* sheet.

h. Press GRAPH to see your graph.

⇒ Answer Questions 6 and 7 on the *Data Collection and Analysis* sheet.

TI-83 and TI-83 Plus

a. Press STAT and use the cursor keys to highlight **CALC**.

b. Press the number adjacent to **LinReg(ax+b)** to copy the command to the home screen.

c. Press 2nd [L1] , 2nd [L2] , to enter the lists containing your data.

d. Press VARS and use the cursor keys to highlight **Y-VARS**.

e. Select **Function** by pressing ENTER .

f.   Press [ENTER] to copy **Y1** to the expression.

On the home screen, you now see the entry **LinReg(ax+b) L1, L2, Y1**. This command will perform a linear regression using the x-values in **L1** and the y-values in **L2**. The resulting regression line will be stored in equation variable **Y1**.

g.   Press [ENTER] to perform the linear regression.

⇒   Answer Question 5 on the *Data Collection and Analysis* sheet.

h.   Press [GRAPH] to see your graph.

⇒   Answer Questions 6 and 7 on the *Data Collection and Analysis* sheet.

Extension

Determine the radius-to-height ratio for the funnel you used. Write an equation relating volume, V and height, h. Differentiate this equation with respect to time. Use your weight versus time graph to find dW/dt. Convert this to dV/dt using the specific gravity of water. Substitute this value into the differential equation. Solve for h as a function of t.

Use this relationship to determine when the water level will be at half its initial value. To test your answer, plug the hole and re-fill the funnel. Unplug the hole and activate a stopwatch simultaneously. Re-plug the hole when the stopwatch reading matches the time you computed above. Is the height of the water in the funnel approximately half its initial value?

Data Collection and Analysis

Name _____

Date _____

Activity 4: Funnel Volumes

Data Table

x_1		x_2	
y_1		y_2	
slope			
x-intercept		y-intercept	

Questions

1. Why is the value of the slope negative?

$$m = \frac{y_2 - y_1}{x_2 - x_1}$$

2. Use the relation in Step 4 to write the equation of the line fitting the data in the traditional $y = mx + b$ form.

3. Is your line a good fit for the data? Does the line pass directly through any particular points? Why?

4. What is the physical interpretation of the x-intercept?

5. Use the parameters a and b that appear on the calculator screen to write the equation of the calculator's best-fit line.

6. Is the line suggested by the regression consistent with your results from Step 4? Why might they be different?

7. What physical characteristics of the funnel could be changed to reduce the rate at which the volume of water in the funnel is changing with time? What would happen to the slope of the fitted line to data taken with the modified funnel?

Teacher Notes
Funnel Volumes: Volume and Weight

1. The various force sensors read in units of Newtons, the SI unit of force. Weight is measured in Newtons. The weight of the water remaining in the funnel is thus measured in Newtons. If you want to convert to cm^3 of water, multiply the force readings by 102 cm^3/N.

2. Hold the probe and funnel so that both are level while data is being collected. Be careful not to touch the funnel during data collection.

Sample results

Actual data will vary.

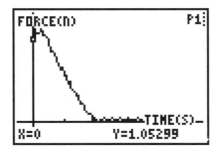

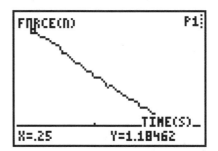

Raw data in DATAMATE   After selection of linear region

Data Table

Sample data; actual data may vary.

x_1	0.25 s	x_2	1.00 s
y_1	1.18 N	y_2	0.60 N
slope	-0.61 N/s		
x-intercept	2.05 s	y-intercept	1.33 N

Answers to Questions

1. The slope is negative because the weight of the water-filled funnel is decreasing with time.

2. answers may vary

3. Yes, the line is a good fit. The fitted line passes directly through the point used in the point-slope formula.

4. The x intercept is the time the funnel was first empty.

5. $y = {}^-0.68x + 1.33$

6. The new line is nearly the same as the one found using two points, but could be closer to the data as a whole since the whole line is used to determine the slope and intercept.

7. Making the opening smaller would slow the release of the water, so that the rate of change of the volume of water would be smaller. The slope of the fitted line would then be smaller in magnitude.

EXPLORATIONS

Activity 5

Keep It Bottled Up: Linear Rates of Pressure Increase

Objective

- Record pressure versus time data as a chemical reaction proceeds.

- Model pressure data using a linear function.

- Use the concept of slope to describe the effect of temperature on chemical reaction rates.

Materials

- TI-83 Plus, TI-83, or TI-73

- CBL 2™ or LabPro® data collection device

- DATAMATE software

- Vernier Gas Pressure Sensor or Pressure Sensor with plastic tubing

- Empty 500 mL container

- One-hole rubber stopper

- Water, both room temperature and warmed

- Effervescent antacid tablets

- Safety goggles

When two or more chemicals react, other substances such as gases may be produced. The rate at which the reaction takes place can be affected by a number of different factors including temperature. In this activity, you will see how temperature affects the rate at which an effervescent antacid tablet reacts with water and releases a gas. The rate at which the reaction occurs is measured by the rate of gas production.

You will measure this rate by recording the pressure variation in a closed container as the reaction proceeds using a pressure sensor. Then you can use a mathematical model relating pressure and time to describe how water temperature affects chemical reaction rates.

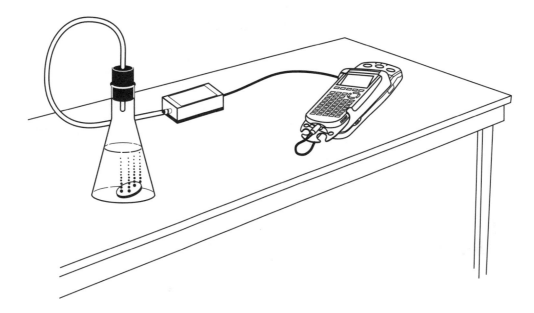

Procedure

1. Obtain and wear safety goggles.

2. Connect the pressure sensor to CH 1 of the CBL 2™ or LabPro® data collection device. Use the unit-to-unit cable to connect the TI graphing calculator to the data collection device. Firmly press in the cable ends.

3. Attach the tubing to the connector or valve of the pressure sensor. Attach the other end of the tubing to a rubber stopper that tightly fits the container.

    ◆ Newer Vernier Gas Pressure Sensors have a white stem protruding from the end of the sensor box. Attach the tube directly to the white stem with a gentle half-turn.

    ◆ Older Vernier Pressure Sensors have a 3-way valve at the end of a plastic tube leading from the sensor box. Before attaching the tube, align the blue handle with the stem of the 3-way valve that will *not* have the tube connected to it, as shown in the figure at the right, closing this stem. Then attach the tube directly to the remaining open stem of the 3-way valve.

4. Turn on the calculator and start the DATAMATE software. Press ⌈CLEAR⌉ to reset the software.

5. Set up the calculator and data collection device for a gas pressure sensor or pressure sensor.

    a. Select **SETUP** from the main screen.

    b. If the calculator displays a pressure sensor in units of kPa in CH 1, proceed directly to Step 6.

   c. Press ENTER to select CH 1.

   d. Select **PRESSURE** from the SELECT SENSOR menu.

   e. Select the correct pressure sensor (**GAS PRESSURE SENSOR** or **PRESSURE SENSOR**) from the PRESSURE menu.

   f. Select the calibration listing for units of (KPA).

6. Set up the data-collection mode.

   a. To select **MODE**, press ⬜▲ once and press ENTER.

   b. Select **TIME GRAPH** from the SELECT MODE menu.

   c. Select **CHANGE TIME SETTINGS** from the TIME GRAPH SETTINGS menu.

   d. Enter **0.2** (0.4 on the TI-73) as the time between samples and press ENTER.

   e. Enter **100** (50 on the TI-73) as the number of samples and press ENTER.

   f. Select **OK** twice to return to the main screen.

7. You are now ready to collect pressure as a function of time data.

   a. Put 200 mL of room-temperature water in the container. In rapid sequence, put the tablet in the container, seal the container with the stopper, and select **START** to begin data collection in order to capture the start of the pressure change. Data collection will run for 20 seconds.

   b. After data collection is complete, point the container away from all people and carefully remove the stopper. Discard the water and any remains of the tablet.

8. Examine the displayed graph. If you achieved a good seal between the container and stopper, you should see a uniformly increasing pressure graph.

   If you need to repeat data collection, press ENTER and return to the previous step. If the run was good, press ENTER and then select **TOOLS** from the main screen. Then select **STORE LATEST RUN** from the TOOLS menu.

9. Now prepare to repeat the experiment with warm water.

   a. Put 200 mL of warm water in the container. In rapid sequence, put the tablet in the container, seal the container with the stopper, and select **START** to begin data collection in order to capture the start of the pressure change. Data collection will run for 20 seconds.

   b. After data collection is complete, point the container away from all people and carefully remove the stopper. Discard the water and any remains of the tablet.

10. Examine the displayed graph. If you achieved a good seal between the container and stopper, you should see a uniformly increasing pressure graph. If you need to repeat data collection, press [ENTER] and return to the previous step.

11. If you are happy with the data, return to the main screen and select **QUIT** to leave DATAMATE. Follow any instructions to return to the calculator's home screen.

12. Next you can view both runs together.

▶ **TI-73**

a. Press [2nd] [PLOT] and press [ENTER] to select **Plot 1**.

b. Change the **Plot1** settings to match the screen shown here. Press [ENTER] to select any of the settings you change.

    This means that the warm-water data will be plotted with the box □ symbol.

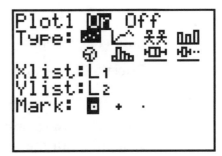

c. Press [2nd] [PLOT] and press [▼] [ENTER] to select **Plot 2**.

d. Change the **Plot2** settings to match the screen shown here. Press [ENTER] to select any of the settings you change.

    The room-temperature water data will then be plotted with + symbol.

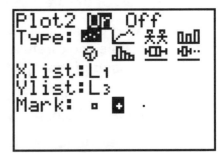

e. Press [ZOOM] and then select **ZoomStat** (use cursor keys to scroll to **ZoomStat**) to draw a graph with the x and y ranges set to fill the screen with data.

f. Press [TRACE] to read values off of the plots. Press [◄] and [►] to trace along each plot. Switch between plots by pressing [▲] and [▼].

▶ **TI-83 and TI-83 Plus**

a. Press ⌐2nd⌐ [STAT PLOT] and press ⌐ENTER⌐ to select **Plot 1**.

b. Change the **Plot1** settings to match the screen shown here. Press ⌐ENTER⌐ to select any of the settings you change.

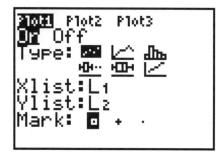

This means that the warm-water data will be plotted with the box ▫ symbol.

c. Use the cursor keys to position the cursor back up at the top of the screen, highlighting the **Plot2** icon. Press ⌐ENTER⌐ to switch the screen to Plot2.

d. Change the **Plot2** settings to match the screen shown here. Press ⌐ENTER⌐ to select any of the settings you change.

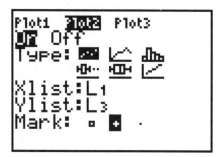

The room-temperature water data will then be plotted with + symbol.

e. Press ⌐ZOOM⌐ and then select **ZoomStat** (use cursor keys to scroll to **ZoomStat**) to draw a graph with the x and y ranges set to fill the screen with data.

f. Press ⌐TRACE⌐ to read values off of the plots. Press ⌐◄⌐ and ⌐►⌐ to trace along each plot. Switch between plots by pressing ⌐▲⌐ and ⌐▼⌐.

Analysis

1. Position the cursor at the beginning of the room-temperature water plot and find the y-intercept. Repeat for the warm-water plot. Round all values to three significant digits and record both y-intercepts in the Data Table on the *Data Collection and Analysis* sheet.

⇒ Answer Question 1 on the *Data Collection and Analysis* sheet.

2. Position the cursor on the room-temperature water plot. Use the cursor keys to identify two points (x_1, y_1) and (x_2, y_2) separated by at least five seconds. Record the coordinates in the Data Table on the *Data Collection and Analysis* sheet.

3. Switch to the warm water plot and identify two points from this line. Record the coordinates in the Data Table on the *Data Collection and Analysis* sheet.

4. When the coordinates of two points on a line are known, the slope of the line can be computed by finding the difference in y values divided by the difference in x values:

$$\text{slope} = \frac{y_2 - y_1}{x_2 - x_1}$$

Use this formula to compute the slope for each plot. Record your answers in the Data Table.

⇒ Answer Questions 2 and 3 on the *Data Collection and Analysis* sheet.

5. Now, have the calculator plot these two lines with the data.

   a. Press [Y=].

   b. Press [CLEAR] to remove any existing equation.

   c. Enter the equation for the warm-water plot. For example, if the slope and intercept were 4 and 5 respectively, enter 4*x+5.

   d. Press [ENTER] to move to the Y2 field, press [CLEAR], and enter the equation for the room-temperature plot.

   e. Press [GRAPH] to see the data with the model graphs superimposed.

⇒ Answer Questions 4-8 on the *Data Collection and Analysis* sheet.

Data Collection and Analysis

Name _____

Date _____

Activity 5: Keep It Bottled Up

Data Table

	x_1	y_1	x_2	y_2	y-intercept	slope
Room temp water						
Warm water						

Questions

1. What is the physical meaning of the y-intercept? Why is this value nearly same for both plots?

2. What is the physical meaning of the slopes of the pressure versus time plots?

3. The slope-intercept form of a linear equation is $y = mx + b$, where m is the slope of the line and b is the y-intercept. Use the information you found above to write linear equations to model the pressure versus time data:

   Equation for room-temperature water data _____

   Equation for warm water data _____

4. How well do the equations fit the data? You may wish to adjust the slope and/or intercept values slightly if you are not satisfied with the way the lines fit the data. If you adjust these values, rewrite the modeling equations below.

5.   What do you think the pressure versus time plot would look like after several minutes, if the stopper were left in the container?

     Would pressure continue to increase at a steady rate? Explain why or why not.

6.   What would the pressure versus time graph look like if the stopper popped off in the middle of the data collection?

7.   For a given water temperature, how do you think the plot would be affected if you used half a tablet?

     What if you used two tablets?

8.   Which plot indicates a faster rate of reaction? How can you tell?

Teacher Notes
Keep It Bottled Up: Linear Rates of Pressure Increase

1. An empty 500 mL soda bottle works well as the container.

2. If a smaller container is used, use less water and half a tablet.

3. Supervise the students as they take the container apart after a reaction. You may want to release the pressure by removing the plastic tubing from the pressure sensor connector before removing the stopper.

4. The gas producing ingredient in the effervescent tablet is sodium bicarbonate. Antacids that do not contain ingredient this cannot be used for the activity.

Sample Results

Actual data will vary.

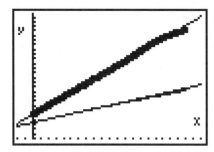

Raw data with both models

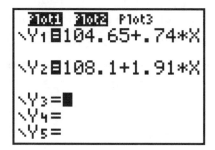

Model expressions

Data Table

Sample data; actual data may vary.

	x_1	y_1	x_2	y_2	y-intercept	slope
Room temp water	0	104.65	5.0	108.35	104	0.74
Warm water	0	108.10	5.0	117.65	108	1.91

Answers to Questions

1. The y-intercept is the initial pressure for both plots and is about 100 kPa. This is due to atmospheric pressure. That is the same for both experiments.

2. The slope of the pressure versus time plots measures the rate of pressure change. Presumably the pressure is due to the chemical reaction of the tablets.

3. Warm water equation: $y = 104.65 + 0.74x$
   Room-temperature water equation: $y = 108.1 + 1.91x$

4. The fit is good.

5. Once the chemical reaction stops (when the tablet is used up), the pressure would stop increasing. That is, the graphs would level off to a constant value.

6. If the stopper popped off, the measured pressure would drop back down to atmospheric pressure.

7. Half a tablet would have half the substance reacting, and so the rate of pressure increase would be lower than observed with a full tablet. For two tablets the rate of pressure increase would be higher than observed with one tablet.

8. The pressure increase is more rapid with the warm water; we can tell this from the higher slopes.

Activity 6

Graph It in Pieces: Piecewise-defined Functions

Objective

♦ Record motion data for a walker.

♦ Describe segments of the walker's motion using linear functions.

♦ Model the motion data using a piece-wise continuous function assembled from linear functions.

Materials

♦ TI-83 Plus, TI-83, or TI-73

♦ CBL 2™ or LabPro® data collection device

♦ DATAMATE software

♦ TI CBR™ or Vernier Motion Detector

♦ Meter stick

♦ Masking tape

Graphs of real-world data cannot always be described with one simple equation. Often the graph is made up of separate pieces which together describe an event. If you move back and forth in front of a motion detector, your motion could be described in separate pieces which together would describe the total motion. Functions which are defined in pieces are called *piecewise-defined functions*.

In this activity, you will create a graph by moving back and forth in front of a motion detector. You will then describe your motion by writing a piecewise-defined function for the motion.

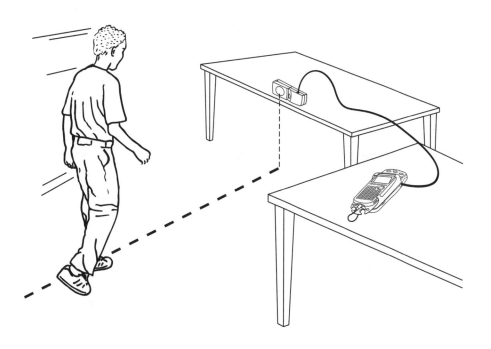

Procedure

1. Set up the motion detector on a table or desk. The detector should be aimed horizontally at a height of about 1.2 m. Use the meter stick and masking tape to mark ½ meter intervals from the detector. Write the distance from the detector on each piece of masking tape.

2. Plug the motion detector into the DIG/SONIC port of the CBL 2™ or the DIG/SONIC 1 port of the LabPro® interface. Use the link cable to connect the TI graphing calculator to the interface. Firmly press in the cable ends.

3. Turn on the calculator and start the DATAMATE software. Press CLEAR to reset the software.

4. Adjust the data collection time so you will have ten seconds to walk.

    a. Select **SETUP** from the main screen.

    b. Press ▲ to select mode.

    c. Press ENTER to change the data collection mode.

    d. Select **TIME GRAPH** from the SELECT MODE screen.

    e. Select **CHANGE TIME SETTINGS**.

    f. Enter **0.2** as the time between samples in seconds. Press ENTER.

    g. Enter **50** as the number of samples. Press ENTER.

    h. Select **OK** twice to return to the main screen.

5. Practice walking in the following manner: Stand about 1.5 m from the detector. When you hear the detector start to click, stand still for about four seconds. Then start walking slowly away from the detector at a uniform rate for about three seconds. Turn and walk slowly toward the detector until the clicking stops. Do not get any closer than 0.5 m to the detector.

6. Select **START** to begin data collection. You will hear the data collection device beep and the motion detector will begin to click. Walk as you practiced. Data collection will run for ten seconds.

7. Press ENTER to display the **DISTANCE** graph.

8. Examine the distance versus time graph. The graph should contain a series of three nearly straight-line regions. Check with your teacher if you are not sure whether you need to repeat the data collection.

    To repeat data collection, press ENTER to return to the graph selection screen, and select **MAIN SCREEN**. Select **START** to begin data collection.

9. Once you are satisfied with the graph, press ENTER to return to the graph selection screen, and select **MAIN SCREEN**. Select **QUIT** to leave DATAMATE. Follow any instructions on the calculator to return to the home screen.

Analysis

1. Redisplay the graph outside of DATAMATE.

    a. Press ZOOM .

    b. Press ▼ until **ZoomStat** is highlighted. Press ENTER to display a graph with the x and y ranges set to fill the screen with data.

    c. Press TRACE to determine the coordinates of a point on the graph using the cursor keys.

2. To create an equation that describes the motion shown in the plot, you will first need to write a linear equation for each section of the graph. Then you can put the pieces together to define a piecewise-defined function.

    Your walking instructions were in three parts, each describing uniform motion. So, to model the motion graph you should use three straight-line pieces. Each one will have the linear form $y = mx + b$, each with its own slope m and y-intercept b.

    Trace across the graph and find the x and y coordinates of the first point on the graph (x_1 and y_1). Trace to the end of the first section of the graph and find the coordinates of this point (x_2 and y_2). Record these two points in the Data Table on the *Data Collection and Analysis* sheet.

    ⇒ Answer Questions 1 and 2 on the *Data Collection and Analysis* sheet.

3. Check to see that this equation does fit the data for the first section of the graph. If the equation does not match the data for the first section of the graph, make adjustments to m or b so that it gives a better fit.

    a. Press Y= .

    b. Press CLEAR to remove any existing equation.

    c. Enter the equation for the segment. For example, for a slope of 3 and an intercept of 2, enter 3*x + 2.

    d. Press GRAPH to see the segment and data.

    e. Press 2nd [QUIT] to return to the home screen.

4. You have now matched the first segment of the graph. To do the same for the second segment, first turn off the plotting of the function for the first segment.

    a. Press Y= .

    b. Move to the equation with the cursor keys.

    c. To turn off the plotting of the function, press ◄ until the = sign is highlighted. Press ENTER to deselect the equation.

    d. Press 2nd [QUIT] to return to the home screen.

5. Redisplay the graph and trace across to the end of the second segment to get the coordinates of a point at the end of the segment (x_3 and y_3).

    a. Press GRAPH.

    b. Press TRACE to determine the coordinates of a point on the graph using the cursor keys.

    c. Press 2nd [QUIT].

    Record the point (x_3 and y_3) in the Data Table on the *Data Collection and Analysis* sheet.

6. The equation for the line matching the second segment can be determined from the points you have recorded. Since the point x_2, y_2 is also at the beginning of the second segment, you have enough information to determine the slope of this segment.

⇒ Answer Question 3 on the *Data Collection and Analysis* sheet.

7. You still need to find the y-intercept of this segment, but you cannot just trace to the y axis as you did before because this segment does not go that far. However, using the definition of slope we can write down the point slope form of a line, or $y - y_3 = m(x - x_3)$. Here y and x are variables, m the slope, and x_3 and y_3 are the values of a point on the line.

⇒ Use this relation to answer Question 4 on the *Data Collection and Analysis* sheet.

8. Enter the equation for the second segment in the Y2 equation register using the same method you did in Step 3, but press ▼ to use the Y2 line. Do not clear the Y1 equation. Observe the way the line fits the second segment of the graph, and adjust your slope and intercept values if needed.

9. Use the method from Step 4 to turn off the plotting of equation Y2.

10. Redisplay the graph and trace to the end of the third segment to read the coordinates of a point there (x_4 and y_4). Record the point (x_4 and y_4) in the Data Table.

⇒ Answer Question 5 on the *Data Collection and Analysis* sheet.

11. Enter the equation for the third line segment in the Y3 equation register, display its graph with the data, and adjust the slope and intercept if necessary. Turn off the plotting of equation Y3 when you are done.

12. So far you have created equations that fit the motion data in a piecewise manner. The next step is to combine those equations for plotting, each plotted only over the appropriate x range. Write down the x ranges over which you would like to plot each of your three equations Y1, Y2 and Y3.

13. The calculator can perform tests which will allow you to assemble the functions into one expression. The expression ($x < 1.2$) would be evaluated as 1 if x has a value less than 1.2, and otherwise would be evaluated as zero. Using this, you can force a function to be plotted only over the appropriate range. For example, **Y2**∗ ($x<1.2$) would only be graphed for x less than 1.2, and would be zero everywhere else.

In the following steps you can build an expression to plot the three lines as a piecewise defined function. Where you see x_2 and x_3 substitute the x values from the Data Table. For example, if you were to use values for x_2 and x_3 of 2.2 and 4.5, the expression for equation **Y4** would look something like this:

$$\mathbf{Y4} = \mathbf{Y1}∗(x<2.2) + \mathbf{Y2}∗(x{\geq}2.2 \text{ and } x{\leq}4.5) + \mathbf{Y3}∗(x>4.5)$$

You can understand this expression by looking at each product separately. Only the **Y1** equation will be plotted for $x < 2.2$, since the other equations are multiplied by zero. For x between 2.2 and 4.5, only **Y2** will be plotted, with **Y1** and **Y3** being multiplied by zero.

> ### TI-73

a. Press (Y=).

b. Move to equation **Y4** with the cursor keys.

c. Enter the following expression.

$$\mathbf{Y1}∗(x < x_2) + \mathbf{Y2}∗(x \geq x_2 \text{ and } x \leq x_3) + \mathbf{Y3}∗(x > x_3)$$

Enter the > symbols and the **and** function by pressing (2nd) [CATALOG] and selecting the desired symbol from the list. Enter equation labels like **Y1** by pressing (2nd) [VARS], and select **2:Y-Vars** to display the FUNCTION menu. Select the desired function name from the list. Remember to substitute your own values for x_2 and x_3.

d. Press (◄) until the icon to the left of **Y1** is blinking. Press (ENTER) until a bold diagonal line is shown to display the model with a thick line.

e. Press (GRAPH) to see the piecewise function plotted with the motion data.

f. Press (2nd) [QUIT] to return to the home screen.

⇒ Answer Questions 6-8 on the *Data Collection and Analysis* sheet.

> ### TI-83 and TI-83 Plus

a. Press (Y=).

b. Move to equation **Y4** with the cursor keys.

c. Enter the following expression.

$$Y_1*(x< x_2) + Y_2*(x \geq x_2 \text{ and } x \leq x_3) + Y_3*(x > x_3)$$

Enter the > symbols by pressing ⟨ 2nd ⟩ [TEST] and selecting the desired symbol from the menu. Enter equation labels like Y_1 by pressing ⟨ VARS ⟩, pressing ⟨ ▶ ⟩ to display the Y-VARS menu, and selecting **1:Function**. Select the desired function name from the list. Enter the and function by selecting ⟨ 2nd ⟩ [TEST] and pressing ⟨ ▶ ⟩ to display the LOGIC menu. Select and from the list. Remember to substitute your own values for x_2 and x_3.

d. Press ⟨ ◀ ⟩ until the icon to the left of Y_1 is blinking. Press ⟨ ENTER ⟩ until a bold diagonal line is shown to display the model with a thick line.

e. Press ⟨ GRAPH ⟩ to see the piecewise function plotted with the motion data.

f. Press ⟨ 2nd ⟩ [QUIT] to return to the home screen.

⇒ Answer Questions 6-8 on the *Data Collection and Analysis* sheet.

Extension

1. José created a distance versus time graph by starting at the 2-meter mark on the floor. He walked towards the detector at 0.25 m/s for 4 seconds, stood still for 2 seconds, walked away from the detector at 0.4 m/s for 2 seconds, and then stopped for 2 seconds. Sketch a plot of José's distance versus time graph.

2. What was José's ending position?

Data Collection and Analysis

Name _____

Date _____

Activity 6: Graph It in Pieces

Data Table

x_1		y_1	
x_2		y_2	

x_3		y_3	

x_4		y_4	

Questions

1. The slope of a line is given by the formula shown below. Calculate the slope of the first line segment between the points given.

$$m = \frac{y_2 - y_1}{x_2 - x_1}$$

2. Now determine the y-intercept of the first segment. That is easy this time, as the segment runs into the y axis. Use the y value of your first point to obtain the value for b, and write the equation for the first section of the graph below.

3. Use the method given in Question 1 to find the slope of the second segment.

    slope m_2 =

4. Write the equation of the line fitting the second segment in the traditional $y = mx + b$ form.

5. Use the same slope and point-slope relations to determine the slope and intercept of a line function that fits your third segment.

    slope m_3 =

    y-intercept =

6. Look at the slope values for each of the three functions. What is the physical interpretation of the slope in each section of the graph?

7. Look at the *y*-intercept value for the first equation. What is the physical interpretation of that value?

8. Using the values you just interpreted, describe how you had to walk to create the motion graph.

Teacher Notes
Graph It in Pieces: Piecewise-defined Functions

1. Either a TI CBR™ or a Vernier Motion Detector can be used in this activity. If a CBR is used, it must be connected through a CBL 2™ or a LabPro®, and not directly to the calculator.

2. The students are asked to create a distance versus time graph that contains three straight-line segments. The motion data will not be perfectly linear, so it is important to keep your students from trying again and again to get perfectly straight line segments. If some curvature is present in their graphs, they can still proceed to model the graph with line segments. The fit will be approximate, but the students will still gain experience in creating a piecewise defined function.

3. This activity uses the **TEST** and **LOGIC** functions of the calculators, which may be unfamiliar to your students. You may want to discuss the use of logic functions with your class.

4. The instructions in this activity become briefer as steps are repeated. This will help students generalize the very specific keystroke instructions given earlier, so that they can apply the steps to general problems in the future.

5. In Step 7 of the Analysis, students are using the point-slope form of the line equation. If you have not used this form with your students, you may want to review its use.

6. Some motion detectors will not be automatically identified by DATAMATE. If you are using such a detector, you must manually set up DATAMATE for the detector:

   a. Select **SETUP** from the main screen.

   b. Press ⬇ until the cursor is next to **DIG** (CBL 2) or **DIG1** (LabPro).

   c. Press ENTER to access the **SELECT SENSOR** menu.

   d. Select **MOTION(M)**.

   e. Select **OK** to return to the main screen.

Sample Results

Actual data will vary.

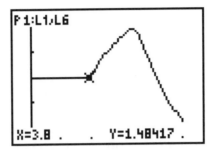

Distance data redisplayed

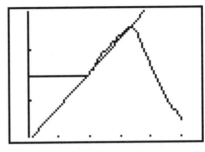

Distance data with second segment line

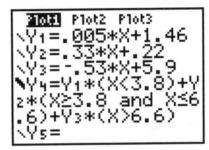

Completed model equations

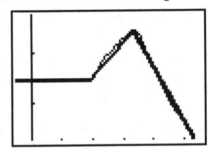

Piece-wise model plotted with motion data

Data Table

Sample data; actual data may vary.

x_1	0	y_1	1.46
x_2	3.8	y_2	1.48

x_3	6.6	y_3	2.41

x_4	10	y_4	0.60

Answers to Questions

1. $m = 0.005$

2. $y = 0.005x + 1.46$

3. $m_2 = 0.33$

4. If we use the third point as the point on the second segment, the point slope form of the line becomes $y - 2.4 = 0.33 (x - 6.6)$ which is rearranged to form $y = 0.33x + 0.22$.

5. $y = {}^-0.53x + 5.90$

6. The slope of each segment corresponds to the velocity of the walker during each segment. The unit of the slope is m/s, or meters/second, consistent with the interpretation of the slope as a velocity.

7. The initial y-intercept is the starting distance from the motion detector. The unit of the intercept is m, or meters.

8. To duplicate the graph shown here, the walker must perform these steps:

    a. Stand at a distance of 1.46 m from the detector for 3.8 s.

    b. Walk away from the detector at 0.33 m/s for 2.8 s.

    c. Walk toward the detector at 0.55 m/s (the negative is implied in the word "toward") for the remaining time.

Activity 7

Mix It Up: Mixing Liquids of Different Temperatures

Objective

♦ Record temperatures of water samples before and after mixing.

♦ Compare the mixing temperatures to a linear prediction.

Materials

♦ TI-83 Plus, TI-83, or TI-73

♦ CBL 2™ or LabPro® data collection device

♦ DATAMATE software

♦ 2 Temperature sensors

♦ Graduated measuring cup (in mL)

♦ Styrofoam™ cups or coffee mugs

♦ Hot and cold water

Suppose that a hot drink and a cold drink are mixed together and you would like to predict the temperature of the mixture. To do this, you need to know the temperatures of the drinks before they are mixed, T_1 and T_2, and the volumes of each used in the mixture, V_1 and V_2. A visual representation of the problem is shown below, where T_m represents the temperature of the mixture:

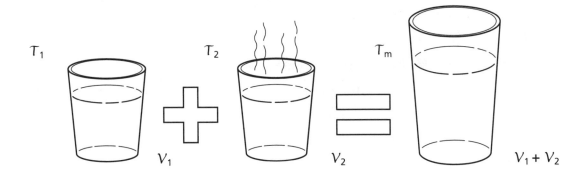

Translated into mathematical symbols, we have:

$$T_1V_1 + T_2V_2 = T_m(V_1 + V_2)$$

In this activity you will use the concepts described above to predict the resulting temperature when two solutions of different temperatures are mixed. The data needed to perform these calculations will be collected using a pair of temperature probes.

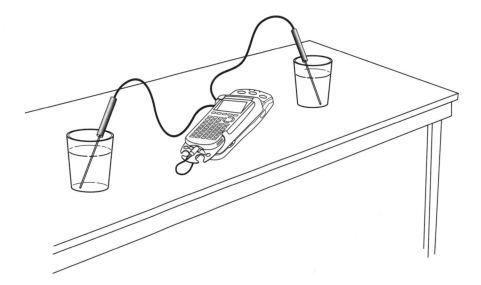

Procedure

1. Connect a temperature probe into each of CH 1 and CH 2 of the CBL 2™ or LabPro® data collection device. Use the unit-to-unit cable to connect the TI graphing calculator to the data collection device. Firmly press in the cable ends.

2. Turn on the calculator and start the DATAMATE software. Press CLEAR to reset the software.

3. Prepare DATAMATE to measure temperatures with the following steps:

    a. Select **SETUP** from the main screen. If CH 1 and CH 2 each display a temperature probe in units of C, skip to Step 4. If they do not, set up DATAMATE for the probes manually.

    b. Press ENTER to select CH 1.

    c. Choose **TEMPERATURE** from the **SELECT SENSOR** list.

    d. Choose the type of temperature probe you are using from the list, with units of C.

    e. Press ▼ to move the cursor to CH 2. Press ENTER to select it.

    f. Choose **TEMPERATURE** from the **SELECT SENSOR** list.

    g. Choose the type of temperature probe you are using from the list, with units of C.

4. Set DATAMATE to record temperature data in single points. In this mode DATAMATE will report a ten-second average on command.

    a. Press ▲ until the **MODE** option is highlighted.

    b. Press ENTER to enter the **SELECT MODE** screen.

    c. Select **SINGLE POINT** from the SELECT MODE menu.

    d. Select **OK** from the setup screen.

5. To test the expression $T_1V_1 + T_2V_2 = T_m(V_1 + V_2)$, you will record the temperature of water in two cups and then find the temperature when the contents of the cups are mixed together. Label one cup or mug as "Cup 1" and the other as "Cup 2."

6. Fill Cup 1 with 100 mL of cold water (about 10 °C) and Cup 2 with 150 mL of hot water (about 50 °C). Do not put any ice in the cold water cup.

7. Put the CH 1 probe in Cup 1, and the CH 2 probe in Cup 2. Observe the temperature readings on the main screen. When the readings are stable (0.1-level fluctuations are acceptable) select **START** from the main screen.

8. After ten seconds the averaged temperature readings will be displayed. Record the averaged temperature readings in the Data Table on the *Data Collection and Analysis* sheet.

   Press ENTER to return to the main screen.

9. Mix the water. Work quickly through the next steps.

   a. Remove the temperature probe from Cup 1 and set the probe aside.

   b. Quickly pour the contents of Cup 1 into Cup 2, keeping the probe in Cup 2.

   c. Watch the temperature reading on CH 2 on the main screen. When it stops changing rapidly, select **START** to make a ten-second measurement. Record the average value in the Data Table on the *Data Collection and Analysis* sheet.

   d. Press ENTER to return to the main screen, and select **QUIT** to leave DATAMATE. Follow any instructions on the screen to return to the calculator's home screen.

   e. Remove the probe from the water, and discard the water.

Analysis

⇒ Answer the Questions 1-7 on the *Data Collection and Analysis* sheet.

Extension

Repeat the activity, this time starting with equal amounts of water in Cup 1 and Cup 2. Summarize the volumes used and temperatures measured in a data table. Based on your explanation in Question 7, how might you predict the mixture temperature, given that Cup 1 and Cup 2 contained equal volumes and knowing the temperatures T_1 and T_2? Is your prediction consistent with the measured mixture value?

Data Collection and Analysis

Name _____

Date _____

Activity 7: Mix It Up

Data Table

Volumes Used (in mL)		Temperatures Measured (in °C)	
Cup 1 (V_1)		Cup 1 (T_1)	
Cup 2 (V_2)		Cup 2 (T_2)	
		Mixture (T_m)	

Questions

1. Consider the equation $T_1V_1 + T_2V_2 = T_m(V_1 + V_2)$ relating volumes and temperatures for mixed solutions. Solve this equation for the mixture temperature T_m.

2. Use this result, along with the values for the initial temperatures and volumes for the water samples, to predict the temperature of the mixture.

3. How does this value compare to the measured value of T_m listed in the Data Table? What might have caused the difference between the calculated and measured mixture temperature values?

4. What is the average of the cold and warm water temperatures, T_1, and T_2, used in this activity? Calculate this value and record it below:

5. Suppose that you wish to repeat this activity under identical conditions, this time adding exactly the right amount of warm water to Cup 1 so that the mixture temperature, T_m, equals the average temperature value recorded above. Should more or less warm water be added to Cup 1 for this trial compared to the amount you used in the original trial? Why?

6. Exactly what volume of warm water, V_2, should be added to Cup 1 so that the mixture temperature equals the average of T_1 and T_2?
    Hint: To do this, you will need to solve the mixture equation for V_2.

7. How does the value of V_2 found in Question 6 compare to the Cup 1 water volume, V_1?

    Why does using equal volumes of water ensure that the mixture temperature will be the average of the cold and warm water temperatures? Justify your answer algebraically. **Hint:** Let $V_1 = V_2$.

Applications

1. The directions on a box of instant cocoa tell you to prepare the drink by adding 150 mL of hot water to the package contents. What amounts of cold water (8 °C) and boiling water (100 °C) should be combined to add 150 mL of 68 °C water to the cocoa mix?

2. Suppose the thermostat of your school's swimming pool malfunctions, causing the water temperature to climb to 34 °C. The recommended temperature for competition is 25 °C. If the pool holds 750,000 liters of water, how many liters must be drained from the pool and replaced with tap water (6 °C) to make it ready for competition?

3. Some types of mixture problems involve combining solutions made up of different percentages of a substance in order to get a mixture with the desired percentage of that substance. The method is the same as that used in the activity you just completed. Solve the following mixture problem.

    Solution A is 5% acid. Solution B is 17% acid. A chemist wants to mix the two to get 500 mL of a solution that is 12% acid. How much of each should be used?

Teacher Notes
Mix it Up: Mixing Liquids of Different Temperatures

1. There should be a significant temperature difference between the water in the two cups. For best results, one cup should contain water that is above room temperature and the other should contain water that is below room temperature. This will minimize errors due to heat transfer between the room and the water.

2. Cold and hot tap water will work well for this activity. It is important that there be no ice in the cold water, as the phase change makes the formula given inapplicable.

3. You may wish to use different amounts of water than those specified in the instruction section. Be sure that the cups you are using are large enough to hold the combined mixture volume.

4. Have the students work quickly as soon as they begin to collect data to minimize heat transfer errors.

Data Table

Sample data; actual data may vary.

Volumes Used (mL)		Temperatures Measured (°C)	
Cup 1 (V_1)	100	Cup 1 (T_1)	16.7
Cup 2 (V_2)	150	Cup 2 (T_2)	64.8
		Mixture (T_m)	45.2

Answers to Questions

1. $$V_2 = \frac{V_1(T_1 - T_m)}{T_m - T_2}$$

2. From the expression above, we get $T_m = 45.6$ °C.

3. The measured value is a little lower than the predicted value. Perhaps this is due to the warm water cooling as we worked.

4. The average is 40.75 °C.

5. If the goal is to get a sample of water of this temperature, we would need to add less warm water than before since the mixture we created was warmer than this average.

6. Solving the expression for V_2 we get $V_2 = \frac{V_1(T_1 - T_m)}{T_m - T_2}$. If $T_m = (T_1 + T_2)/2$, then a little algebra shows that $V_2 = V_1$.

7. Going back to the original expression of $T_1V_1 + T_2V_2 = T_m(V_1 + V_2)$, if we let $V_2 = V_1$, then a little more algebra shows that $T_m = (T_1 + T_2)/2$.

EXPLORATIONS

Activity 8

Spring Thing: Newton's Second Law

Objective

♦ Collect force and motion data for a bob moving at the end of a light spring.

♦ Compare the force and acceleration data to test Newton's second law.

♦ Use Newton's second law to estimate the mass of an object.

Materials

♦ TI-83 Plus, TI-83, or TI-73

♦ CBL 2™ or LabPro® data collection device

♦ DATAMATE software

♦ TI CBR™ or Vernier Motion Detector

♦ Vernier Dual-Range Force Sensor or Student Force Sensor

♦ Ring stand

♦ Light spring or Slinky™

♦ Standard mass hanger

If you push or pull an object (and yours is the only force on the object), the way it changes its motion depends on two things: the *force* you apply, and the object's *mass*. Sir Isaac Newton was the first to recognize that an object's acceleration is directly proportional to the total force applied (the larger the force, the more rapidly it speeds up or slows down), and inversely proportional to its mass (massive objects have a greater tendency to resist efforts to make them speed up or slow down). Stated mathematically, that is $F = ma$ where F is the force applied to the object, m is its mass, and a is its acceleration. This expression is known as Newton's second law.

In this activity, you will use a force sensor and a motion detector to record force and acceleration data for an object (called the *bob*) moving up and down hanging from a light spring. This data will be used to test the mathematical relationship of Newton's second law.

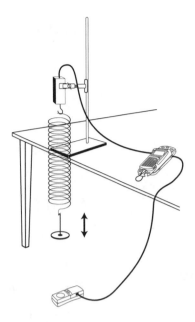

Procedure

1. Set up the apparatus.

    a. Attach the force sensor to a ring stand so that the sensor hangs well over the edge of the table. The hook must be pointing straight down.

    b. Hang the spring from the hook, and hang the bob from the spring.

    c. Position the motion detector directly under the bob so that the disc is pointing upward. When the bob is at rest, the distance from the bob to the detector should be between 0.7 and 1.0 m.

2. Prepare the force sensor and the motion detector for data collection.

    a. Connect the force sensor into CH 1 of the CBL 2™ or LabPro® data collection device.

    b. If you are using a Dual Range Force Sensor, set the range switch to 10 N.

    c. Connect the motion detector to the DIG/SONIC port of the CBL 2 or the DIG/SONIC1 port of the LabPro.

    d. Use the unit-to-unit cable to connect the TI graphing calculator to the data collection device. Firmly press in the cable ends.

3. Turn on the calculator and start the DATAMATE software. Press CLEAR to reset the software.

4. Set up DATAMATE for the force sensor.

    a. Select **SETUP** from the main screen. If the setup screen shows both force and motion, skip to Step 5.

    b. Press ENTER to select **CH 1**.

    c. Select **FORCE** from the SELECT SENSOR menu.

    d. Select the correct force sensor (**DUAL R FORCE 10(N)** or **STUDENT FORCE(N)**) from the FORCE menu.

5. In this activity you only want to measure the force it takes to accelerate the bob, as opposed to just support it while hanging motionless. To account for the weight of the spring and bob, you need to zero the force sensor.

   a. Check to see that the bob is not moving.

   b. Select **ZERO** from the setup screen.

   c. Select **CH1:FORCE** from the select channel screen.

   d. Wait until the bob stops moving. Press ENTER to zero the force sensor. All subsequent force measurements will be referenced from the current force on the sensor.

6. You are now ready to collect distance, velocity, acceleration, and force versus time data.

   a. Lift the bob no more than 10 cm and release it. Wait until the bob is moving up and down smoothly.

   b. Select **START** to begin data collection, which will run for five seconds.

7. After data collection is done, press ENTER from the graph selection screen to see a distance versus time graph. You should see a smooth sinusoidal function. If you want to repeat data collection, press ENTER, select **MAIN SCREEN**, and return to Step 6.

Analysis

1. View each of the force, distance, velocity and acceleration graphs in turn by pressing ENTER and selecting the desired graph from the DATAMATE graph selection screen. Pay particular attention to the times that each function reaches a maximum, minimum and a zero.

   ⇒ Sketch these graphs in the spaces shown in Question 1 on the *Data Collection and Analysis* sheet.

   When you are done sketching, select **MAIN SCREEN** and select **QUIT** to leave DATAMATE. Follow any instructions on the calculator to return to the home screen.

   ⇒ Answer Questions 2-4 on the *Data Collection and Analysis* sheet.

2. The graphs are all a quantity versus time. However, that is not the only way the data can be graphed. To predict what a graph of force versus acceleration would look like, consider any specific time on your graphs. What values do the force and acceleration have? Imagine plotting a point on a new force versus acceleration graph using the values at that particular time. Now consider other times. As you build up the graph using all times, what would the resulting graph look like?

   ⇒ Answer Question 5 on the *Data Collection and Analysis* sheet.

3. Display a new graph of force versus acceleration.

     a. Press ⌈2nd⌉ [STAT PLOT] ([PLOT] on the TI-73) and press ⌈ENTER⌉ to select **Plot 1**.

     b. Change the **Plot1** settings to match the screen shown here. Press ⌈ENTER⌉ to select any of the settings you change.

        On the TI-73 press ⌈2nd⌉ [STAT] and scroll down to highlight **L8**. Press ⌈ENTER⌉ to paste **L8** to the **Plot1** settings screen. **L8** contains your acceleration data, and **L2** contains the force data.

        On the TI-83 series, enter **L8** by pressing ⌈2nd⌉ [LIST] and scroll down to highlight **L8**. Press ⌈ENTER⌉ to paste **L8** to the **Plot1** settings screen.

     c. Press ⌈ZOOM⌉ and then select **ZoomStat** (use cursor keys to scroll to **ZoomStat**) to draw a graph with the x and y ranges set to fill the screen with data.

⇒ Answer Questions 6 and 7 on the *Data Collection and Analysis* sheet.

4. You can fit a model of $y = mx$ to the force versus acceleration data using trial and error for the parameter m.

     a. Press ⌈Y=⌉.

     b. Press ⌈CLEAR⌉ to remove any existing equation.

     c. Enter **M∗X** on the **Y1** line. (On the TI-73, access the alphabetic entry screen by pressing ⌈2nd⌉ [TEXT].)

     d. Press ⌈2nd⌉ [QUIT] to return to the home screen.

5. Set a value for the parameter m, and then look at the resulting graph. To obtain a good fit, you will need to try several values for m. Use the steps below to store different values to the parameter m. Start with $m = 0.2$.

     a. Enter the value for the parameter m. Press ⌈STO▶⌉ M ⌈ENTER⌉ to store the value in the variable **M**.

     b. Press ⌈GRAPH⌉ to see your data with the model graph superimposed.

     c. Press ⌈2nd⌉ [QUIT] to return to the home screen.

     d. Repeat Steps a through c using different values. Experiment until you find one that provides a good fit for the data. Record this optimized value of m in the Data Table.

⇒ Answer Questions 8-10 on the *Data Collection and Analysis* sheet.

Extension

For a spring, the force *F* applied by the spring, and the amount of stretch, x, are related by Hooke's law, or $F = -kx$. The constant k is called the spring constant. The spring constant measures the stiffness of the spring—a stiff spring with a large k applies a large force when it is stretched or compressed even a little bit. An example of a spring with a large k is a suspension spring on an automobile, while the spring in a retractable pen has a small k.

Make a plot of force (**L2**) versus position (**L6**) and determine the value of k that fits the data. What are the units of k?

Data Collection and Analysis

Name _____

Date _____

Activity 8: Spring Thing

Data Table

m	
bob mass (kg)	

Questions

1. In the spaces below, make a sketch of each of the force, distance, velocity and acceleration graphs. You may want to start your sketch by marking the times of each maximum, minimum and zero crossings on the graph. Then you can fill in the remaining details of the graphs.

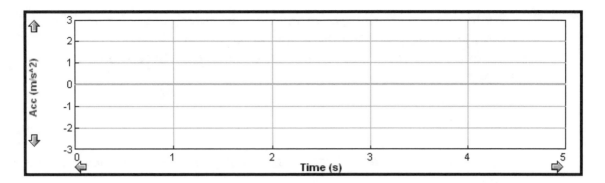

2. Inspect the graphs of distance, velocity and acceleration versus time. Where is the bob located when acceleration is greatest? What is the velocity at that time?

3. Can the velocity be zero at the same time that the acceleration is non-zero? Explain why or why not.

   Do you have evidence from the graphs? _____

4. Inspect the four graphs. All four should be variations on a sinusoidal function, with varying phases and amplitudes. Which two graphs share the same phase? That is, which two are always in step?
   Hint: Which two variables are addressed by Newton's second law?

5. As you build up the graph of force versus acceleration using all times, what would the resulting graph look like?

6. What does the graph tell you about the way force and acceleration are related? Is the graph consistent with your prediction in Question 5?

7. Is the data consistent with Newton's second law, which reads $F = ma$. That is, Newton's second law says that force and acceleration are directly proportional. Does your graph show proportionality between force and acceleration?

8. What is the mass of the bob? Enter this value in the Data Table shown above, in units of kg.

9. How does the mass of the bob compare to the optimized value of the parameter m for the force versus acceleration graph? In what way does this comparison of values confirm Newton's second law?

10. It is likely that the value of the parameter m is somewhat larger than the mass of the bob. How can you explain this difference?
    Hint: Is anything bouncing up and down with the bob?

Teacher Notes
Spring Thing: Newton's Second Law

1. Suspend the hanging bob directly above the motion detector. Do not allow the bob to come closer than 50 cm to the motion detector during data collection.

2. You may want to place a wire basket over the motion detector to protect it from falling weights.

3. Although it is possible to acquire good data with a hand-held force sensor, data will be more consistently high quality if the force sensor is suspended from a ring stand or other rigid support.

4. It is useful to have high-quality sketches of the four graphs so that students can accurately determine the phase relationship between the four functions. The calculator cannot display four graphs simultaneously, so the students are asked to sketch their data. You may choose to have students transfer data to a computer using TI InterActive!™ or Vernier Graphical Analysis. The sample data shown here are graphed with Graphical Analysis.

5. Either a Slinky™ with a light bob (about 50 g) or a slightly stiffer spring (about 3 N/m stiffness) with a larger bob (200 g) can be used. The key is that the combination of spring and bob yields several cycles during the 5 s data collection. One spring that works well is the Harmonic Motion Spring from VWR International, http://www.vwrsp.com/.

6. If the acceleration data is too noisy, try making the reflection from the bob stronger. An old CD or an index card can be taped to the bottom of the bob, although too large a surface will add damping forces.

7. The values obtained for the slope parameter m are almost always larger than the mass of the bob due to the moving mass of the spring. In the limit of a mass-less spring, then the bob mass and the slope would be the same. Detailed analysis shows that 1/3 of the mass of a uniform spring should be added to the mass of the bob for comparison to the slope m.

8. Either a TI CBR™ or a Vernier Motion Detector can be used. The CBR must be connected to an data collection device and not directly to the calculator.

9. Some motion detectors will not be automatically identified by DATAMATE. If you are using such a detector, you must manually set up DATAMATE for the detector:

    a. Select **SETUP** from the main screen.

    b. Press ⬇ until the cursor is next to DIG (CBL 2™) or DIG1 (LabPro®).

    c. Press ENTER to access the **SELECT SENSOR** menu.

    d. Select **MOTION(M)**.

    e. Select **OK** to return to the **MAIN SCREEN**.

Sample Results

Actual data will vary.

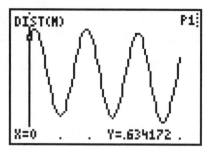

Distance data in DATAMATE

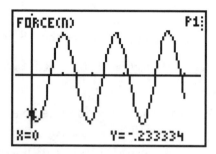

Force data in DATAMATE

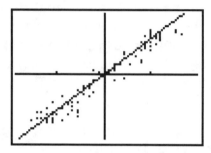

Force versus acceleration data
with model

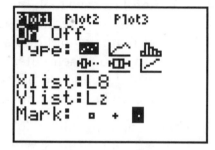

Graph settings for force versus
acceleration

Data Table

Sample data; actual data may vary.

m	0.22
bob mass (kg)	0.200 kg

Answers to Questions

1. Motion and force data graphed in Vernier Graphical Analysis. Note that the
    time cursor is at the same time in each graph, clearly showing the phase
    relationship between graphs.

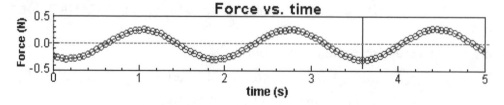

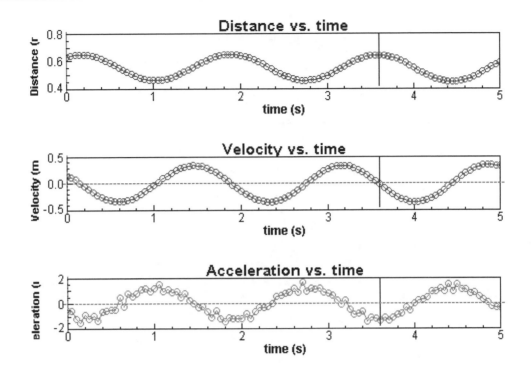

2. When the acceleration is at a maximum, the bob is located at a minimum position. The velocity at that time is zero.

3. The velocity can clearly be zero when there is a non-zero acceleration—the time discussed in the previous question is an example. The acceleration is calculated from the rate of change of velocity, not the value of the velocity.

4. The force and acceleration graphs are in the same phase.

5. Since the force and acceleration graphs are in phase, a graph of force versus acceleration would be a straight line going through the origin. When force is at a positive maximum, so is the acceleration, and vice versa.

6. The graph of force versus acceleration shows points generally on a line going through the origin. That is consistent with my prediction in Question 5.

7. Yes, the data is consistent with Newton's second law, $F = ma$. Newton's second law is a simple proportionality, so a graph of force versus acceleration should be a line passing through the origin of slope m.

9. The bob mass is slightly less than the optimum value for the parameter m, but they are still within 10%.

10. The spring has mass, so that perhaps the mass of the spring is combined with the mass of the bob.

EXPLORATIONS

Activity 9

Stretch It to the Limit: The Linear Force Relation for a Rubber Band

Objective

♦ Record force versus stretch data for a rubber band.

♦ Model force versus stretch data with a proportional relationship.

Materials

♦ TI-83 Plus, TI-83, or TI-73

♦ CBL 2™ or LabPro® data collection device

♦ DATAMATE software

♦ TI CBR™ or Vernier Motion Detector

♦ Vernier Dual-Range Force Sensor or Student Force Sensor

♦ Ring stand

♦ 1 Long rubber band (or 3 smaller rubber bands)

When a force is applied to a rubber band, it stretches a certain amount. Exactly how much it stretches depends on the applied force and the characteristics of the rubber band. In general, the more force that is applied, the more it stretches. For rubber bands that are not stretched too much, if you double the force applied, it turns out that the stretch doubles as well. Two quantities, x and y, that change in this way are said to be *proportional*. x and y are related by the constant K in the equation

$$y = Kx$$

In this activity you will use a force sensor and a motion detector to investigate the relationship between the force applied to a rubber band and the distance that the rubber band stretches. To measure how much a rubber band has stretched, we will use the stretched length of the band minus the relaxed length of the band.

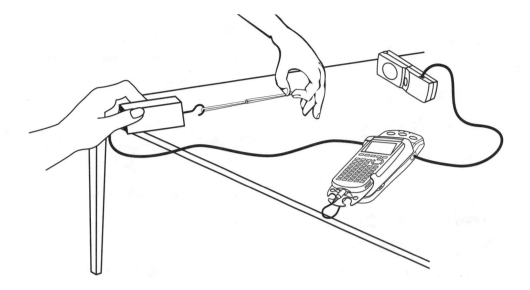

Procedure

1. For this activity, you will stretch and relax a rubber band with your hand. A motion detector records the amount the rubber band is stretched while a force sensor measures the force of your pull. Be sure not to get closer than 50 cm to the motion detector during data collection. The rubber band being used should be flexible enough to stretch at least 15 cm. Several smaller rubber bands linked together also work well for this activity.

2. Prepare the force sensor and motion detector for data collection.

    a. Connect the force sensor to CH 1 of the CBL 2™ or LabPro® data collection device.

    b. If you are using a Dual Range Force Sensor, set the range switch to 10 N.

    c. Connect the motion detector to the DIG/SONIC port of the CBL 2 or the DIG/SONIC 1 port of the LabPro data collection device.

    d. Use the unit-to-unit link cable to connect the TI graphing calculator to the interface. Firmly press in the cable ends.

3. Turn on the calculator and start the DATAMATE software. Press CLEAR to reset the software.

4. Set up the calculator and data collection device for the force sensor.

    a. Select **SETUP** from the main screen.

    b. If the setup screen lists the force sensor, skip to Step 5.

    c. Press ENTER to select **CH 1**.

    d. Select **FORCE** from the SELECT SENSOR menu.

    e. Select the correct force sensor (**DUAL R FORCE 10(N)** or **STUDENT FORCE(N)**) from the FORCE menu.

5. To account for the relaxed length of the rubber band, you need to zero both sensors. To do this you have to hold your hands in the position they will be in when data collection begins. You may need to have another person operate the calculator during these steps. Keep in mind that your hand must never get closer than 50 cm to the motion detector during data collection, so allow enough room to stretch the rubber band during the activity.

   a. Hold the force sensor with your right hand as shown in the drawing, or fix it to a ring stand. The force sensor should not move during data collection. With your left hand hold the rubber band so that it is just barely taut. Your left hand must be directly between the force sensor and the motion detector. Keep your hands in this position for now.

   b. Select **ZERO** from the setup screen.

   c. Select **ALL CHANNELS** from the SELECT CHANNEL screen.

   d. Keep your left hand still, and press (ENTER) to zero the sensors. This will measure all future distance measurements from the position of your left hand, and all force measurements from the current force, which will be near zero. Do not move your hand from this position until you begin taking data in the next step.

6. You are now ready to collect force versus stretch distance data.

   a. Select **START** to begin data collection. Data collection will run for five seconds.

   b. Gently stretch and relax the rubber band, moving your left hand along a line between the force sensor and the motion detector. Do not let your hand get any closer than 50 cm from the motion detector.

7. After data collection is complete, a menu of available graphs will be displayed. Press (ENTER) to see a graph of the force as a function of time. Press (ENTER) to return to the graph selection screen, and press (▼) (ENTER) to see the distance versus time graph.

   If you want to repeat data collection, press (ENTER), select **MAIN SCREEN**, and return to Step 6.

8. If you are satisfied with the data, press (ENTER) and select **MAIN SCREEN**. Select **QUIT** to leave DATAMATE. Follow instructions on the screen to return to the calculator home screen.

9. The graphs shown by DATAMATE are functions of time. That is not what you need, however, since you want force versus distance. To display that graph, you will need to change your graph settings.

   The distance data reflects the additional stretch of the rubber band. However, because the motion detector measures distances as increasing *away* from the detector, you will need to change the sign of the distance data stored in **L6**.

▷ **TI-73**

a. Press ⸨(−)⸩ ⸨2nd⸩ [STAT].

b. Select the list **L6** by pressing the digit next to **L6** (usually 6).

c. Press ⸨STO▸⸩ ⸨2nd⸩ [STAT].

d. Again select the list **L6** by pressing the digit next to **L6** (usually 6) to complete the expression **– L6** → **L6**.

e. Press ⸨ENTER⸩ to complete the operation.

▷ **TI-83 and TI-83 Plus**

a. Press ⸨(−)⸩ ⸨2nd⸩ [**L6**] ⸨STO▸⸩ ⸨2nd⸩ [**L6**] to enter the expression **– L6** → **L6**.

b. Press ⸨ENTER⸩ to complete the operation.

10. Now you can plot the force used to stretch the rubber band versus the distance the band was stretched.

a. Press ⸨2nd⸩ [STAT PLOT] ([PLOT] on the TI-73) and press ⸨ENTER⸩ to select **Plot 1**.

b. Change the **Plot1** settings to match the screen shown here. Press ⸨ENTER⸩ to select any of the settings you change.

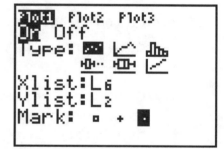

c. Press ⸨ZOOM⸩ and then select **ZoomStat** (use cursor keys to scroll to **ZoomStat**) to draw a graph with the x and y ranges set to fill the screen with data.

Analysis

As mentioned earlier, an approximate model for force and stretch holds that they are proportional. To test this, try plotting the line of proportionality $y = Kx$ with the data.

1. First, enter the equation.

a. Press ⸨Y=⸩.

b. Press ⸨CLEAR⸩ to remove any existing equation.

c. Enter **K∗x** in the **Y1** line. (On the TI-73, access the alphabetic entry screen by pressing ⸨2nd⸩ [TEXT].)

d. Press ⸨2nd⸩ [QUIT] to return to the home screen.

2. Next set a value for the parameter K, and then look at the resulting graph. Begin by using a slope of one, so $K = 1$.

a.   Enter a value for the parameter K. Press `STO ▸` K `ENTER` to store the value in the variable **K**.

b.   Press `GRAPH` to see your data with the model graph superimposed.

c.   Press `2nd` [QUIT] to return to the home screen.

To obtain a good fit, you will need to try several values for K. Repeat Steps a-c to store different values to the parameter K. Experiment until you find one that provides a good fit for the data.

⇒ Answer Question 1 on the *Data Collection and Analysis* page.

3.   The K value may also be determined algebraically by substituting the x and y values of one point into the variation equation, $y = Kx$.

a.   Press `GRAPH` `TRACE` to enter trace mode.

b.   Use the cursor keys to move the cursor to a point near the middle of the graph. If the cursor is on the line rather than the data points, press `▲` to shift the focus to the data points. Round the x and y values of this point to the nearest hundredth and record them in the Data Table on the *Data Collection and Analysis* sheet. Use these values to solve for K, and write this value in the Data Table.

⇒ Answer Question 2 on the *Data Collection and Analysis* sheet.

4.   In addition to your two estimates of the parameter K, you can use the calculator to automatically determine the slope and intercept of a straight line. This line can be fit to the data using the steps below.

TI-73

a.   Press `2nd` [STAT] and use the cursor keys to highlight **CALC**.

b.   Press the number adjacent to **LinReg(ax+b)** to copy the command to the home screen.

c.   After the **LinReg(ax+b)** command, press `2nd` [STAT] and select **L6** by pressing the number next to **L6** . Then press `,`. Repeat the procedure to select **L2**.

d.   After selecting **L2**, press `,` then press `2nd` [VARS].

e.   Use the cursor keys to select **Y-Vars** and press `ENTER` .

f.   Press `ENTER` to select **Y1** and copy it to the expression.

On the home screen, you will now see the entry **LinReg(ax+b) L6, L2, Y1**. This command will perform a linear regression with **L6** as the x-values and **L2** as the y-values. The resulting regression line will be stored in equation variable **Y1**.

g.   Press ENTER to perform the linear regression.

⇒   Record the regression equation with its parameters in Question 3 on the *Data Collection and Analysis* sheet.

h.   Press GRAPH to see the graph.

⇒   Answer Questions 4-7 on the *Data Collection and Analysis* sheet.

TI-83 and TI-83 Plus

a.   Press STAT and use the cursor keys to highlight **CALC**.

b.   Press the number adjacent to **LinReg(ax+b)** to copy the command to the home screen.

c.   Press 2nd [L6] , 2nd [L2] , to enter the lists containing your data.

d.   Press VARS and use the cursor keys to highlight **Y-VARS**.

e.   Select **Function** by pressing ENTER.

f.   Press ENTER to copy **Y1** to the expression.

On the home screen, you will now see the entry **LinReg(ax+b) L6, L2, Y1**. This command will perform a linear regression using the x-values in **L6** and the y-values in **L2**. The resulting regression line will be stored in equation variable **Y1**.

g.   Press ENTER to perform the linear regression.

⇒   Record the regression equation with its parameters in Question 3 on the *Data Collection and Analysis* sheet.

h.   Press GRAPH to see the graph.

⇒   Answer Questions 4-7 on the *Data Collection and Analysis* sheet.

Extension

As you were recording motion and force data for the stretched and relaxed rubber band, time values were being recorded simultaneously by the data collection device. In fact, this data was shown to you immediately after data collection.

Restart DATAMATE and inspect the force versus time graph. This plot shows how force values varied with time while you were pulling on the rubber band.

Make a prediction about what a plot of stretch distance versus time would look like. Check your prediction by displaying the distance graph. How is the stretch distance versus time plot related to the force versus time plot? Be specific.

Data Collection and Analysis

Name _____

Date _____

Activity 9: Stretch It to the Limit

Data Table

x	
y	
K	

Questions

1. Record the value of K that fits the data best.

   $K =$ _____

2. Are the K values in Question 1 and the Data Table consistent? What might cause them to be slightly different?

3. Record the regression equation with its parameters from Step 4.

4. How does the slope in the linear regression compare with the K values in Question 1 and the Data Table? What should be the value of the y-intercept from the regression? Explain.

5. Which equation seems to fit better? Which equation is a better direct variation model? Why?

6. Explain why the graph is linear even though you stretched the rubber band back and forth in front of the motion detector.

7. How would the data be affected if you used a stiffer, less flexible rubber band? How would this change the K value?

Teacher Notes
Stretch It to the Limit: The Linear Force Relation for a Rubber Band

1. A TI CBR™ can be used in place of a Vernier Motion Detector in this experiment. The CBR must be connected to the data collection device, and not directly to the calculator.

2. To stretch and relax the rubber band, grasp it with your fingertips or loop it around one finger. The back of your hand should be facing the motion detector. During data collection your hand must remain perpendicular to the table surface.

3. The rubber band must remain taut during data collection. If it goes slack the linear relationship between force and distance will not hold.

4. Some motion detectors will not be automatically identified by DATAMATE. If you are using such a detector, you must manually set up DATAMATE for the detector:

   a. Select **SETUP** from the main screen.

   b. Press ⟨ ▼ ⟩ until the cursor is next to DIG (CBL 2™) or DIG1 (LabPro®).

   c. Press ⟨ENTER⟩ to access the SELECT SENSOR menu.

   d. Select **MOTION(M)**.

   e. Select **OK** to return to the main screen.

Sample Results

Actual data will vary.

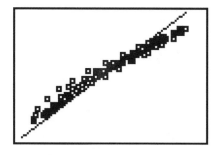

Raw data with proportional model

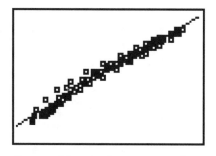

Data with calculator regression

Data Table

Sample data; actual data may vary.

x	0.13
y	3.14
K	24

Answers to Questions

1. Optimal value for K will depend on the rubber band used.

2. The slope obtained by using all the points in the previous step may well be different from the slope obtained by using a single point. The new line passes through one point exactly, and may pass near other points.

3. $y = 0.68 + 18.7x$

4. The slope from the linear regression is close to that of the model and single point K. The y-intercept should be close to zero since a line of proportionality passes through the origin.

5. The linear regression is a slightly better fit due to the extra parameter. The $y = Kx$ model fits the physical experiment better, however, since at zero stretch the band requires zero force.

6. The force versus stretch graph does not show time. The band was stretched back and forth in time.

7. A stiffer rubber band requires more force to stretch, so its K would be larger. The same proportional relationship between force and distance should hold, however.

EXPLORATIONS

Activity 10

What Goes Up: Position and Time for a Cart on a Ramp

Objective

- ♦ Record position versus time data for a cart rolling up and down a ramp.

- ♦ Determine an appropriate parabolic model for the position data using the x- and y-intercept information.

Materials

- ♦ TI-83 Plus, TI-83, or TI-73

- ♦ CBL 2™ or LabPro® data collection device

- ♦ DATAMATE software

- ♦ TI CBR™ or Vernier Motion Detector

- ♦ 4-wheeled cart

- ♦ Board or track at least 1.2 m

- ♦ Books to support ramp

When a cart is given a brief push up a ramp, it will roll back down again after reaching its highest point. Algebraically, the relationship between the position and elapsed time for the cart is quadratic in the general form

$$y = ax^2 + bx + c$$

where y represents the position of the cart on the ramp and x represents the elapsed time. The quantities a, b, and c are parameters which depend on such things as the inclination angle of the ramp and the cart's initial speed. Although the cart moves back and forth in a straight-line path, a plot of its position along the ramp graphed as a function of time is parabolic.

Parabolas have several important points including the vertex (the maximum or minimum point), the y-intercept (where the function crosses the y-axis), and the x-intercepts (where the function crosses the x-axis). The x- and y-intercepts are related to the parameters a, b, and c given in the equation above according to the following properties:

1. The y-intercept is equal to the parameter c.

2. The product of the x-intercepts is equal to the ratio $\dfrac{c}{a}$.

3. The sum of the x-intercepts is equal to $-\dfrac{b}{a}$.

These properties mean that if you know the x- and y-intercepts of a parabola, you can find its general equation.

In this activity, you will use a motion detector to measure how the position of a cart on a ramp changes with time. When the cart is freely rolling, the position versus time graph will be parabolic, so you can analyze this data in terms of the key locations on the parabolic curve.

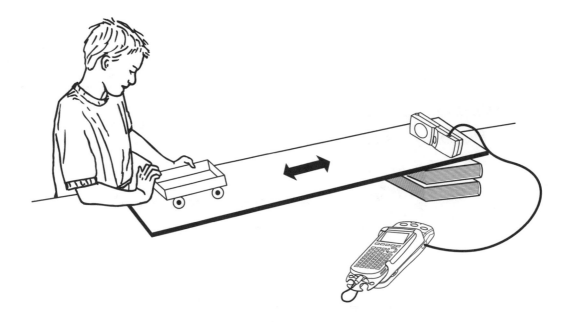

Procedure

1. Place one or two books beneath one end of the board to make an inclined ramp. The inclination angle should be only a few degrees. Place the motion detector at the top of the ramp. Remember that the cart must never get closer than 0.4 m to the detector, so if you have a short ramp you may want to use another object to support the detector.

2. Connect the motion detector into the DIG/SONIC port of the CBL 2™ or the DIG/SONIC 1 port of the LabPro® data collection device. Use the unit-to-unit cable to connect the TI graphing calculator to the data collection device. Firmly press in the cable ends.

3. Turn on the calculator and start the DATAMATE software. Press CLEAR to reset the software.

4. So that the zero reference position of the motion detector will be about a quarter of the way up the ramp, you will zero the detector while the cart is in this position.

    a. Select **SETUP** from the main screen.

    b. Select **ZERO** from the setup screen.

    c. Select **DIG-DISTANCE** from the SELECT CHANNEL screen.

d. Hold the cart still, about a quarter of the way up the ramp. The exact position is not critical, but the cart must be freely rolling through this point in Step 6.

e. Press (ENTER) to zero the motion detector.

5. Practice rolling the cart up the ramp so that you release the cart below the point where you zeroed the detector, and so that the cart never gets closer than 0.4 m to the detector. Be sure to pull your hands away from the cart after it starts moving so the motion detector does not detect your hands.

6. Select **START** to begin data collection. You will hear the data collection device beep. Wait for about a second, and then roll the cart as you practiced earlier. Data collection will run for five seconds.

7. Press (ENTER) to display the **DISTANCE** graph.

8. Examine the distance versus time graph. The graph should contain an area of smoothly changing distance. The smoothly changing portion must include two $y = 0$ crossings.

    Check with your teacher if you are not sure whether you need to repeat the data collection. To repeat data collection, press (ENTER) to return to the graph selection screen, select **MAIN SCREEN**, then return to Step 6.

Analysis

1. Since the cart may not have been rolling freely on the ramp the whole time data was collected, you need to remove the data that does not correspond to the free-rolling times. In other words, you only want the portion of the graph that appears parabolic. DATAMATE allows you to select the region you want using the following steps.

    a. Starting from the distance graph, press (ENTER).

    b. Select **SELECT REGION** from the graph selection screen.

    c. Move the left bound cursor to the left edge of the parabolic region using the cursor keys.

    d. Press (ENTER) to record the left bound.

    e. Move the right bound cursor to the right edge of the parabolic region using the cursor keys.

    f. Press (ENTER) to record the right bound. Once the calculator finishes performing the selection, you will see the selected portion of the graph filling the width of the screen.

2. Since the cart was not rolling freely when data collection started, adjust the time origin for the graph so that it starts with zero. To do this, you will need to leave DATAMATE.

    a. Press [ENTER] to return to the graph selection screen.

    b. Select **MAIN SCREEN** from the graph selection screen.

    c. Select **QUIT** to leave DATAMATE. Follow the instructions on the calculator screen to return to the calculator home screen.

3. To adjust the time origin, subtract the minimum time in the time series from all the values in the series. That will start the time series from zero.

    ### ▶ TI-73

    a. Access lists by pressing [2nd] [STAT]. Press the number next to L1; this enters **L1** on the home screen.

    b. Press [—].

    c. To enter the **min()** function press [MATH], use [▶] to highlight the NUM menu, and press the number adjacent to **min(** to paste the command to the home screen.

    d. Enter **L1** again, as you did before, and press [ )] to close the minimum function.

    e. Press [STO▶], and enter **L1** a third time to complete the expression **L1 − min(L1) → L1**. Press [ENTER] to perform the calculation.

    ### ▶ TI-83 and TI-83 Plus

    a. Press [2nd] [L1].

    b. Press [—].

    c. To enter the **min()** function press [MATH], use [▶] to highlight the NUM menu, and press the number adjacent to **min(** to paste the command to the home screen.

    d. Press [2nd] [L1] again and press [ )] to close the minimum function.

    e. Press [STO▶], and press [2nd] [L1] a third time to complete the expression **L1 − min(L1) → L1**. Press [ENTER] to perform the calculation.

4. You can find the two x-intercepts and the y-intercept by tracing across the parabola. Redisplay the graph with the individual points highlighted.

    a. Press [2nd] [STAT PLOT] ([PLOT] on the TI-73) and press [ENTER] to select **Plot 1**.

b. Change the **Plot1** settings to match the screen shown here. Press ENTER to select any of the settings you change.

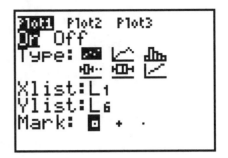

c. Press ZOOM and then select **ZoomStat** (use cursor keys to scroll to **ZoomStat**) to draw a graph with the x and y ranges set to fill the screen with data.

d. Press TRACE to determine the coordinates of a point on the graph using the cursor keys.

Trace across the graph to determine the y-intercept along with the first and second x-intercepts. You will not be able to get to exact x-intercepts because of the discrete points, but choose the points closest to the zero crossing. Round these values to 0.01, and record them in the first Data Table on the *Data Collection and Analysis* sheet.

5. Determine the product and sum of the x-intercepts. Record these values in the second Data Table on the *Data Collection and Analysis* sheet.

6. Use the intercept values, along with the three intercept properties discussed in the introduction, to determine the values of a, b, and c for the general form parabolic expression $y = ax^2 + bx + c$. Record these values in the third Data Table.
   Hint: Write an equation for each of the three properties, and then solve this system of equations for a, b, and c.

⇒ Answer Question 1 on the *Data Collection and Analysis* sheet.

7. Now that you have determined the equation for the parabola, plot it along with your data.

   a. Press Y=.

   b. Press CLEAR to remove any existing equation.

   c. Enter the equation for the parabola you determined in the **Y1** field. For example, if your equation is $y = 5x^2 + 4x + 3$, enter **5∗x2+4∗x+3** on the **Y1** line.

   d. Press GRAPH to see the data with the model graph superimposed.

⇒ Answer Question 2 on the *Data Collection and Analysis* sheet.

8. You can also determine the parameters of the parabola using the calculator's quadratic regression function, as shown on the next page.

▶ **TI-73**

a. Press ⌑2nd⌑ [STAT] and use the cursor keys to highlight **CALC**.

b. Press the number adjacent to **QuadReg** to copy the command to the home screen.

c. After the **QuadReg** command, press ⌑2nd⌑ [STAT] and select **L1** by pressing the number next to **L1** . Then press ⌑,⌑. Repeat the procedure to select **L6**.

d. After selecting **L6**, press ⌑,⌑ then press ⌑2nd⌑ [VARS].

e. Press the number next to **Y-Vars**.

f. Press ⌑ENTER⌑ to select **Y1** and copy it to the expression.

  On the home screen, you will now see the entry **QuadReg L1, L6, Y1**. This command will perform a quadratic regression with **L1** as the x-values and **L6** as the y-values. The resulting regression line will be stored in equation variable **Y1**.

g. Press ⌑ENTER⌑ to perform the quadratic regression.

⇒ Record the regression equation with its parameters in Question 3 on the *Data Collection and Analysis* sheet.

h. Press ⌑GRAPH⌑ to see the graph.

⇒ Answer Questions 4-6 on the *Data Collection and Analysis* sheet.

▶ **TI-83 and TI-83 Plus**

a. Press ⌑STAT⌑ and use the cursor keys to highlight **CALC**.

b. Press the number adjacent to **QuadReg** to copy the command to the home screen.

c. Press ⌑2nd⌑ [L1] ⌑,⌑ ⌑2nd⌑ [L6] ⌑,⌑ to enter the lists containing the data.

d. Press ⌑VARS⌑ and use the cursor keys to highlight **Y-VARS**.

e. Select **Function** by pressing ⌑ENTER⌑.

f. Press ⌑ENTER⌑ to copy **Y1** to the expression.

  On the home screen, you will now see the entry **QuadReg L1, L6, Y1**. This command will perform a quadratic regression using the x-values in **L1** and the y-values in **L6**. The resulting regression line will be stored in equation variable **Y1**.

g. Press ⌑ENTER⌑ to perform the quadratic regression.

⇒ Record the regression equation with its parameters in Question 3 on the *Data Collection and Analysis* sheet.

h. Press ⌑GRAPH⌑ to see the graph.

⇒ Answer Questions 4-6 on the *Data Collection and Analysis* sheet.

Data Collection and Analysis

Name _____

Date _____

Activity 10: What Goes Up

Data Tables

y-intercept	First x-intercept	Second x-intercept

Product of x-intercepts	
Sum of x-intercepts	

a	
b	
c	

Questions

1. Substitute the values of a, b, and c you just found into the equation $y = ax^2 + bx + c$. Record the completed modeling equation here.

2. Is your parabola a good fit for the data?

3. Record the regression equation from Step 8 with its parameters.

4. Are the values of a, b, and c in the quadratic regression equation above consistent with your results from your earlier calculation?

5. In the experiment you just conducted, the vertex on the parabolic distance versus time plot corresponds to a minimum on the graph even though this is the position at which the cart reaches its maximum distance from the starting point along the ramp. Explain why this is so.

6. Suppose that the experiment is repeated, but this time the motion detector is placed at the bottom of the ramp instead of at the top. Make a rough sketch of your predicted distance versus time plot for this situation. Discuss how the coefficient a would be affected, if at all.

Teacher Notes
What Goes Up: Position and Time for a Cart on a Ramp

1. A four-wheeled dynamics cart is the best choice for this activity. (Your physics teacher probably has a collection of dynamics carts.) A toy car such as a HotWheels® or Matchbox® car is too small, but a larger, freely-rolling car can be used.

2. A ball can be used, but it is very difficult to have the ball roll directly up and down the ramp. As a result, the data quality is strongly dependent on the skill of the experimenter when a ball is used. If a channeled track which forces a ball to roll along a line is used as the ramp, a ball will yield satisfactory data.

3. A TI CBR™ or a Vernier Motion Detector can be used in this activity. If a CBR is used, it must be connected through a CBL 2™ or a LabPro®, and not directly to the calculator.

4. Note that the ramp angle should only be a few degrees above horizontal. We suggest an angle of five degrees. Most students will create ramps with angles much larger than this, so you might want to have them calculate the angles of their tracks. That will serve both as a trigonometry review and ensure that the ramps are not too steep.

5. It is critical that the students zero the motion detector in a location that will be crossed by the cart during its roll. If the cart does cross the zero location (both on the way up and the way down), there will be two x-axis crossings as required by the analysis. If the students do not zero the motion detector, or zero it in a location that is not crossed by the cart during data collection, then the analysis as presented is not possible.

6. If the experimenter uses care, it is possible to have the cart freely rolling throughout data collection. In this case (as in the sample data below) there is no need to select a region or adjust the time origin, saving several steps.

7. Some motion detectors will not be automatically identified by DATAMATE. If you are using such a detector, you must manually set up DATAMATE for the detector:

    a. Select **SETUP** from the main screen.

    b. Press ⬛▼ until the cursor is next to DIG (CBL 2) or DIG1 (LabPro).

    c. Press ⌈ENTER⌋ to access the SELECT SENSOR menu.

    d. Select **MOTION(M)**.

    e. Select **OK** to return to the main screen.

Sample Results

Actual data will vary.

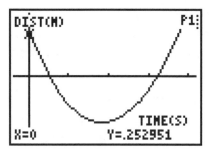

Raw data in DATAMATE

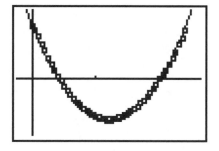

Data with parabolic model

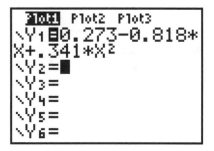

Model equation

Data Tables

Sample data; actual data may vary.

y-intercept	First x-intercept	Second x-intercept
0.273	0.40	2.0

Product of x-intercepts	0.8
Sum of x-intercepts	2.4

a	0.341
b	-0.818
c	0.273

Answers to Questions

1. Model equation is $y = 0.273 - 0.818 x + 0.341 x^2$. (depends on data collected)

2. Model parabola is an excellent fit, as expected since the vertices were taken from the experimental data.

3. Regression quadratic equation is $y = 0.285 - 0.797 x + 0.326 x^2$, or nearly the same as that obtained using the vertex form.

4. The parameters in the calculator's regression are nearly the same as those determined from the vertex form of the equation.

5. The motion detector records distance *away* from itself. Since the detector was at the top of the ramp, the cart was at its closest (minimum distance) to the detector when the cart was at its highest point.

6. If the experiment were repeated with the motion detector at the bottom of the ramp, the distance data would still be parabolic. However, the parabola would open downward, and the coefficient *a* would change sign.

EXPLORATIONS

Activity 11

That's the Way the Ball Bounces: Height and Time for a Bouncing Ball

Objective

♦ Record height versus time data for a bouncing ball.

♦ Model a single bounce using both the general and vertex forms of the parabola.

Materials

♦ TI-83 Plus, TI-83, or TI-73

♦ CBL 2™ or LabPro® data collection device

♦ DATAMATE software

♦ TI CBR™ or Vernier Motion Detector

♦ Ball (racquetball or basketball size)

Picture a bouncing ball. Between impacts with the floor, the ball rises and slows, then descends and speeds up. For any particular bounce, if the ball's height is plotted as a function of time, the resulting graph has a parabolic shape. In other words, the relationship between height and time for a single bounce of a ball is quadratic. This relationship is expressed mathematically as

$$y = ax^2 + bx + c$$

where y represents the ball's height at any given time x. Another form of a quadratic equation is

$$y = a(x - h)^2 + k$$

where h is the x-coordinate of the vertex, k is the y-coordinate of the vertex, and a is a parameter. This way of writing a quadratic is called the *vertex form*.

In this activity, you will record the motion of a bouncing ball using a motion detector. You will then analyze the collected data and model the variations in the ball's height as a function of time during one bounce using both the general and vertex forms of the quadratic equation.

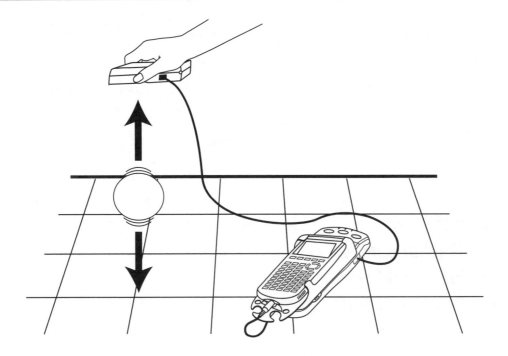

Procedure

1. Position the motion detector about 1.5 m above the floor, so that the disc is pointing straight downward.

2. Plug the motion detector into the DIG/SONIC port of the CBL 2™ or the DIG/SONIC 1 port of the LabPro®. Use the unit-to-unit cable to connect the TI graphing calculator to the data collection device. Press in the cable ends firmly.

3. Turn on the calculator and start the DATAMATE software. Press CLEAR to reset the software.

4. Zero the motion detector so that the detector's origin will be the floor.

    a. Select **SETUP** from the main screen.

    b. Select **ZERO** from the setup screen.

    c. Select **DIG-DISTANCE** from the SELECT CHANNEL screen.

    d. Confirm that there are no targets in the region below the motion detector, and press ENTER to zero the motion detector.

5. Practice dropping the ball so that it bounces straight up and down beneath the motion detector. Minimize the ball's sideways travel. Dropping the ball from about waist high works well. The ball must never get closer than 0.5 m from the detector. Be sure to pull your hands away from the ball after you drop it so the motion detector does not detect your hands.

6. Select **START** to begin data collection. You will hear the data collection device beep. Wait for about a second, and then drop the ball as you practiced earlier. Data collection will run for five seconds.

7. Press (ENTER) to display the **DISTANCE** graph.

8. Examine the distance versus time graph. It should contain a series of parabolic regions. Check with your teacher if you are not sure whether you need to repeat the data collection.

   To repeat data collection, press (ENTER) to return to the graph selection screen, and select **MAIN SCREEN**. Return to Step 6.

9. Once you are satisfied with the graph, press (ENTER) to return to the graph selection screen.

Analysis

1. Select the data corresponding to the ball's position between two bounces.

   a. Select **SELECT REGION** from the graph selection screen.

   b. Move the left bound cursor to the left edge of a parabolic region of your choice using the cursor keys.

   c. Press (ENTER) to record the left bound.

   d. Move the right bound cursor to the right edge of the same parabolic region using the cursor keys.

   e. Press (ENTER) to record the right bound. After a moment you will see the selected portion of the graph filling the width of the screen.

2. Remember that you zeroed the motion detector on the floor of the room. Since the motion detector measures increasing values *away* from itself your data will all be negative, and your graph will appear upside down. To change the sign of the data, you can exit the DATAMATE software and multiply the distance data by ⁻1.

   a. Press (ENTER) to return to the graph selection screen.

   b. Select **MAIN SCREEN** from the graph selection screen.

   c. Select **QUIT** to leave DATAMATE. Follow the instructions on your calculator screen to return to the calculator home screen.

   ▶ _____ TI-73 _____

   d. Press ((−)) (2nd) [STAT].

   e. Select the list **L6** by pressing the digit next to **L6** (usually 6).

   f. Press (STO▶) (2nd) [STAT].

g. Again select the list **L6** by pressing the digit next to **L6** (usually 6) to complete the expression **–L6 → L6**.

h. Press ENTER to complete the operation.

▶ **TI-83 and TI-83 Plus**

d. Press (–) 2nd [L6] STO▶ 2nd [L6] to enter the expression **–L6 → L6**.

e. Press ENTER to complete the operation.

3. Now redisplay the graph with the sign change and with the individual points highlighted.

a. Press 2nd [STAT PLOT] ([PLOT] on the TI-73) and press ENTER to select **Plot 1**.

b. Use the cursor keys to position the cursor on each of the following **Plot1** settings. Press ENTER to select any of the settings you change:

Type = ∟⋰
Mark = ▫

c. Press ZOOM and then select **ZoomStat** (use cursor keys to scroll to **ZoomStat**) to draw a graph with the x and y ranges set to fill the screen with data.

d. Press TRACE to determine the coordinates of a point on the graph using the cursor keys.

4. Trace across the graph to determine the x- and y-coordinates of the vertex of the parabola (in this case, the maximum point on the curve). Round these values to the nearest hundredth, and record them in the first Data Table on the *Data Collection and Analysis* sheet.

⇒ Answer Question 1 on the *Data Collection and Analysis* sheet.

5. The model from physics for the distance versus time motion of a ball in free fall is quadratic. Fit a quadratic model $y = a(x – h)^2 + k$ to your data. In this vertex form, h is the x-coordinate of the vertex, k is the y-coordinate of the vertex, and a is a parameter.

Since you have values for the parameters h and k of your model, you can try plotting the model using a guess for the a parameter. First, enter your model equation for graphing.

a. Press Y=.

b. Press CLEAR to remove any existing equation.

c. Enter the vertex form of the parabola using your values for the parameters h and k. For example, if your equation is $y = a(x – 4)^2 + 5$, enter A∗(x–4)²+5 in the **Y1** field. (On the TI-73, access the alphabetic entry screen by pressing 2nd [TEXT].)

d. Press 2nd [QUIT] to return to the home screen.

6. Next, set a value for the parameter a and then look at the resulting graph. To obtain a good fit, try several values for a. Use the steps below to store different values to the parameter a. Start with $a = 1$. Experiment until you find one that provides a good fit for the data. *Test both positive and negative values for* a.

   a. Enter a value for the parameter a. Press (STO▶) A (ENTER) to store the value in the variable A.

   b. Press (GRAPH) to see your data with the model graph superimposed.

   c. Press (2nd) [QUIT] to return to the home screen.

   Use your optimized value for a and the values of h and k you determined earlier to complete the vertex form of the equation.

⇒ Answer Question 2 on the *Data Collection and Analysis* sheet.

7. It is also possible to express any quadratic function in the standard form of $y = ax^2 + bx + c$, where the coefficient a is the same as the coefficient you just found for the vertex form, and b and c are other parameters related to the h and k you already know. To determine the coefficients b and c, expand the vertex form of your equation and collect like terms.

   Round the corresponding values of a, b, and c to the nearest tenth and record them in the middle column of the second Data Table on the *Data Collection and Analysis* sheet.

8. Another way to determine the parameters is to use the calculator to perform a quadratic regression on the data to determine the parabola that fits the data best.

   ▶___ **TI-73** _____

   a. Press (2nd) [STAT] and use the cursor keys to highlight **CALC**.

   b. Press the number next to **QuadReg** to copy the command to the home screen.

   c. After the **QuadReg** command, press (2nd) [STAT] and select **L1** by pressing the number next to **L1**. Then press (,). Repeat the procedure to select **L6**.

   d. After selecting **L6**, press (,) then press (2nd) [VARS].

   e. Press the number next to **Y-Vars.**

   f. Press (ENTER) to select **Y1** and copy it to the expression.

   g. On the home screen, you will now see the entry **QuadReg L1**, **L6**, **Y1**. This command will perform a quadratic regression with **L1** as the x-values and **L6** as the y-values. The resulting regression curve will be stored in equation variable **Y1**. Press (ENTER) to perform the regression.

   Copy the parameters a, b and c that appear on the calculator screen to the third column of the second Data Table.

h. Press GRAPH to see the graph.

⇒ Answer Questions 3-5 on the *Data Collection and Analysis* sheet.

▶ **TI-83 and TI-83 Plus**

a. Press STAT and use the cursor keys to highlight **CALC**.

b. Press the number adjacent to **QuadReg** to copy the command to the home screen.

c. Press 2nd [L1] , 2nd [L6] , to enter the lists containing the data.

d. Press VARS and use the cursor keys to highlight **Y-VARS**.

e. Select **Function** by pressing ENTER.

f. Press ENTER to copy **Y1** to the expression.

g. On the home screen, you will now see the entry **QuadReg L1**, **L6**, **Y1**. This command will perform a quadratic regression with **L1** as the *x*-values and **L6** as the *y*-values. The resulting regression curve will be stored in equation variable **Y1**. Press ENTER to perform the regression.

Copy the parameters *a*, *b* and *c* that appear on the calculator screen to the third column of the second Data Table.

h. Press GRAPH to see the graph.

⇒ Answer Questions 3-5 on the *Data Collection and Analysis* sheet.

Extension

How does the value of *a* vary from one parabolic section to the next? Collect another run of data, and determine a new value of the parameter *a* using any method you like. Explain why the values of *a* are in close agreement for both bounces. What does *a* measure?

Calculus Extension

Take the second derivative of the modeling equation. What is the physical significance of this value?

Data Collection and Analysis

Name _____

Date _____

Activity 11: That's the Way the Ball Bounces

Data Tables

Vertex	
x-coordinate	**y-coordinate**

Parameters	Values calculated from vertex form	Values from regression
a		
b		
c		

Questions

1. In this activity, the ball bounced straight up and down beneath the detector, yet the plot you see might seem to depict a ball that is moving sideways as it bounces up and down. Explain why the graph looks the way it does.

2. Write the vertex form of the parabola from Step 6.

3. Are the values of a, b, and c in the quadratic regression equation consistent with the values you determined earlier?

4. Describe how the parameter a affects the graph of $y = a(x - h)^2 + k$.
    Specifically, how do the magnitude of a and the sign of a change the graph?

5. Suppose you had chosen the parabolic section for the bounce just to the right
    of the one you actually used in this activity. Describe how the parameters h
    and k would change, if at all, if this different parabolic section were to be fit
    with the equation $y = a(x - h)^2 + k$.

Teacher Notes
That's the Way the Ball Bounces: Height and Time for a Bouncing Ball

1. A basketball works well for this activity. Avoid using a soft or felt-covered ball such as a tennis ball as the surface prevents good detection by the motion detector.

2. The motion detector cord must not get between the ball and the detector during data collection.

3. A TI CBR™ or a Vernier motion detector a can be used in this activity. If a CBR is used, it must be connected through a CBL 2™ or a LabPro®, and not directly to the calculator.

4. The activity is best done by a group of three students: one to hold the detector, another to release the ball, and a third to operate the calculator.

5. Hold the ball from the sides and release it by quickly, moving hands outward and out of the detection cone of the motion detector.

6. Some motion detectors will not be automatically identified by DATAMATE. If you are using such a detector, you must manually set up DATAMATE for the detector:

   a. Select **SETUP** from the main screen.

   b. Press ⬛▼⬛ until the cursor is next to DIG (CBL 2) or DIG1 (LabPro).

   c. Press ⬛ENTER⬛ to access the SELECT SENSOR menu.

   d. Select **MOTION(M)**.

   e. Select **OK** to return to the main screen.

Sample Results

Actual data will vary.

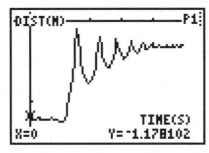

Raw distance data

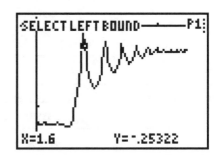

First step of data selection

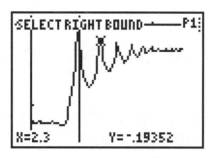

Second step of data selection

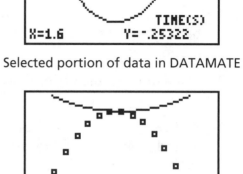

Selected portion of data in DATAMATE

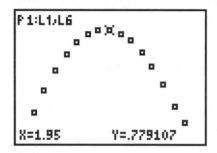

Data graphed with sign inversion

First attempt to fit vertex form of quadratic; $a=1$

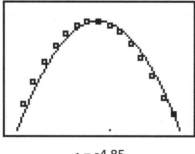

$a = {}^-4.85$

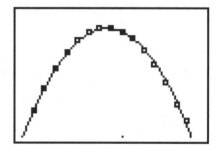

Fit of calculator regression

Data Tables

Sample data; actual data may vary.

Vertex	
x-**coordinate**	*y*-**coordinate**
1.95	0.78

Parameters	Values calculated from vertex form	Values from regression
a	${}^-4.8$	${}^-4.6$
b	18.9	17.8
c	${}^-19.2$	${}^-16.4$

Answers to Questions

1. The graph we are using is vertical distance versus time, not vertical distance versus horizontal distance. That is, the horizontal axis is not horizontal distance, so the appearance of the graph has nothing to do with a side-ways moving ball.

2. Vertex model equation: $y = -4.85\,(x - 1.95)^2 + 0.78$.

3. The parameters of the standard form quadratic as determined by calculator regression and by the vertex fit are similar.

4. The magnitude of a determines how sharply curved the parabola is, while the sign of a determines whether the parabola is open upward (positive a) or downward (negative a).

5. Since the vertex of the new parabola would be to the right of the one originally used, the time value h would be larger. The y coordinate of the vertex would be smaller than before, as the ball does not bounce as high each time.

EXPLORATIONS

Activity 12

Walk This Way: Definition of Rate

Objective

♦ Measure distance and velocity versus time information for a walker.

♦ Compute the area under the velocity versus time graph, with units.

♦ Compare that area to the distance traveled by the walker.

Materials

♦ TI-83 Plus, TI-83, or TI-73

♦ CBL 2™ or LabPro® data collection device

♦ DATAMATE software

♦ TI CBR™ or Vernier Motion Detector

A *rate* is defined as some quantity divided by a time interval. For walking, we would define the rate of walking (commonly called speed, if we just consider walking in one direction) as the ratio of the distance walked divided by the time interval taken to do the walking.

$$\text{rate} \equiv \frac{\text{distance traveled}}{\text{time interval}}$$

From this definition you can also work backward. If you know the rate, or speed, of walking, as well as the time interval walked, you can find the distance traveled using:

rate x time interval = distance traveled

Strictly, the rate defined above is the average rate, so for non-constant speeds we will need to find the average speed for use with the formula.

A motion detector will give you the speed of a walker versus time. (The motion detector will actually give you velocity versus time, but for motion away from the detector speed and velocity are the same.) The product of rate and time interval is the *area* under the curve of the speed versus time graph.

The area is easy to calculate when the speed is constant, but it turns out that you can even use the area under the curve when the speed is not constant. One way to calculate that area is to use the average velocity during the time interval, where the average is calculated by using many velocities at evenly spaced times. When you are using many, many velocities, you are performing an *integral*, which is one of the key concepts in *calculus*, a topic in advanced mathematics.

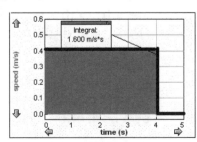

In this activity you will record a speed versus time graph, find the area under it, and compare that result to the actual distance traveled as read by the distance versus time graph.

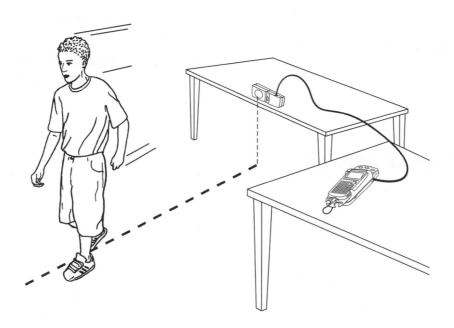

Procedure

1. Place the motion detector on the edge of a table pointing to an open area. Prepare to walk *away* from the detector at a uniform pace, starting at a distance of about 1 meter.

2. Connect the motion detector into the DIG/SONIC port of the CBL 2™ or the DIG/SONIC 1 port of the LabPro® data collection device. Use the unit-to-unit cable to connect the TI graphing calculator to the data collection device. Firmly press in the cable ends.

3. Turn on the calculator and start the DATAMATE software. Press `CLEAR` to reset the software.

4. Select **START** to begin data collection. You will hear the data collection device beep. Wait for approximately one second after you hear the beep. Then walk away from the detector at a slow, uniform pace for two to three seconds. Finally, stand still again until you hear the data collection device beep again. Data collection will run for five seconds.

5. Press `ENTER` to display the **DISTANCE** graph. The distance graph should consist of a horizontal section, followed by a uniformly increasing function, followed by a horizontal section.

   If necessary, repeat data collection by pressing `ENTER`, selecting **MAIN SCREEN**, and returning to the previous step.

Analysis

1. Use the cursor keys to trace across the distance graph to read time and distance values. The x values correspond to time in seconds, and the y values correspond to distance from the motion detector in meters. Record the time when the distance values started to change, as well as the starting distance, in the Data Table on the *Data Collection and Analysis* sheet. Round these values to three significant digits.

   Advance the cursor to the right side of the increasing region of the graph, and record the ending time and distance. Include units with your entries. Round these values to three significant digits.

2. Press ENTER to return to the graph selection screen. Press ▼ to select **VELOCITY**, and press ENTER to see the velocity versus time graph.

3. Trace across the graph and select what looks like a typical velocity during the period when you were walking. Do not be too concerned with this choice; just find a representative velocity value. Later you will find a true average value. Record this velocity (including units) as the estimated average velocity in the Data Table on the *Data Collection and Analysis* sheet.

4. You can use DATAMATE to find a better average velocity.

   a. Press ENTER, and return to the main screen by selecting **MAIN SCREEN**.

   b. Select **ANALYZE** from the main screen.

   c. Select **STATISTICS** from the analyze screen.

   d. Select **2:DIG–VELOCITY** from the SELECT GRAPH screen.

   e. You will see a prompt to select the left bound. Press ▶ to move the cursor to the same starting time you found from the distance graph, at the beginning of the region when you were walking. Press ENTER to select the left edge of the graph.

   f. You will see a new prompt to select the right bound. Press and hold ▶ until the cursor is at the right side of the walking region of the graph, at the same ending time you found from the distance graph. Press ENTER to have DATAMATE find statistics about the velocity graph.

   g. DATAMATE will display a number of statistics, including the mean, or average, speed. Record the mean value in the Data Table on the *Data Collection and Analysis* sheet.

⇒ Answer Question 1 on the *Data Collection and Analysis* sheet.

5. Now that you have found the necessary values from the graphs, calculate the distance walked in several different ways.

   a. Find the time interval by subtracting the time when you started to walk from the time when you stopped walking. You will use this time interval in the following rate calculations. Record the time interval in seconds in the Data Table.

   b. Find the distance walked using the rate definition and the estimated average velocity. To do this, multiply your estimated average velocity by the time interval. Enter the result in the Data Table. Include units.

   c. Find the distance walked using the rate definition and the calculator's average velocity. To do this, multiply the calculator's average velocity by the time interval. Enter this value in the Data Table next to the average velocity. Include units.

   d. Find the distance walked directly from the starting and ending distance information you obtained from the distance versus time graph. Subtract the starting distance from the ending distance to get the distance traveled. Record this value in the Data Table next to the distance graph values. Include units.

⇒ Answer Questions 2 and 3 on the *Data Collection and Analysis* sheet.

Extensions

1. From the main screen of DATAMATE choose **ANALYZE**, and find the **INTEGRATE** option. Use this command to find the area under the velocity time graph and compare to the values calculated previously. What are the units of the integral result?

2. In the main exercise you used the entire walking period. Since the definition of rate depends on the time interval, as opposed to time, you can use any time interval you like. Repeat the analysis using just a portion of the walking period. Be sure you use the same time end points to find the change in position and the average velocity.

3. As long as the average velocity (as opposed to speed) is used, the motion need not be all in one direction for these calculations to work. The velocity is negative when the motion is toward the detector.

   Collect new data for a back-and-forth walk where you start about a meter from the detector, walk slowly away for three seconds and then return for two, ending a little farther away than when you started.

   Find the displacement from the distance graph as you did before. Note that the displacement is the net distance traveled (the difference between the ending and starting positions only), and is not the total path distance. Also, the area under the velocity versus time graph is positive when the velocity is positive, and negative when the velocity is negative. As a result, the area under the entire velocity versus time graph may be smaller than the area under only the early portion of the graph.

Data Collection and Analysis

Name _____

Date _____

Activity 12: Walk This Way

Data Table

starting time	
ending time	
time interval	
starting distance	
ending distance	
estimated average velocity	
average velocity from calculator	
distance traveled (from est. velocity)	
distance traveled (from average velocity)	
distance traveled (from distance graph)	

Questions

1. Compare your estimated average velocity to that supplied by the calculator. Does the calculator value make sense? Why might the two values be different?

2. How do the three distance values compare? Which one is the most direct measure of distance? **Hint:** which one did not use the rate definition? Does the rate definition give reasonable distance values?

3. Sometimes areas are expressed in square distance units, such as m^2. Notice that the areas under the velocity versus time graphs had units of meters, not square meters. Explain why this is so.
    Hint: What are the units of the x and y axes?

Teacher Notes
Walk This Way: Definition of Rate

1. Either a TI CBR™ or a Vernier Motion Detector can be used in this activity. If a CBR is used, it must be connected through a CBL 2™ or a LabPro®, and not directly to the calculator.

2. This activity is different from many in that most of the analysis is done within DATAMATE. Since the analysis is largely reading values from graphs, we felt it unnecessary to re-graph the data outside of DATAMATE.

3. A common trap for students is to use the clock time (as read from the horizontal axis) as opposed to the time interval. That is why we never write the rate equation as "distance = rate × time." That expression is misleading, since the time is not the same as the time interval except in the special case that the time interval starts at $t = 0$. The subtlety of the time interval calculation is explored further in the second extension.

4. In Step 1 of the Analysis, the student must choose two times from the distance graph and then use the same two times in selecting a region of the velocity graph in Step 4. The actual times chosen are not critical, as long as the *same* times are used in both Steps 1 and 4.

5. Some motion detectors will not be automatically identified by DATAMATE. If you are using such a detector, you must manually set up DATAMATE for the detector:

   a. Select **SETUP** from the main screen.

   b. Press ⬇ until the cursor is next to DIG (CBL 2) or DIG1 (LabPro).

   c. Press ENTER to access the **SELECT SENSOR** menu.

   d. Select **MOTION(M)**.

   e. Select **OK** to return to the **MAIN SCREEN**.

Sample Results

Actual data will vary.

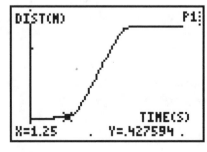

Distance data in DATAMATE

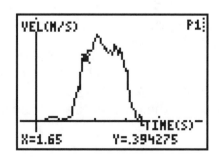

Velocity data

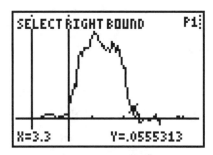

Right bound selection
for velocity average

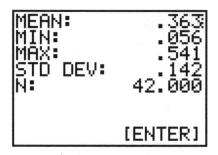

Velocity average result

Data Table

Sample data; actual data may vary.

starting time	1.25 s
ending time	3.30 s
time interval	2.05 s
starting distance	0.428 m
ending distance	1.19 m
estimated average velocity	0.390 m/s
average velocity from calculator	0.363 m/s
distance traveled (from est. velocity)	0.808 m
distance traveled (from average velocity)	0.744 m
distance traveled (from distance graph)	0.762 m

Answers to Questions

1. The estimated average velocity is close to, but a little larger than, the calculator's value. I do not expect a perfect match since the estimated value is just an eyeball guess. Since the values are close, the calculator's value certainly makes sense.

2. The distances calculated from the rate equations are very close to the actual distance traveled as determined by the distance graph. The rate expression makes sense.

3. The velocity versus time graph has units of m/s on the y axis, and s on the x axis. The product of m/s $\times$ s is just m, or a distance. The units of area depend on the units of the two dimensions of the area.

EXPLORATIONS

Activity 13

Velocity Test: Interpreting Velocity Graphs

Objective

- ◆ Record distance versus time data for a simple motion of a walker.

- ◆ Analyze the distance versus time data to sketch the form of a corresponding velocity versus time graph.

- ◆ Compare this velocity graph with the velocity graph determined by the calculator.

Materials

- ◆ TI-83 Plus, TI-83, or TI-73

- ◆ CBL 2™ or LabPro® data collection device

- ◆ DATAMATE software

- ◆ TI CBR™ or Vernier Motion Detector

When you walk, ride a bike, or travel in a car, you are often interested in the distance traveled, the time it took, and the speed or velocity of your motion. In this activity, you will learn more about how these four quantities are related.

Speed and velocity are often confused since the terms are sometimes used interchangeably, but they are not the same thing. So what is the difference? *Speed* is how far you have gone, divided by the time it took to move. In other words, speed tells how fast you are traveling, but without regard to direction. Since the distance you have traveled is always positive, speed is always positive.

On the other hand, *velocity* is the rate of change of position. Position is the directed distance from a chosen starting point, or origin. If we consider only motion on the positive side of the origin, motion away from the origin is a positive change in position, while motion toward the origin is a negative change in position. Velocity can, therefore, be either positive or negative depending upon your direction of motion. The data from a motion detector is a directed distance, so it can easily be used to calculate velocity.

Velocity is defined as the change in position divided by the change in time, or

$$v \equiv \frac{\Delta d}{\Delta t} = \frac{d_2 - d_1}{t_2 - t_1}$$

Here, d_1 and d_2 are your positions at two particular times t_1 and t_2. This definition should look familiar, for it has exactly the same form as that of slope for a y versus x graph, or

$$\text{slope} = \frac{\Delta y}{\Delta x} = \frac{y_2 - y_1}{x_2 - x_1}$$

If you look at a plot of distance from the detector, which is position as a function of time, the velocity is the slope of that graph. For simple distance graphs you can find the slope of a segment of the graph to find the corresponding velocity during that time interval. In this activity, you will calculate a few velocities from a distance graph and compare them to the velocity graph produced by the calculator.

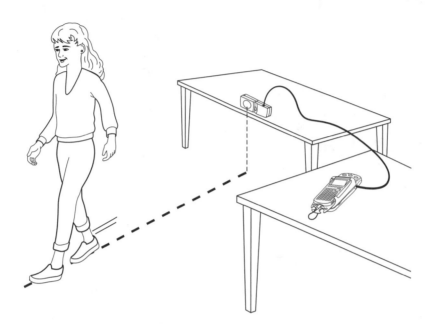

Procedure

1. Place the motion detector on the edge of a table about waist level, pointing into an open area. You will need at least 2 meters unobstructed space to walk in front of the detector.

2. Connect the motion detector into the DIG/SONIC port of the CBL 2™ or the DIG/SONIC 1 port of the LabPro® data collection device. Use the unit-to-unit cable to connect the TI graphing calculator to the data collection device. Press in the cable ends firmly.

3. Turn on the calculator and start the DATAMATE software. Press CLEAR to reset the software.

4. For this activity you need a position versus time graph that shows both positive and negative slope, but you do not want it to be too complicated. Stand about 1 m in front of the motion detector. After you hear the clicking start, stand still for about a second. Then walk slowly away for about two seconds at a uniform rate, and then walk toward the detector for the remaining time. Do not get any closer than 50 cm from the detector.

   When you are ready, select **START** to begin data collection. You will hear the data collection device beep. Data collection will run for five seconds.

5. The graph selection screen will appear. Press (ENTER) to display the **DISTANCE** graph. Examine the distance versus time graph. This graph should start with a nearly horizontal region, followed by a fairly linear increase, followed by a fairly linear decrease.

    Check with your teacher if you are not sure whether you need to repeat the data collection. To repeat data collection, press (ENTER) to return to the graph selection screen. Select **MAIN SCREEN** and then return to Step 4.

Analysis

1. Use the cursor keys and the distance versus time plot to determine the time interval when the velocity is positive. In other words, when is the slope of the distance versus time graph positive?

⇒ Record the starting and ending times in Question 1 on the *Data Collection and Analysis* sheet. Answer Questions 2 and 3.

2. The several time intervals you just identified will let you describe the distance versus time graph using just four points. There should be three roughly linear segments:

    *   The first segment runs from $t_1 = 0$ s to some time later that we will call t_2.
    *   The next segment starts at t_2 and runs to time t_3 when you changed direction.
    *   The last segment runs from t_3 to the end of the data collection, which we will call t_4.

    The distance information at each of these four times will allow you to calculate a velocity for each time interval.

    Trace across the distance graph using the cursor keys, and find the x and y coordinates of the four points. Round all values to two decimal places and record the values in the Data Table on the *Data Collection and Analysis* sheet.

⇒ Answer Questions 4-6 on the *Data Collection and Analysis* sheet.

3. The DATAMATE software can display its velocity versus time graph. Press (ENTER) to return to the graph selection screen. Press (▼) to highlight **VELOCITY**, and press (ENTER).

⇒ Answer Questions 7-10 on the *Data Collection and Analysis* sheet.

Data Collection and Analysis

Name _____

Date _____

Activity 13: Velocity Test

Data Table

	t	d		
point 1				
			slope segment 1	
point 2				
			slope segment 2	
point 3				
			slope segment 3	
point 4				

Questions

1. Record the starting and ending times when the velocity is positive.

2. Identify all intervals where the velocity is negative. Explain how you know the velocity values are negative for these intervals.

3. What portions of the graph represent a velocity of zero? Explain your answer.

4. Make a sketch of the distance versus time graph using just the three segments you have extracted from the raw data. Use the frame provided below for your sketch.

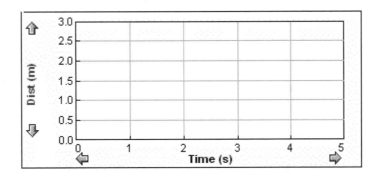

5. Calculate the slope of the each of the three segments and enter them in the Data Table. Note that the slope is just the velocity during the corresponding time interval. What are the units of the slope?

6. Now use the slopes of the three segments to sketch a velocity versus time graph. Since each slope is also a velocity value for that time interval, the velocity graph will consist of three horizontal lines at various heights.

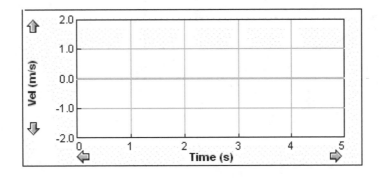

7. How does the calculator's graph compare to yours?

8. Why might the calculator's graph and your graph be different?
   Hint: Does the calculator use just three segments to find slopes?

9. Complete the following table showing characteristics of a velocity graph for each specific kind of motion.

Actual Motion	Velocity Graph Characteristic
Person moves towards the detector	
Person stands still	
Person moves away from the detector	

10. Look at the distance versus time plot of a walker (below, left). Describe the motion of the walker in as much detail as possible in the space below. Sketch the corresponding velocity versus time graph in the axes provided.

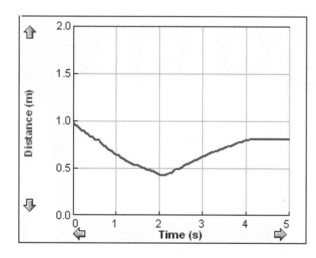 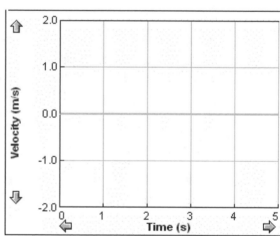

Teacher Notes
Velocity Test: Interpreting Velocity Graphs

1. Place the motion detector at waist-high level for the walker. The walker should not be closer than 0.5 meter to the detector when data collection begins. Clear the area of other materials such as desks or chairs.

2. The instructions ask the student to walk in a particular motion: Stand still, walk away from the detector for two seconds, and then back to the detector for two more seconds. The objective of this particular walk is to create a graph that is simple to analyze in terms of slopes of segments. A more general graph can be used, but the analysis will be more complicated.

3. In order to keep the distance graph simple, the walker must maintain a constant rate while walking directly away and toward the motion detector.

4. Either a TI CBR™ or a Vernier Motion Detector can be used. The CBR must be connected to a data collection device and not directly to the calculator.

5. Some motion detectors will not be automatically identified by DATAMATE. If you are using such a detector, you must manually set up DATAMATE for the detector:

    a. Select **SETUP** from the main screen.

    b. Press ⬇ until the cursor is next to **DIG** (CBL 2) or **DIG1** (LabPro).

    c. Press [ENTER] to access the **SELECT SENSOR** menu.

    d. Select **MOTION(M)**.

    e. Select **OK** to return to the main screen.

Sample Results

Actual data will vary.

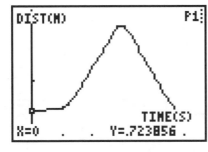

Typical distance versus time graph

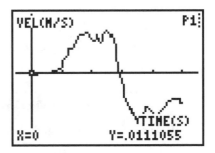

Velocity versus time data
for the same run

Data Table

Sample data; actual data may vary.

	t	d		
point 1	0 s	0.73 m		
			slope segment 1	0.01 m/s
point 2	1.00 s	0.74 m		
			slope segment 2	0.42 m/s
point 3	2.80 s	1.50 m		
			slope segment 3	⁻0.39 m/s
point 4	5.00 s	0.64 m		

Answers to Questions

1. Using the distance graph, the velocity is positive from 1.00 to 2.90 s, as judged by the positive slope.

2. The slope is negative from 2.90 to 5.00 s, so the velocity is negative in this region.

3. The first 1.00 s has a velocity near zero, since the graph is nearly horizontal.

4. Sketches will vary; you can compare them to the original distance graph.

5. Since the y-axis has units of meters, and the x-axis has units of seconds, the slope must have units of meters per second, or m/s.

6. Sketches will vary; you can compare them to the original velocity graph.

7. The calculator's graph is similar to my sketch, but is more irregular.

8. The calculator will have no way to choose landmark points for slope calculation (as I did) but must instead use many points. So, the calculator's graph holds more detailed velocity information.

9.

Actual Motion	Velocity Graph Characteristic
Person moves towards the detector	negative slope
Person stands still	zero slope
Person moves away from the detector	positive slope

10. The walker started out standing just closer than 1.0 m from the detector, and was moving toward the detector when data collection began. The walker continued to move toward the detector for 2.0 s, at which time he or she turned around and walked away from the detector for two seconds. The speed away from the detector was a bit smaller than the speed toward the detector. Starting at t = 4.0 s, the walker stood still for the remaining time.

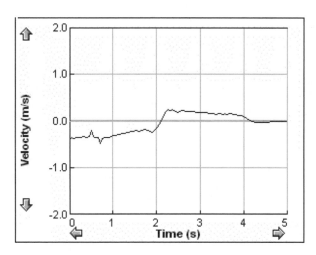

EXPLORATIONS

Activity 14

From Here to There: Applications of the Distance Formula

Objective

♦ Record the x- and y-coordinates of a rod moving in a star pattern.

♦ Use the recorded coordinates to calculate the distances moved between the vertices of the star.

♦ Compare the calculated distances with direct measurement on the star pattern.

Materials

♦ TI-83 Plus, TI-83, or TI-73 (two if using CBL 2™, one if using LabPro®)

♦ Two CBL 2 or one LabPro data collection devices

♦ DATAMATE software

♦ Two TI CBR™ or Vernier Motion Detectors

♦ Meter stick

♦ Dowel rod or plastic pipe about 50 cm by 1 cm

♦ Masking tape

Many problems in applied mathematics involve finding the distance between points. If we know the coordinates of a pair of points (x_1, y_1) and (x_2, y_2), it is easy to find the distance between them by using the distance formula, which is a restatement of the Pythagorean Theorem.

$$d = \sqrt{(x_2 - x_1)^2 + (y_2 - y_1)^2}$$

In this activity you will use a pair of motion detectors. They will record the Cartesian x, y coordinates of a rod moving in a star-shaped pattern. The data collected by the detectors will be used to test the distance formula.

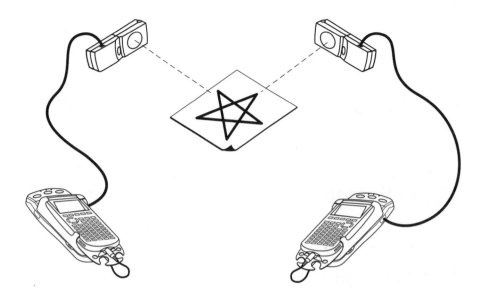

Procedure

This activity can be performed using two CBL 2™ data collection devices with two identical calculators, or one LabPro® data collection device with one calculator. The instructions address both configurations, so read carefully to find which steps to follow.

1. Remove the star figure sheet from your activity packet. It is a pattern sheet of a star with the vertices marked with letters. Tape the pattern to the table to keep the sheet from moving.

2. Set up the motion detectors on a table or desk as shown in the picture. Use the meter stick to place each detector 50 cm from the points indicated on the star pattern sheet. Make note of which detector will collect x-data and which will collect y-data. Each detector must have an unobstructed view of the star region.

3. Connect the motion detectors to the DIG/SONIC port of each CBL 2 data collection device or the DIG/SONIC 1 and DIG/SONIC 2 ports of the LabPro data collection device (use Port 1 for the x-detector). Use the unit-to-unit link cable to connect the TI graphing calculator to the data collection device. Firmly press in the cable ends.

4. Turn on the calculator(s) and start the DATAMATE software. Press [CLEAR] to reset the software.

5. Adjust the data collection time so you will have ten seconds to move the rod. If you are using CBL 2 data collection devices, do this on both calculators.

   a. Select **SETUP** from the main screen.

   b. Press [▲] to select mode.

c. Press (ENTER) to change the data collection mode.

d. Select **TIME GRAPH** from the SELECT MODE screen.

e. Select **CHANGE TIME SETTINGS**.

f. Enter **0.2** as the time between samples in seconds and press (ENTER). (Use **0.4** for the TI-73.)

g. Enter **50** as the number of samples and press (ENTER). (Use **25** for the TI-73.)

h. Select **OK** twice to return to the main screen.

6. Hold the rod vertically with the tip resting on point **A** of the star pattern. Keep your hands and arms out of the beams of the motion detectors. Practice moving the rod along the star pattern, point **A** to point **B** to point **C** and so forth, keeping the rod vertical the entire time.

7. Select **START** (on both calculators simultaneously if you are using two) to begin data collection. You will hear the data collection device(s) beep and the motion detectors will begin to click. Move the rod as you practiced. You will have ten seconds to complete the motion; it is all right if you end the pattern with a few seconds to go. Keep the rod at point A until data collection ends.

8. Press (ENTER) to display a **DISTANCE** graph. (If you are using LabPro® with one calculator, to see the second graph, press (ENTER) and use the cursor keys to select the second distance channel. Press (ENTER) to view the graph.)

9. Examine the distance versus time graphs. The graphs should show smooth back-and-forth motions with no large spikes. Check with your teacher if you are not sure whether you need to repeat the data collection.

   To repeat data collection, press (ENTER) to return to the graph selection screen, and select **MAIN SCREEN**. Select **START** and go back to Step 7.

10. Once you are satisfied with the graph, press (ENTER) to return to the graph selection screen, and select **MAIN SCREEN**. Select **QUIT** to leave DATAMATE, and follow any instructions to return to the calculator home screen.

11. Use the meter stick to measure the distance from the *y*-motion detector to point **A** on the star. Record this value in the Data Table on the *Data Collection and Analysis* sheet. Round this (and all other data) to three significant figures.

Analysis

1. (*Skip this step if you are using LabPro with one calculator.*)

    To complete the analysis, you need to move the distance data from one calculator to another. To avoid overwriting data, you will first copy the data to a new location in the calculator and then send it to the receiving calculator. The following transfer instructions assume that you are moving data between two calculators of the same model. Use the *y*-data calculator as the sending calculator, and the *x*-data unit as the receiving calculator. Be sure you know which is which!

    ▶ _____TI-73_____

    a. Disconnect the calculators from the data collection devices, and directly connect the two calculators with a black link cable. Firmly press in the cable ends.

    b. On the sending calculator, copy the distance data to a new list name. To do this, press ⟨ 2nd ⟩ [STAT] and press the number adjacent to **L6**.

    c. Press ⟨ STO▶ ⟩.

    d. Press ⟨ 2nd ⟩ [STAT] and press the number adjacent to **L2**. You will now have the expression **L6 → L2** on the home screen. Press ⟨ENTER⟩ to copy the distance data in **L6** to **L2**.

    e. Press ⟨ APPS ⟩ and press the number adjacent to **Link**.

    f. Press the number adjacent to **List** to select a data list.

    g. Press ⟨ ▼ ⟩ until **L2** is highlighted. Press ⟨ENTER⟩ to select it.

    h. Press ⟨ ▶ ⟩ to highlight the **TRANSMIT** menu.

    i. On the receiving calculator, press ⟨ APPS ⟩ and press the number adjacent to **Link**.

    j. Press ⟨ ▶ ⟩ to highlight **RECEIVE**, and press ⟨ENTER⟩. The receiving calculator will show **Waiting**.

    k. On the sending calculator, press ⟨ENTER⟩ to actually transmit the list.

    l. The receiving calculator may display a message screen headed **DuplicateName**. If it does, press the number adjacent to **Overwrite**. The receiving calculator will show **Done**.

▶ **TI-83 and TI-83 Plus**

a. Disconnect the calculators from the data collection devices, and directly connect the two calculators with a black link cable. Firmly press in the cable ends.

b. On the sending calculator, copy the distance data to a new list name. To do this, press ⌈ 2nd ⌉ [L6] ⌈ STO▶ ⌉ ⌈ 2nd ⌉ [L2].

c. You will now have the expression **L6** → **L2** on the home screen. Press ⌈ ENTER ⌉ to copy the distance data in **L6** to **L2**.

d. Press ⌈ 2nd ⌉ [LINK].

e. Press the number adjacent to **List** to select a data list.

f. Press ⌈ ▼ ⌉ until **L2** is highlighted. Press ⌈ ENTER ⌉ to select it.

g. Press ⌈ ▶ ⌉ to highlight the **TRANSMIT** menu.

h. On the receiving calculator, press ⌈ 2nd ⌉ [LINK].

i. Press ⌈ ▶ ⌉ to highlight **RECEIVE**, and press ⌈ ENTER ⌉. The receiving calculator will show **Waiting**.

j. On the sending calculator, press ⌈ ENTER ⌉ to actually transmit the list.

k. The receiving calculator may display a message screen headed **DuplicateName**. If it does, press the number adjacent to **Overwrite**. The receiving calculator will show **Done**.

2. Display a graph of the *y*-values versus the *x*-values. If you collected data using two data collection devices, use the receiving calculator.

a. Press ⌈ 2nd ⌉ [STAT PLOT] ([PLOT] on the TI-73) and press ⌈ ENTER ⌉ to select **Plot 1**.

b. Change the **Plot1** settings to match the screen shown here. Press ⌈ ENTER ⌉ to select any of the settings you change.

(On the TI-73, enter list names by pressing ⌈ 2nd ⌉ [STAT] and selecting the desired list.)

(If you are using LabPro® with one calculator, use **L9** instead of **L2**. To enter **L9**, press ⌈ 2nd ⌉ [LIST], scroll to **L9**, and press ⌈ ENTER ⌉ to paste it to the stat plot screen.)

c. Press ⌈ ZOOM ⌉ and then select **ZoomStat** (use cursor keys to scroll to **ZoomStat**) to draw a graph with the *x* and *y* ranges set to fill the screen with data. The graph you get is nearly, but not quite, what you want, for the proportions of the *x* and *y* scales are not the same.

d.   Press ⌈ZOOM⌉ and select **ZSquare** to re-plot your data with equal-size x-pixels and y-pixels.

e.   Press ⌈TRACE⌉ to determine the coordinates of a point on the graph using the cursor keys.

3.   Trace across your graph to display the coordinates of the five vertices. Record the x- and y-coordinates of the vertices in the Data Table on the *Data Collection and Analysis* sheet.

⇒   Answer Questions 1 and 2 on the *Data Collection and Analysis* sheet.

4.   The star on the pattern sheet is composed of a number of line segments. Since you know the coordinates of each vertex, find the length of each segment using the distance formula. These lengths can be verified by direct measurement with a meter stick.

a.   Use the values in the Data Table, together with the distance formula, to find the length of each of the line segments listed in the Data Table. Record these measurements in the second column of the Data Table.

b.   Then use a meter stick to measure the length of each segment of the star on the pattern sheet. Round these measurements to the nearest 0.001 meter and record them in the last column of the Data Table.

⇒   Answer Question 3 on the *Data Collection and Analysis* sheet.

Place one motion detector (to collect x data) about 50 cm from this point

·

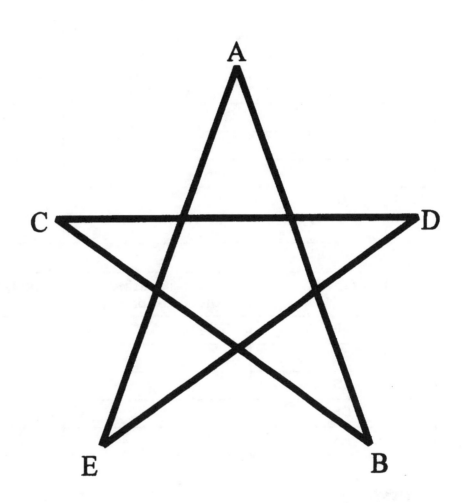

Place one motion detector (to collect y data) about 50 cm from this point

·

Data Collection and Analysis

Name _____

Date _____

Activity 14: From Here to There

Data Table

Distance to point A from y-detector	_____ m

Point	x-coordinate	y-coordinate
A		
B		
C		
D		
E		

Segment	Length using distance formula	Length using direct measurement
AB		
BC		
CD		
DE		
EA		

Questions

1. Compare the distance from the y-detector to point A (recorded in the Data Table) against the y-coordinate of point A. Are they similar? Should they be similar? Why?

2. Based on your answer to the previous question, what is the physical interpretation of the y-coordinates of the data? What is the physical interpretation of the x-coordinates?

3. How do the segment lengths calculated using the distance formula compare with those you found by direct measurement? Which method do you think is more accurate? Why?

Teacher Notes
From Here to There: Applications of the Distance Formula

1. This activity requires two motion detectors. Either TI CBR™s or Vernier Motion Detectors can be used. The TI CBR must be connected through a data collection device, and cannot be connected directly to the calculators. If the TI CBL 2™ is used, you must use two data collection devices and two calculators, and then transfer data to a single calculator for analysis. If a Vernier LabPro® is used, both motion detectors can be connected to a single data collection device.

    LabPros must have ROM version number 6.2 or newer. ROM versions 6.12 and older do not fully support two motion detectors. To determine ROM version, notice the numbers shown on the title screen as DATAMATE is launched. For updates to ROM (also called firmware), see www.vernier.com/calc/flash.html.

2. Some motion detectors will not be automatically identified by DATAMATE. If you are using such a detector, you must manually set up DATAMATE for the detector:

    a. Select **SETUP** from the main screen.

    b. Press ⬛▼ until the cursor is next to DIG (CBL 2) or DIG1 (LabPro).

    c. Press ENTER to access the **SELECT SENSOR** menu.

    d. Select **MOTION(M)**.

    e. Select **OK** to return to the main screen.

3. A wooden dowel or a section of plastic PVC pipe works well. A very small diameter rod (less than 0.5 cm) will result in noisy distance data.

4. Arrange the motion detectors so that their faces are parallel to the edges of the pattern sheet.

5. The raw x- and y-data are shown below in sample data. The exact shape will depend on the speed of the rod during the movement.

Sample Results

Actual data will vary.

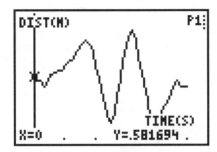

Raw *x* data in DATAMATE

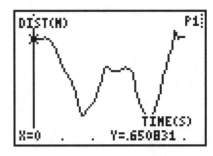

Raw *y* data in DATAMATE

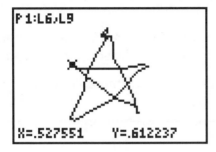

y versus *x* distance data

Data Table

Sample data; actual data may vary.

Distance to point **A** from *y*-detector	0.642 m

Point	*x*-coordinate	*y*-coordinate
A	0.581	0.650
B	0.623	0.547
C	0.527	0.612
D	0.634	0.609
E	0.521	0.538

Segment	Length using distance formula	Length using direct measurement
AB	0.111 m	0.108 m
BC	0.116 m	0.101 m
CD	0.107 m	0.104 m
DE	0.128 m	0.108 m
EA	0.124 m	0.110 m

Answers to Questions

1. The values are essentially the same, as they should be if the motion detector is reading the true distance from itself to the rod.

2. The y-coordinate is the distance from the y-motion detector to the rod, and the x-coordinate is the distance from the x-motion detector to the rod.

3. The segment lengths as calculated by the distance formula are nearly the same as the direct measurement values. The direct measurement values are more reliable, since they do not depend on the rod motion. My lab partner may not have moved the rod carefully!

EXPLORATIONS

Activity 15

Under Pressure: The Inverse Relationship Between Pressure and Volume

Objective

◆ Record pressure versus volume data for a sample of air.

◆ Fit an inverse function model to the data.

◆ Use the table calculation feature of the TI handheld.

◆ Re-plot the data using linearization.

Materials

◆ TI-83 Plus, TI-83, or TI-73

◆ CBL 2™ or LabPro® data collection device

◆ DATAMATE software

◆ Vernier Gas Pressure Sensor or Pressure Sensor with syringe included

Take a sample of air in a closed container and keep it at room temperature. If you change the volume of the container, what will happen to the air pressure inside? You can feel this by squeezing a small balloon in your hand. As the balloon gets smaller, you have to push harder. That is, as the volume decreases, the pressure increases. Two quantities that change this related way could be *inversely* related. If pressure and volume are inversely related, even if both quantities change, then their product stays the same.

Suppose that x and y represent the quantities that are inversely related. Then

$$xy = k, \text{ or } x = \frac{k}{y}$$

where k is a constant in both equations. Maybe you can think of some other quantities that also behave this way. For air and other gases, this relation has a name: *Boyle's law*.

In this activity, you will use a pressure sensor to investigate the relationship between pressure and volume for air contained within a closed syringe.

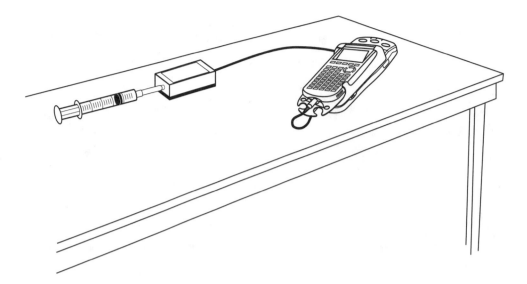

Procedure

1. Prepare the pressure sensor and an air sample for data collection.

   a. Connect the pressure sensor to CH 1 of the CBL 2™ or the LabPro®. Use the unit-to-unit link cable to connect the TI graphing calculator to the data collection device. Firmly press in the cable ends.

   b. With the syringe disconnected from the pressure sensor, move the piston of the syringe until the leading edge of the inside black ring is positioned at the 10.0 mL mark.

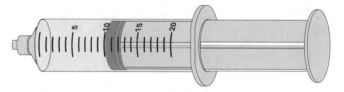

   c. Attach the syringe to the pressure sensor.

   ◆ Newer Vernier Gas Pressure Sensors have a white stem protruding from the end of the sensor box. Attach the tube directly to the white stem with a gentle half-turn.

   ◆ Older Vernier Pressure Sensors have a 3-way valve at the end of a plastic tube leading from the sensor box. Before attaching the tube, align the blue handle with the stem of the 3-way valve that will *not* have the tube connected to it, as shown in the figure at the right, closing this stem. Then attach the tube directly to the remaining open stem of the 3-way valve.

   The air in the syringe/pressure sensor system is now sealed, so that as you move the piston, the air volume and pressure both change.

2. To obtain the best data possible, you will need to correct the volume readings from the syringe. Look at the syringe; its scale reports its own internal volume. However, that volume is not the total volume of trapped air in your system since there is a little bit of space in the tubing and internal to the pressure sensor.

   To account for the extra volume in the system, you will need to add a small and constant volume to your syringe readings. If your sensor does not have a valve and tubing attached to it, the correction is **0.8 mL**. If your sensor does have attached tubing, the correction is **1.5 mL**. For example, with the 0.8 mL correction and a 5.0 mL syringe volume, the total volume would be 5.8 mL. *It is that total volume that you will need for the analysis.*

3. Turn on the calculator and start the DATAMATE software. Press [CLEAR] to reset the software.

4. Set up the calculator and data collection device for a gas pressure sensor or pressure sensor.

   a. Select **1: SETUP** from the main screen.

   b. If the calculator displays a pressure sensor with units of kPa in CH 1, proceed directly to Step 5. If it does not, continue with this step to set up the sensor manually.

   c. Press [ENTER] to select **CH 1**.

   d. Select **PRESSURE** from the SELECT SENSOR menu.

   e. Select the correct pressure sensor (**GAS PRESSURE SENSOR** or **PRESSURE SENSOR**) from the PRESSURE menu.

   f. Select the calibration listing for units of kPa.

5. Set up the data collection mode.

   a. To select **MODE**, press [▲] once and press [ENTER].

   b. Select **EVENTS WITH ENTRY** from the SELECT MODE menu.

   c. Select **OK** to return to the main screen.

6. You are now ready to collect pressure and volume data. It is best for one person to handle the gas syringe and for another to operate the calculator.

   a. Select **START** to begin data collection.

   b. Move the piston so the front edge of the inside black ring is positioned at the 5 mL line on the syringe. Hold the piston firmly in this position until the pressure value displayed on the calculator screen stabilizes.

c. Press ENTER. (The person holding the syringe can relax after ENTER is pressed.) Type in the total gas volume (in mL) on the calculator. That is, enter either **5.8** or **6.5**, as appropriate for your sensor. Remember, you are adding the constant volume to the apparent volume of the syringe. Press ENTER to store this pressure-volume data pair.

d. To collect another data pair, move the piston to 7.0 mL. When the pressure reading stabilizes, press ENTER and enter the total volume, remembering to add the appropriate correction to the syringe volume.

e. Continue with this procedure using syringe volumes of 10.0, 12.0, 15.0, 17.0, and 20.0 mL.

f. Press STO▶ when you have finished collecting data. A graph of pressure versus volume will be shown.

7. In order to work directly with the data, you need to leave the DATAMATE software. Press ENTER to return to the main screen, and select **QUIT** to leave the software. Follow any instructions on the screen to return to the calculator home screen.

Analysis

1. Redisplay the graph.

    a. Press ZOOM.

    b. Press ▼ until **ZoomStat** is highlighted; press ENTER to display a graph with the x and y ranges set to fill the screen with data.

    c. Press TRACE to determine the coordinates of a point on the graph using the cursor keys.

2. Examine the data pairs on the displayed graph. As you move the cursor right or left, the volume (x) and pressure (y) values of each data point are displayed below the graph. Record the pressure (round to the nearest 0.1 kPa) and volume data values in the first Data Table on the *Data Collection and Analysis* sheet.

3. To test Boyle's law you can plot the inverse function $y = k/x$ with the data. You will see this equation with the data, and can then adjust the value for k to improve the fit. First, enter the inverse function and then, in the next step, explore values of k.

    a. Press Y=.

    b. Press CLEAR to remove any existing equation.

    c. Enter **k/x** in the **Y1** field. (On the TI-73, access the alphabetic entry screen by pressing 2nd [TEXT].)

    d. Press 2nd [QUIT] to return to the home screen.

4. Set a value for the parameter k, and then look at the resulting graph. To obtain a good fit, you will need to try several values. Use the steps below to store different values to the parameter k. Start with k = 500. Experiment until you find one that provides a good fit for the data.

   a. Enter a value for the parameter k. Press [STO▸] K [ENTER] to store the value in the variable **K**.

   b. Press [GRAPH] to see the data with the model graph superimposed.

   c. Press [2nd] [QUIT] to return to the home screen.

⇒ Answer Question 1 on the *Data Collection and Analysis* sheet.

5. Find the products of the data coordinates and record them in the third column of the Data Table.

⇒ Answer Question 2 on the *Data Collection and Analysis* sheet.

6. The modeling equation you have determined in this activity can be used to predict syringe pressure values for given volumes. The second Data Table on the *Data Collection and Analysis* sheet lists a number of volumes. Fill in the corresponding pressures. Although it would not take long to do this by hand, try using the table feature of the calculator to do the calculation.

   a. Press [2nd] [TBLSET] to display **Table Setup**.

   b. Use the cursor keys to highlight **Ask** on the **Indpnt:** line, and press [ENTER] to select this mode.

   c. Use the cursor keys to highlight **Auto** on the **Depend:** line, and press [ENTER] to select this mode.

   d. Press [2nd] [TABLE] to display the table.

   e. Enter **2.5** for the first x value, and finish the entry with [ENTER]. Note how the calculator has determined the y value from the model. Complete the Data Table for the remaining three entries.

⇒ Answer Questions 3 and 4 on the *Data Collection and Analysis* sheet.

7. Another way to see if two quantities are inversely related is to plot the one quantity versus the inverse of the other. For this pressure activity, that would be pressure versus the inverse of the volume. If the new plot shows a line of proportionality, then the original data is inversely related. You can see this by noting the simple rearrangement of the equation $y = k/x$ as $y = kx\,(1/x)$. Written this way, you can see that y is proportional to the quantity $(1/x)$. The process of graphing calculated quantities to obtain a straight-line graph is sometimes called *linearization*.

To see if the data is inversely related using this test, you need to define a new column containing the inverse of the volume data. The volume data is in **L1**; **L3** is available for the inverse volume information. **L2** will continue to hold the pressure data.

▶ **TI-73**

a.   Press [2nd] [QUIT] to return to the home screen.

b.   Press **1/ L1** [STO▶] **L3** [ENTER]. To enter list names on the TI-73, press [2nd] [STAT] to see a menu of list names. **L3** will now hold the inverse of the values in **L1**.

▶ **TI-83, TI-83 Plus**

a.   Press [2nd] [QUIT] to return to the home screen.

b.   Press **1/** [2nd] **[L1]** [STO▶] [2nd] **[L3]** [ENTER]. **L3** will now hold the inverse of the values in **L1**.

8.   You can plot the pressure versus inverse volume data on a new graph using the following commands.

a.   Press [2nd] [STAT PLOT] ([PLOT] on the TI-73) and press [ENTER] to select **Plot 1**.

b.   Change the **Plot1** settings to match the screen shown here. Press [ENTER] to select any of the settings you change.

c.   Press [ZOOM] and then select **ZoomStat** (use cursor keys to scroll to **ZoomStat**) to draw a graph with the *x* and *y* ranges set to fill the screen with data.

⇒ Answer Question 5 on the *Data Collection and Analysis* sheet.

Extension

1.   An alternate way to find a model for the data you collected involves a process known as *regression analysis*. The calculator will select the best parameters for the power function $y = ax^b$. (The TI-73 cannot perform this analysis.)

*Note: Before performing this extension, the **Stat Plot 1** settings must first be restored to graph **L1** and **L2** using the plotting setup of Step 8, with **L2** replacing **L3**.*

a.   Press [STAT] and use the arrow keys to highlight **CALC**.

b.   Press the number adjacent to **PwrReg** to copy the command to the home screen.

c.   Press [2nd] **[L1]** [,] [2nd] **[L2]** [,] to enter the lists containing your data.

d.   Press [VARS] and use the cursor keys to highlight **Y-VARS**.

e.   Select **Function** by pressing [ENTER].

f. Press ENTER to copy **Y1** to the home screen.

g. On the home screen, you will now see the entry **PwrReg L1, L2, Y1**. This command will perform a power regression with **L1** as the x and **L2** as the y values. The resulting regression line will be stored in equation variable **Y1**. Press ENTER to perform the regression.

h. Press ZOOM and then select **ZoomStat** (use cursor keys to scroll to **ZoomStat**) to draw a graph with the x and y ranges set to fill the screen with data.

Does the power law model provide a good fit to the pressure versus volume data? How many parameters are adjusted to achieve a good fit compared to the inverse model?

2. It is possible to deduce the internal volume of the sensor rather than using the supplied values. If you assume Boyle's law, you can determine the internal volume from the y-intercept value. For example, if the internal volume of the sensor is d, then the total volume of air in the system is $v + d$. From Boyle's law, we have $P*(v + d) = k$, which can be rearranged to $v = k*(1/P) - d$. From the form of this equation, we can see that the y-intercept of a v (y-axis) versus $1/P$ (x-axis) graph is the negative of the internal volume.

Note that this is not the same graph setup as used in the activity. Collect a new data set, but do not correct the volumes; just enter the syringe volume directly. Create a graph of v versus $1/P$. Fit a straight line to the data, and from the y-intercept determine the internal volume of your particular sensor. For comparison to your results, the internal volume of the Vernier Gas Pressure Sensor (model without attached tubing and value) is about 0.8 mL, while for the Vernier Pressure Sensor (with tubing and valve) the aggregate internal volume is about 1.5 mL.

Data Collection and Analysis

Name _____

Date _____

Activity 15: Under Pressure

Data Tables

Volume in mL (x values)	Pressure in kPa (y values)	Product (x * y)

Volume in mL (x values)	Pressure in kPa (y values)
2.5	
17.8	
520	
0.0012	

Questions

1. In the space below, use the value for k to record the model equation that gives the best fit to the data.

2. Notice that the values in the third column of the first Data Table are closely related to the value of k you found in Step 4. Explain why this is so.

3. Could the volume ever be zero? Why or why not? What would be the corresponding pressure?

4. Complete the following statement:
    As the volume of a gas sample decreases, its pressure _____.

5. Based on your graph of pressure versus inverse volume, are pressure and volume inversely proportional?

Teacher Notes
Under Pressure: The Inverse Relationship Between Pressure and Volume

1. Do not use any extra tubing in attaching the syringe to the sensor. Attach the syringe directly to the Gas Pressure Sensor. Attach the syringe directly to the valve on the Pressure Sensor. Using any extra plastic tubing will degrade the results because of additional volume not counted in the syringe volume.

2. The product of the pressure and volume values, determined in Step 5 of the Analysis, can also be done directly using list calculations. You may choose to have students do the analysis that way.

Sample Results

Actual data will vary.

P1:L1,L2
(pressure versus volume curve graph)
X=7.8 . . . . . Y=131 . . . . .

Pressure versus volume graph

L1	L2	L3	2
5.8	179	1038.2
7.8	131	1021.8
10.8	94.6	1021.7
12.8	80.3	1027.8
15.8	65.9	1041.2
17.8	58.9	1048.4
20.8	50.6	1052.5
L2(1)=179		

Raw data

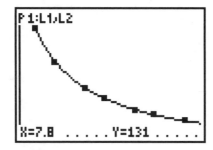

X	Y₁	
2.5	414	
17.8	58.146	
520	1.9904	
.0012	862500	
X=		

Table calculation

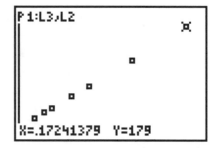

Pressure versus inverse volume

Data Tables

Sample data; actual data may vary.

Volume in mL (x values)	Pressure in kPa (y values)	Product (x * y)
5.8	179	1039
7.8	131	1018
10.8	94.6	1022
12.8	80.3	1028
15.8	65.9	1041
17.8	58.9	1048
20.8	50.6	1053

Volume in mL (x values)	Pressure in kPa (y values)
2.5	414
17.8	58
520	2.0
0.0012	863,000

Answers to Questions

1. The model equation $y = 1035/x$ gave an excellent fit to the experimental data.

2. The products are all near 1035. This is as expected, since the model equation $y = 1035/x$ can be rearranged to $xy = 1035$.

3. From the model, the volume can't ever be zero because that would imply an infinite pressure.

4. As the volume of a gas sample decreases, its pressure increases.

5. Based on the graph of pressure versus inverse volume, pressure and volume are indeed inversely proportional. The graph of pressure versus inverse volume is very nearly a straight line.

EXPLORATIONS

Activity 16

Light at a Distance: Distance and Light Intensity

Objective

♦ Collect light intensity versus distance data for a point light source.

♦ Compare data to an inverse-square model.

♦ Compare data to a power law model.

♦ Discuss the difference between an inverse-square model and a power law model.

Materials

♦ TI-83 Plus, TI-83, or TI-73

♦ CBL 2™ or LabPro® data collection device

♦ DATAMATE software

♦ Meter stick or tape measure

♦ Light sensor

♦ DC-powered point light source

While traveling in a car at night, you may have observed the headlights of an oncoming vehicle. The light starts as a dim glow in the distance, but as the vehicle gets closer, the brightness of the headlights increases rapidly. This is because the light spreads out as it moves away from the source. As a result, light intensity decreases as the distance from a typical light source increases. What is the relationship between distance and intensity for a simple light bulb?

In this activity you can explore the relationship between distance and intensity for a light bulb. You will record the intensity at various distances between a light sensor and the bulb. The data can then be analyzed and modeled mathematically.

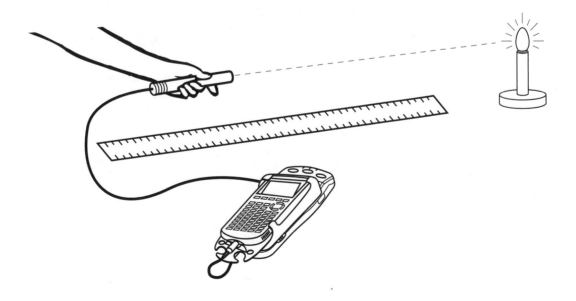

Procedure

1. Arrange the equipment. There must be no obstructions between the bulb and the light sensor during data collection. Remove any surfaces near the bulb, such as books, people, walls or tables. There should be no reflective surfaces behind, beside, or below the bulb. The filament and light sensor should be at the same vertical height. This makes the light bulb look more like a point source of light as seen by the light sensor. While you are taking intensity readings, the light sensor must be pointed directly at the light bulb.

2. Attach the light sensor to CH 1 on the CBL 2™ or LabPro® data collection device. Use the unit-to-unit cable to connect the data collection device to the TI graphing calculator. Firmly press in the cable ends.

    Note: If the sensor has a range switch, set it to 600 lux for a small light source, or 6000 lux for a larger, brighter source.

3. Turn on the calculator and start the DATAMATE software. Press [CLEAR] to reset the software.

4. Set up DATAMATE and the data collection device for the light sensor.

    a. Select **SETUP** from the main screen.

    b. If CH 1 displays the light sensor, skip to Step 5.

    c. Press [ENTER] to select **CH 1**.

    d. Choose **LIGHT** from the SELECT SENSOR list.

    e. Choose **600 LUX** or **6000 LUX** from the LIGHT list to match the switch setting you used. The sensor will read in units of lux.

5. Set up the calculator and the data collection device for the events with entry data collection mode.

    a. Press [▲] to select MODE and press [ENTER].

    b. Select **EVENTS WITH ENTRY** from the SELECT MODE menu to collect light intensity data as a function of distance. In this mode you will trigger the data collection device to record the light intensity for each position you choose.

    c. Select **OK** to return to the main screen.

6. Dim the lights to darken the room. A very dark room is critical to obtain good results.

7. Hold the light sensor about 10 cm from the light bulb filament. Move the sensor away from the bulb and watch the displayed intensity values on the calculator screen.

⇒ Answer Question 1 on the *Data Collection and Analysis* sheet.

8. To account for the particular brightness of the light source, choose a starting distance that gives a reading less than the maximum reading for the sensor (600 or 6000 lux for the Vernier sensor, or 1 for the TI sensor), but as large as possible. However, do not get any closer than 5 cm for small (<5 mm) bulbs, or 10 cm otherwise. Choose the starting distance, and enter it as x_L in the Data Table on the *Data Collection and Analysis* sheet.

9. Again place the light sensor the planned starting distance from the light bulb filament.

    Important: The distance must be measured carefully. Be sure you measure from the filament of the lamp to the sensor tip on the light sensor.

10. Select **START** from the main screen to prepare for data collection.

11. Wait for the value displayed on the calculator to stabilize. Press (ENTER), and then enter the distance between the light sensor and the light source in meters on the calculator. Press (ENTER) to conclude the entry.

12. Move the light sensor 1 cm farther away from the light source and repeat the previous step.

13. Continue moving the sensor in 1-cm increments until the readings fall to less than 10% of the initial reading, collecting data as before. After the final data point, press (STO▶) to end data collection.

14. Inspect the graph of light intensity versus distance. Trace to read the x and y values of the left-most point, round the values to three significant figures, and record them as x_L and y_L in the Data Table.

15. Press (ENTER) to return to the main screen, and select **QUIT** to leave DATAMATE. Follow any instructions on the calculator to return to the home screen.

Analysis

1. Redisplay the graph outside of DATAMATE.

    a. Press (ZOOM).

    b. Press (▼) until **ZoomStat** is highlighted. Press (ENTER) to display a graph with the x and y ranges set to fill the screen with data.

2. Inspect the graph of the light intensity versus distance.

⇒ Answer question 2 on the *Data Collection and Analysis* sheet.

3. One model for light intensity holds that the intensity is proportional to the inverse square of the distance from a point light source; that is, a graph would be of the form $y = C/x^2$, where C is an adjustable parameter. Does the data follow this model? You can check it out by finding an approximate value for C and then graphing the model with the data. First, enter the model equation.

    a. Press (Y=).

b. Press [CLEAR] to remove any existing equation.

c. Enter **C/x²** in the **Y1** field. (On the TI-73, access the alphabetic entry screen by pressing [2nd] [TEXT].)

d. Press [2nd] [QUIT] to return to the home screen.

4. Set a value for the parameter C and then look at the resulting graph. To obtain a good fit, you will need to try several values for C. Use the steps below to determine an initial guess for the parameter. One way to find an approximate value for the parameter is to use the left-most point. If you solve for C, then $C = yx^2$. Use the x and y values for the left-most point to calculate an initial value for C. Record this value in the Data Table on the *Data Collection and Analysis* sheet.

    a. Enter a value for the parameter C. Press [STO▶] **C** [ENTER] to store the value in the variable **C**.

    b. Press [GRAPH] to see the data with the model graph superimposed.

    c. Press [2nd] [QUIT] to return to the home screen.

5. If the model is systematically high or low, you may want to adjust the value of C to improve the fit. As you did before, store a new value in **C**, and then display the graph and model. Once you have optimized the model, record the complete equation in the Data Table.

⇒ Answer Question 3 on the *Data Collection and Analysis* sheet.

6. Another model can be used to compare to the data. The general power law of $y = ax^b$ may provide a better fit than the inverse-square function, especially if the light source is not small or if there are reflections from walls or other surfaces. The difference between this new model and the inverse-square model is that the exponent is not fixed at -2. Instead, the exponent is now an adjustable parameter. The calculator can be used to automatically determine the parameters a and b in the general power law relation to the data.

    ### TI-73

    (The TI-73 cannot perform this analysis.)

    ### TI-83 and TI-83 Plus

    a. Press [STAT] and use the cursor keys to highlight **CALC**.

    b. Press [▼] repeatedly to scroll down to **PwrReg**. When it is highlighted, press [ENTER] to copy the command to the home screen.

    c. Press [2nd] [L1] [,] [2nd] [L2] [,] to enter the lists containing the data.

d. Press `VARS` and use the cursor keys to highlight **Y-VARS**.

e. Select **Function** by pressing `ENTER`.

f. Press `ENTER` to copy **Y1** to the home screen.

g. On the home screen, you will now see the entry **PwrReg L1, L2, Y1**. This command will perform a power law regression with **L1** as the x and **L2** as the y values. The resulting regression curve will be stored in equation variable **Y1**. Press `ENTER` to perform the regression. Use the parameters a and b, rounded to two significant figures, to write the power law model equation in the Data Table.

h. Press `GRAPH` to see the graph of the data and the power regression function.

⇒ Answer Questions 4 and 5 on the *Data Collection and Analysis* sheet.

Extension

1. Suppose that your patio is illuminated by an overhead light fixture with two bulbs. You decide to save on electricity by removing one of the bulbs. If the light is currently mounted 5 m off the ground, to what height should the light fixture be moved in order to retain the same amount of light on the patio with one bulb? Does your answer depend on the model you use?

2. Two identical light bulbs shine on your favorite reading chair from different locations in the room. The first bulb is 3 m from the chair and provides an intensity of 0.6 mW/cm^2. The second is 2 m from the chair. What intensity does this bulb provide? Does your answer depend on the model you use?

Data Collection and Analysis

Name _____

Date _____

Activity 16: Light at a Distance

Data Table

Left-most point x value x_L	
Left-most point y value y_L	
Initial model parameter C	
Optimized inverse-square model $y = C/x^2$	
Power law model $y = ax^b$	

Questions

1. What is your prediction for the relationship between intensity and the distance to a light source?

2. Is the graph of the light intensity versus distance consistent with your earlier prediction?

3. How well does the inverse-square model $y = C/x^2$ fit the experimental data?

4. How well does the power law model fit the data? Could it fit any better than the inverse-square model? Could it fit more poorly?

5. How would using a brighter light bulb affect the parameters a, b, and C in the two models?

Teacher Notes
Light at a Distance: Distance and Light Intensity

1. If you obtain readings of more than 600 or 6000 lux (Vernier sensor, depending on setting) or 1 (TI sensor), move farther away from the light source. Students may need to adjust the range of distances used for data collection, depending on the brightness of the light source. Some students may need help with this in Step 8 of the procedure. Because of the different light sources that could be used in the lab, the optimum range for data collection will vary.

2. Only a true point light source exhibits an inverse-square dependence of intensity on distance. It is very difficult in a classroom to achieve a true point light source with no reflective surfaces nearby. As a result, you and your students should not consider results incorrect if you do not get an exponent of nearly -2 in the power law fit. In fact, it is unlikely you will obtain a -2 exponent. An extended light source will yield an exponent between -1 and -2. A long straight light, such as a fluorescent tube, will yield an exponent of about -1 at typical distance ranges.

3. An excellent light source for this experiment is the AA-cell size Mini Maglite® flashlight (www.maglite.com). The reflector can be unscrewed and removed completely, revealing a very small and intense near-point light. If another kind of flashlight is used, it is essential that it *not* have a reflector around the bulb or the source will not behave at all like a point source.

4. It is important that the light be powered by DC (direct current), such as by a battery source. AC-powered lamps exhibit a time-varying flicker that is not detectable by eye, but that may substantially reduce the quality of the data.

5. The quantity measured by the light sensors is not strictly called *intensity*, but we use this common term for convenience.

6. You may want to have students adjust the window range to replot the data to include the origin. The inverse-square nature of the model is more readily visible when plotted this way. (See sample data below.)

Sample Results

Actual data will vary.

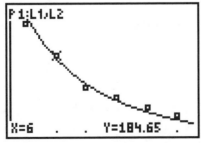

Sample data with inverse-square model

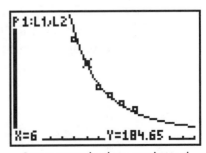

Same sample data replotted over a wider range

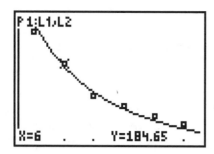

Sample data with power law model

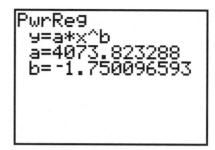

Power law fit parameters

Data Table

Sample data; actual data may vary.

Left-most point x value x_L	5
Left-most point y value y_L	244
Initial model parameter C	6100
Optimized inverse-square model $y = C/x^2$	$y = 6300/x^2$
Power law model $y = ax^b$	$y = 4100x^{-1.8}$

Answers to Questions

1. The intensity of the light appears to get smaller with increasing distance. The relationship could be an inverse relationship, or it could be something else.

2. Yes, the data are consistent with a decreasing function such as an inverse function, as the graph is always decreasing but it never crosses the horizontal axis.

3. The inverse-square model fits the data very well.

4. The fit of the general power law looks very similar to the inverse-square fit. The power law fit has to be at least as good as the inverse-square fit, since the power law fit includes the possibility of the inverse-square fit with the exponent taking a value of -2. The fit of the power law model could be better than the inverse-square model *if* the data does not actually have an inverse-square behavior.

5. A brighter bulb would shift increase all readings proportionately. So, a and C would increase, but b would stay the same.

EXPLORATIONS

Activity 17

Chill Out: How Hot Objects Cool

Objectives

♦ To record temperature versus time cooling data.

♦ To model cooling data with an exponential function.

Materials

♦ TI-83 Plus, TI-83, or TI-73

♦ CBL 2™ or LabPro® data collection device

♦ DATAMATE software

♦ Temperature probe

♦ Hot water

When you have a hot drink, you know that it gradually cools off. Newton's law of cooling provides us with a model for cooling. It states that the temperature difference T_{diff} between a hot object and its surroundings decreases exponentially with time.

$$T_{diff} = T_0\,e^{-kt}$$

In the model T_0 is the initial temperature difference, and k is a positive constant.

In this activity you will use a temperature probe to collect data as the warmed probe cools. You can then fit several mathematical models to the data.

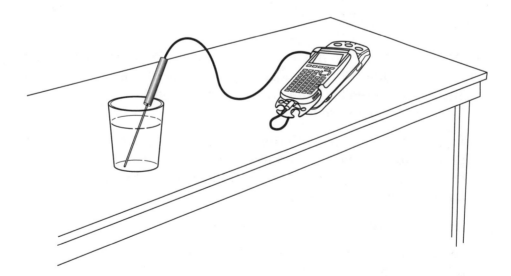

Procedure

1. Connect a temperature probe to CH 1 on the CBL 2™ or LabPro®. Use the unit-to-unit cable to connect the data collection device to the calculator. Press in the cable ends firmly.

2. Turn on the calculator and start the DATAMATE software. Press $\boxed{\text{CLEAR}}$ to reset the software.

3. If CH 1 displays a temperature probe in units of °C, proceed to Step 4. If it does not, set up DATAMATE for the sensor manually. To do this,

   a. Select **SETUP** from the main screen.

   b. Press $\boxed{\text{ENTER}}$ to select **CH 1**.

   c. Choose **TEMPERATURE** from the SELECT SENSOR list.

   d. Choose the type of temperature probe (with units of °C) you are using from the list.

   e. Select **OK** to return to the main screen.

4. Obtain a cup of hot water at 45 to 55 °C. Place the temperature probe in the water, and wait about 20 seconds for the probe to reach the temperature of the water. Rather than waiting for the water to cool, just remove the temperature probe from the water and observe the cooling of the probe itself. Remove the probe from the water and rest it on the edge of a table. Do not let anything touch the tip of the probe.

5. Collect the cooling data. Select **START** from the main screen. Data collection will run for three minutes, after which a graph of temperature versus time will display.

6. Newton's law of cooling models the temperature difference between the warm object and its surroundings. As an estimate of the room temperature, use the minimum temperature on the graph. Inspect the graph to determine its minimum temperature reading.

   a. Trace along the graph with the $\boxed{\blacktriangleright}$ key and determine the minimum temperature reached. Round this temperature down to the next whole degree (as in 24.54 → 24) and record the value in the Data Table on the *Data Collection and Analysis* sheet.

   b. Press $\boxed{\text{ENTER}}$ to return to the main screen.

   c. Select **QUIT** from the main screen. Follow any instructions on the screen to return to the calculator home screen.

Analysis

1. Since the model for Newton's law of cooling uses the difference between the temperature of the warm object and its surroundings, subtract the minimum temperature from the measured temperature before comparing data to the model.

   ### TI-73

   a. Access lists by pressing [2nd] [STAT]. Press the number next to **L2** to copy **L2** to the home screen.

   b. Press [−] then key in the (minimum temp), where (minimum temp) is the numerical value you entered in the Data Table on the *Data Collection and Analysis* sheet.

   c. Press [STO▸], and enter **L2** a second time. The expression will look like **L2 − 24 → L2**, depending on the particular minimum temperature. Press [ENTER] to perform the calculation.

   ### TI-83 and TI-83 Plus

   a. Press [2nd] [L2].

   b. Press [−] then key in the (minimum temp), where (minimum temp) is the numerical value you entered in the data table.

   c. Press [STO▸], and press [2nd] [L2] a second time. The expression will look like **L2 − 24 → L2**, depending on the particular minimum temperature. Press [ENTER] to perform the calculation.

2. Redisplay the graph of temperature difference versus time.

   a. Press [ZOOM].

   b. Press [▼] until **ZoomStat** is highlighted; press [ENTER] to display a graph with the x and y ranges set to fill the screen with data.

   c. Press [TRACE] to determine the coordinates of a point on the graph using the cursor keys.

⇒ Answer Question 1 on the *Data Collection and Analysis* sheet.

3. Plot an exponential model of $y = Te^{-kx}$ to the data. Use these new variable names to match what the calculator can use. You can determine the value for T (the initial temperature difference T_0) by tracing the graph to the point at $x = 0$. Record this parameter as T in the Data Table.

4. Since you have values for the parameter T of the model, you can try plotting the model using a guess for the k parameter. First, enter the model equation for graphing.

   a. Press [Y=].

   b. Press [CLEAR] to remove any existing equation.

   c. Enter the exponential model using the value for the parameter T. For example, if the equation is $y = 25e^{-kt}$, enter **25*e^(-K*x)** on the **Y1** line. (On the TI-73, access the exponential function by pressing [MATH] and selecting the LOG menu; access the alphabetic entry screen by pressing [2nd] [TEXT].)

   d. Press [◄] until the icon to the left of **Y1** is blinking. Press [ENTER] until a bold diagonal line is shown which will display the model with a thick line.

   e. Press [2nd] [QUIT] to return to the home screen.

5. Set a value for the parameter k, and then look at the resulting graph. To obtain a good fit, you will need to adjust the value of k. Use the steps below to store different values to the parameter k, starting with $k = 0.01$.

   a. Enter a value for the parameter k. Press [STO▶] **K** [ENTER] to store the value in the variable **K**.

   b. Press [GRAPH] to see the data with the model graph superimposed. The model line is bold.

   c. Press [2nd] [QUIT] to return to the home screen.

   Experiment until you find one that provides a good fit for the data. Record the k value that works best in the Data Table.

   ⇒ Using this k value and the value of T you determined earlier, complete the model equation and record it in Question 2 on the *Data Collection and Analysis* sheet.

6. You can also use the calculator to fit an exponential to the data. The calculator uses the exponential form of $y = ab^x$. This is slightly different from the form you used in the modeling of the previous step, but it is still an exponential.

   TI-73

   a. Press [2nd] [STAT] and use the cursor keys to highlight **CALC**.

   b. Press the number adjacent to **ExpReg** to copy the command to the home screen.

   c. After the **ExpReg** command, press [2nd] [STAT] and select **L1** by pressing the number next to **L1**. Then press [,]. Repeat the procedure to select **L2**.

d. After selecting **L2**, press [,] then press [2nd] [VARS].

e. Use the cursor keys to select **Y-Vars** and press [ENTER] .

f. Press [ENTER] to copy **Y1** to the expression.

On the home screen, you will now see the entry **ExpReg L1, L2, Y1**. This command will perform an exponential regression with **L1** as the x and **L2** as the y values. The resulting regression equation will be stored in equation variable **Y1**. Press [ENTER] to perform the regression. Copy the parameters a and b that appear on the calculator screen to the Data Table.

g. Press [GRAPH] to see the graph.

⇒ Answer Questions 3-9 on the *Data Collection and Analysis* sheet.

TI-83 and TI-83 Plus

a. Press [STAT] and use the cursor keys to highlight **CALC**.

b. Press the number adjacent to **ExpReg** to copy the command to the home screen.

c. Press [2nd] [L1] [,] [2nd] [L2] [,] to enter the lists containing the data.

d. Press [VARS] and use the cursor keys to highlight **Y-VARS**.

e. Select **Function** by pressing [ENTER].

f. Press [ENTER] to copy **Y1** to the expression.

On the home screen, you will now see the entry **ExpReg L1, L2, Y1**. This command will perform an exponential regression with **L1** as the x values and **L2** as the y values. The resulting regression equation will be stored in equation variable **Y1**. Press [ENTER] to perform the regression. Copy the parameters a and b that appear on the calculator screen to the Data Table.

g. Press [GRAPH] to see the graph.

⇒ Answer Questions 3-9 on the *Data Collection and Analysis* sheet.

Extension

Newton's law of cooling states that the rate of change of the temperature of a liquid is directly proportional to the difference between its temperature and the temperature of the surroundings. The differential equation is:

$$\frac{dT}{dt} = -k(T - T_{room})$$

where T_{room} represents the surrounding temperature. Solve the differential equation (showing the steps) given above to show that $T = (T_0 - T_{room}) T_0 e^{-kt} + T_{room}$. In this equation, T_0 represents the initial temperature.

Data Collection and Analysis

Name _____

Date _____

Activity 17: Chill Out

Data Table

	Minimum Temperature (°C)	
$y = Te^{-kt}$	T	
	k	
$y = ab^x$	a	
	b	

Questions

1. Is the graph consistent with the model of a decreasing exponential? In what way?

2. Record the model equation from Step 5 of the *Analysis* section here.

3. How does the regression fit compare to the model? How can both models fit the data well when the fit parameters are different?

4. Why are the values for a and T similar, while b and k are quite different? Use the model equations to find the relationship between k and b so you can compare the value to that of the calculator.

5. When $t = 0$, what is the value of e^{-kt}?

6. When t is very large, what is the value of the temperature difference? What is the temperature of the sensor at this time?

7. What could you do to the experimental apparatus to decrease the value of k in another run? What quantity does k measure?

8. Use either the model equation or the regression equation to predict the time it takes the sensor to reach a temperature 1°C above room temperature.

9. If the starting temperature difference is cut in half, does it take half as long to get to 1°C above room temperature? Explain.

Teacher Notes
Chill Out: How Hot Objects Cool

1. As a short-cut you can have students warm the probe by rubbing the tip with their hands. The magnitude of the temperature change will be much smaller, but the analysis is the same.

2. Data collection must be started *after* the probe has started to cool. Do not worry about catching the first few seconds of cooling.

3. The **L2** list must not contain zero or negative values, or the exponential fit will fail. If the student is careless in subtracting the final value, rounded down, from the original list values, then non-positive values could result. Negative values in **L2** are the most likely cause of errors in this activity.

4. Ideally the student would subtract room temperature from the list **L2**. However, if the room temperature measurement is done too quickly with a warmed probe, then the room temperature value will be high, and the **L2** list will contain negative numbers. To make the activity fail-safe from such an error, we have the student subtract the minimum value of the series, as determined by a trace. Some teachers may wish to modify the activity to use a careful room-temperature measurement and subtraction.

Sample Results

Actual data will vary.

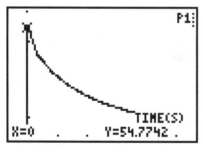

Uncorrected temperature
versus time data

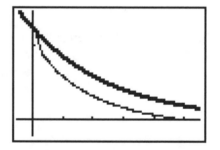

Data and model with first guess
for *k* (0.01)

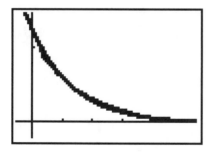

Data and regression line

Data Table

Sample data; actual data may vary.

Minimum Temperature (°C)		24
$y = Te^{-kt}$	T	30
	k	0.02
$y = ab^x$	a	38.03
	b	0.977

Answers to Questions

1. Yes, the data is consistent with a decreasing exponential, as the graph is always decreasing, but it never crosses the horizontal axis.

2. Model equation is $y = 30e^{-0.02x}$.

3. The regression line fits the data well. Both the regression and the model are exponential functions, so they can have the same shape.

4. The bases of the exponential functions are different, leading to different multiplicative terms in the exponent. Comparing the exponential terms, we have $b^x = e^{-kx}$, or $-\ln(b) = k$.

5. When $t = 0$, we have $e^0 = 1$.

6. When t is large, $e^{-\text{large}}$ approaches zero, so the temperature difference approaches zero.

7. A decreasing k would correspond to a longer time to cool. To make the probe take longer to cool, wrap it in insulation.

8. $1 = 30e^{-0.02t}$, or $t = 170$ seconds, using the model.

9. No, it takes more than half as long. Using the model expression, we see that the time to 1°C temperature difference is ln(starting temp difference)/0.02. If the starting temp difference is 15°C, then it takes 135 seconds to reach a 1°C difference.

EXPLORATIONS

Activity 18

Charging Up, Charging Down: Exponential Models

Objective

♦ Record potential versus time data for a discharging capacitor.

♦ Model potential data using an exponential function.

Materials

♦ TI-83 Plus, TI-83, or TI-73

♦ CBL 2™ or LabPro® data collection device

♦ DATAMATE software

♦ Voltage probe

♦ 9-volt battery

♦ 100-kΩ resistor

♦ 220-µF capacitor

A *capacitor* is an electronic component used to store electrical energy. Many of the devices you use on a daily basis, such as your calculator, rely on capacitors as part of their electronic circuitry. Cameras use capacitors, too. Before using an electronic flash, energy is transferred from the camera battery to a capacitor. That energy quickly dissipates in the flash unit when you press the shutter release. The result is a bright flash!

When a capacitor discharges through a resistor, the voltage (or potential) across the capacitor drops off rapidly at first, and then decreases more slowly as the energy dissipates. The action of a discharging capacitor is described by the exponential model

$$y = Ve^{-Kx}$$

where y represents the voltage across the capacitor at any time x; V is the capacitor's initial voltage; K is a positive parameter that depends on the physical characteristics of the capacitor and resistor; and e is a special number called the *base* of the natural logarithm. The number e, about 2.718, is similar to π in that it never repeats and never terminates. It is a common base used in exponential expressions.

In this activity, you will collect voltage data from a discharging capacitor using a voltage probe. The capacitor will be connected to another circuit element called a *resistor*, which controls the rate at which the capacitor discharges. You will then compare the exponential model to the data you collect.

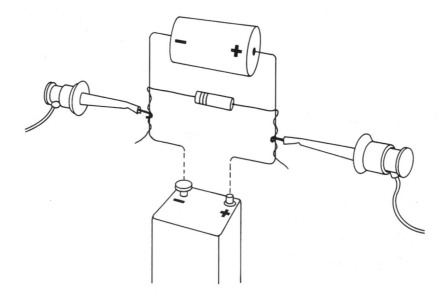

Procedure

1. Connect the circuit as shown with the 220 µF capacitor and the 100 kΩ resistor. Record the values of the resistor (R) and capacitor (C), as well as any tolerance values marked on them, in the Data Table on the *Data Collection and Analysis* sheet.

2. Connect the voltage probe to CH 1 on the CBL 2™ or LabPro® data collection device. Connect the clip leads on the voltage probe across the capacitor, with the red (positive lead) to the positive side of the capacitor. Connect the black lead to the other side of the capacitor. Connect the resistor across the capacitor as shown. Use the unit-to-unit cable to connect the TI graphing calculator to the data collection device. Firmly press in the cable ends.

3. Turn on the calculator and start the DATAMATE software. Press ⌈CLEAR⌉ to reset the software.

4. Set up the calculator and data collection device.

   a. Select **SETUP** from the main screen.

   b. Press ⌈ ▲ ⌋ to select **MODE** and press ⌈ENTER⌋.

   c. Select **TIME GRAPH** from the SELECT MODE menu to collect data as a function of time.

   d. Select **CHANGE TIME SETTINGS** from the TIME GRAPH SETTINGS menu to set the data collection rate.

   e. Enter **0.5** as the time between samples in seconds and press ⌈ENTER⌋.

   f. Enter **100** as the number of samples and press ⌈ENTER⌋.

   g. Select **OK** twice to return to the main screen.

5. Verify that the wires are in the position illustrated, which will confirm that the capacitor is charged.

6. Remove the battery from the circuit, and quickly select **START** to begin data collection. After data collection is complete, a graph of potential versus time will be displayed.

7. Press ENTER to return to the main screen.

8. Select **QUIT** to leave DATAMATE, and then follow any instructions on the screen to return to the calculator's home screen.

9. Print or sketch the graph of potential versus time. To return to a graph of the data outside of DATAMATE,

   a. Press ZOOM.

   b. Press ▼ until **ZoomStat** is highlighted; press ENTER to display a graph with x and y ranges set to fill the screen with data.

   c. Press TRACE to determine the coordinates of a point on the graph using the cursor keys.

Analysis

1. The standard model for the capacitor discharge curve is an exponential. You can now fit a curve of the form $y = Ve^{-Kx}$ to the data, where x is time and y is the capacitor voltage.

   Using the graph now on the calculator screen, find the y-intercept and move the flashing cursor to it to read the value. Round the value to the nearest hundredth, and record this voltage V in the Data Table on the *Data Collection and Analysis* sheet for use in the next step.

2. In order to graph the model with the data, you must enter the model equation and initial values for V and K. As a first guess, use $K = 1$. In a moment you will adjust K to improve the fit of the model to the data.

   a. Press 2nd [QUIT] to return to the home screen.

   b. Enter the value for V. Press STO▸ V ENTER to store the value in the variable V. (On the TI-73, access the alphabetic entry screen by pressing 2nd [TEXT].)

   c. Enter 1, your first guess for K. Press STO▸ K ENTER to store the value in the variable **K**.

   d. Press Y=.

   e. Press CLEAR to remove any existing equation.

   f. Enter **V*e^(–K*X)** in the **Y1** field. Access e^ by pressing 2nd [e^x]. (On the TI-73, access the e^ function by pressing MATH, and then press ▸ three times to get to the LOG menu. Select 4:e^(to enter e^.)

g. Press ⬛◀ until the icon to the left of **Y1** is blinking. Press ⬛ENTER until a bold diagonal line is shown to display the model with a thick line.

h. Press ⬛GRAPH to see the data with the model graph superimposed.

i. Press ⬛2nd [QUIT] to return to the home screen.

3. To obtain a good fit, you will need to adjust the value of K. Enter a new value for K, and display the graph again. Repeat until the model (drawn with a thick line) fits the data well. Record the K value that works best in the Data Table.

   a. Enter a value for the parameter K. Press ⬛STO▶ K ⬛ENTER to store the value in the variable **K**.

   b. Press ⬛GRAPH to see the data with the model graph superimposed.

   c. Press ⬛2nd [QUIT] to return to the home screen.

4. Redisplay the graph and use the calculator's trace function to move the cursor along the data plot. Determine the approximate time at which the capacitor voltage reached half its initial value. This value is sometimes called the *half-life* value, denoted $t_{1/2}$.

   Record the value in the Data Table. It represents the time required for a quantity that is decaying exponentially to reach half its starting value.

   You can compare the value of $t_{1/2}$ to the K parameter you determined in the model, using this formula for determining half-life

$$t_{1/2} = \frac{\ln 2}{K}$$

   Use the formula and the K value determined in Step 3 to compute a value of $t_{1/2}$, and record it in the Data Table.

⇒ Answer Questions 1 - 4 on the *Data Collection and Analysis* sheet.

Extension

1. Another possible model is a fourth-degree polynomial equation. Perform a quartic (fourth power) regression on the data you have collected, and see if the model is a good one.

    #### TI-73

    Note: *Since the TI-73 cannot do a quartic regression, perform a quadratic regression instead.*

    a. Press ⌞2nd⌟ [STAT] and use the cursor keys to highlight **CALC**.

    b. Press the number next to **QuadReg** to copy the command to the home screen.

    c. After the **QuadReg** command, press ⌞2nd⌟ [STAT] and select **L1** by pressing the number next to **L1**. Then press ⌞,⌟. Repeat the procedure to select **L2**.

    d. After selecting **L2**, press ⌞,⌟ then press ⌞2nd⌟ [VARS].

    e. Use the cursor keys to select **Y-Vars** and press ⌞ENTER⌟.

    f. Press ⌞ENTER⌟ to select **Y1** and copy it to the expression.

    g. On the home screen, you will now see the entry **QuadReg L1**, **L2**, **Y1**. This command will perform a quadratic regression with **L1** as the x and **L2** as the y values. The resulting regression curve will be stored in equation variable **Y1**. Press ⌞ENTER⌟ to perform the regression.

    h. Press ⌞GRAPH⌟ to see the graph.

    #### TI-83 and TI-83 Plus

    a. Press ⌞STAT⌟ and use the cursor keys to highlight **CALC**.

    b. Press the number adjacent to **QuartReg** to copy the command to the home screen.

    c. Press ⌞2nd⌟ [L1] ⌞,⌟ ⌞2nd⌟ [L2] ⌞,⌟ to enter the lists containing the data.

    d. Press ⌞VARS⌟ and use the cursor keys to highlight **Y-VARS**.

    e. Select **Function** by pressing ⌞ENTER⌟.

    f. Press ⌞ENTER⌟ to copy **Y1** to the expression.

    g. On the home screen, you will now see the entry **QuartReg L1**, **L2**, **Y1**. This command will perform a quartic regression with **L1** as the x and **L2** as the y values. The resulting regression curve will be stored in equation variable **Y1**. Press ⌞ENTER⌟ to perform the regression.

    h. Press ⌞GRAPH⌟ to see the graph.

⇒ Answer Extension Question 1 on the *Data Collection and Analysis* sheet.

To see just how the model fits the data when a wider range is graphed, change the scale of the graph. This is a more severe test of the model than just graphing the model over the same range as the data.

a. Press ZOOM.

b. Press the number next to **Zoom Out**.

c. Press ENTER to zoom out.

⇒ Answer Extension Question 2 on the *Data Collection and Analysis sheet*.

A more appropriate regression model for the data is an exponential. To perform an exponential regression on the data you collected, use the same method you used above for the quartic regression, but choose **ExpReg** as the regression choice. Obtain a display of the data and the exponential regression curve on the same screen.

⇒ Answer Extension Question 3 on the *Data Collection and Analysis* sheet.

Notice that the exponential regression equation used by the calculator is of the form $y = ab^x$ while the modeling equation used in this activity was $y = Ve^{-Kx}$.

⇒ Answer Extension Question 4 on the *Data Collection and Analysis* sheet.

2. Use the expression

$$y = Ve^{-Kx}$$

to derive the expression

$$t_{1/2} = \frac{\ln 2}{K}$$

Note: *When the voltage across the capacitor has dropped to ½V, the time is called* $t_{1/2}$.

Data Collection and Analysis

Name _____

Date _____

Activity 18: Charging Up, Charging Down

Data Table

R (Ω)	
C (F)	
V	
K	
$t_{1/2}$ (from graph)	
$t_{1/2}$ (from K)	

Questions

1. How does this half-life value compare to the one you extracted from the graph?

2. In your own words, describe how the values of V and K affect the shape of the voltage versus time graph, $y = Ve^{-Kx}$.

3. According to the model, when does the capacitor voltage reach exactly zero?

4. Compare the value of K to the value of $1/RC$. Calculate $1/RC$ from the values of R and C in the Data Table. What could you do to the circuit to make the capacitor take longer to discharge?

Extension Questions

1. How well does the quartic curve fit the data, given the way the graph is now plotted?

2. Now that you have a wider view of the data and the fit, is the quartic equation (quadratic on the TI-73) still a good model for the data?

3. Does this model provide a good fit?

4. How are the values of a and V related? How are the values of b and K related?

Teacher Notes
Charging Up, Charging Down: Exponential Models

1. The activity is written to use the standard base e exponential function
    $y = Ve^{-Kx}$. You may want to use the form $y = ab^x$ instead. The latter form is
    the built-in exponential fit of the calculator, and so would avoid having the
    students convert the base of an expression.

2. As long as the battery produces at least 5 V, it can be used in the activity.
    Retired smoke detector batteries are ideal.

3. The suggested resistor and capacitor values can be changed. As long as the
    RC product is on the order of 15 seconds, the experiment will work. Keep the
    resistor to less than 100 kΩ to avoid measurement problems due to the input
    impedance of the CBL 2™ or LabPro®. If the *RC* product is any shorter than
    1 second, students will have trouble catching the start of the decay. The
    100 kΩ resistor can be obtained from Radio Shack, #271-1347. The 220 μF
    capacitor is Radio Shack #272-1017.

4. With the suggested *RC* value, all of the voltage readings will be positive. If a
    shorter *RC* value is used, and the data collection time is not changed, it is
    possible that some voltage readings will be non-positive after the capacitor is
    discharged. In this case the exponential fit will fail.

5. Try other *RC* products to observe faster and slower decay rates.

6. Typical resistors and capacitors are only nominally the value indicated; they
    may be up to 40% different from the marked value. For this reason, a class
    set of supposedly identical resistors and capacitors may yield quite different
    decay curves.

7. Note that 100 KΩ means 100,000 Ω. The ohm (Ω) is a measure of resistance.
    220 μF means 0.000220 F. The Farad (F) is a measure of capacitance. You may
    want to review metric prefix usage with your students.

Sample Results

Actual data will vary.

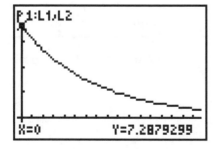

Raw graph from DATAMATE

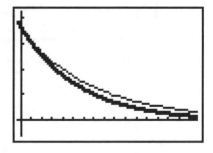

Data and model with *K* a little large

Data Table

Sample data; actual data may vary.

R (Ω)	100,000
C (F)	0.000220
V	7.28
K	0.042
$t_{1/2}$ (from graph)	17 s
$t_{1/2}$ (from K)	16 s

Answers to Questions

1. The two half-life values are nearly the same.

2. The value of V is a simple multiplicative factor that changes the y-intercept. K determines the rate of decay of the exponential function; larger K means the function drops off more quickly.

3. Since the exponential function never reaches zero for any finite time, by the model the capacitor voltage never reaches zero.

4. K is nearly the same as 1/RC. For the same capacitor, a larger resistor would decrease the value of K, and so by the model the capacitor would take longer to discharge.

Extension

Actual data will vary.

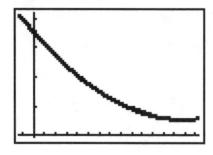

Quartic fit displayed over data

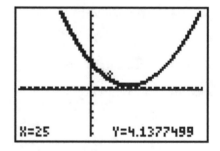

Quartic fit after zooming out

EXPLORATIONS

Activity 19

Bounce Back:
The Exponential
Pattern of
Rebound Heights

Objective

♦ Record the successive maximum heights for a bouncing ball.

♦ Model the bounce height data with an exponential function.

Materials

♦ TI-83 Plus, TI-83, or TI-73

♦ CBL 2™ or LabPro® data collection device

♦ DATAMATE software

♦ TI CBR ™ or Vernier Motion Detector

♦ Ball (a basketball works well)

When a ball bounces up and down on a flat surface, the maximum height it reaches decreases from bounce to bounce. In fact, the maximum height decreases in a very predictable way for most types of balls. The relationship between the maximum height attained by the ball on a given bounce (which we will call the *rebound height*) and number of bounces that have occurred since the ball was released is an exponential

$$y = hp^x$$

where y represents the rebound height, x represents the bounce number, h is the release height, and p is a constant that depends on the physical characteristics of the ball used. It is easy to see where this model comes from: Suppose that the ball is released from height h. Then on each bounce it rebounds to a fraction p of the previous maximum height. After zero, one and two bounces, the ball will attain a maximum height of h, hp, $(hp)p = hp^2$, and so forth. The relation above is generalized for any x number of bounces.

In this exercise, you will collect motion data for a bouncing ball using a motion detector. You will then analyze this data to test the model $y = hp^x$.

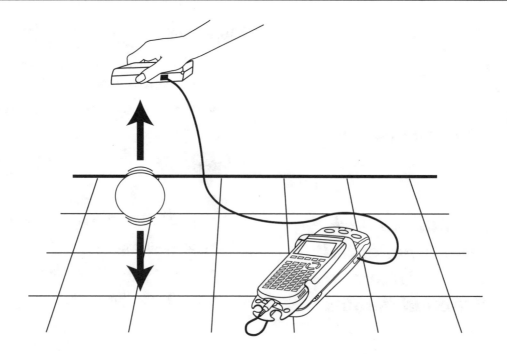

Procedure

1. Plug the motion detector into the DIG/SONIC port of the CBL 2™ or DIG/SONIC 1 port of the LabPro® data collection device. Use the unit-to-unit cable to connect the TI graphing calculator to the data collection device. Firmly press in the cable ends.

2. Turn on the calculator and start the DATAMATE software. Press [CLEAR] to reset the software.

3. Hold the motion detector about 1.5 m above the floor, pointing straight downward. Practice dropping the ball so that it bounces straight up and down beneath the motion detector. Let the ball bounce on a smooth, level surface, and minimize the ball's sideways travel. Dropping the ball from a height of about 1 meter works well.

   Do not allow anything to obstruct the path between the motion detector and the ball while data is being collected. If the ball does move sideways slightly, move the motion detector horizontally to stay above the ball.

4. Select **START** to begin data collection. You will hear the data collection device beep. Drop the ball under the detector as you practiced earlier. Data collection will run for five seconds.

5. Press [ENTER] to display the **DISTANCE** graph.

6. Examine the distance versus time graph. The distance versus time graph should contain a series of at least five smoothly changing parabolic regions. Since the motion detector was pointing downward, and it measures increasing values *away* from itself, the graph will appear to be upside down.

Check with your teacher if you are not sure whether you need to repeat the data collection. To repeat data collection, press [ENTER] to return to the graph selection screen, and select **MAIN SCREEN**. Select **START** to begin data collection.

7. Once you are satisfied with the distance versus time data, leave the DATAMATE software. From a view of the distance versus time graph, press [ENTER] and select **MAIN SCREEN**. Select **QUIT** and follow any instructions to return to the calculator's home screen.

Analysis

1. To make the distance versus time graph a bit easier to work with, you can adjust the coordinate system by subtracting all the distance values from the maximum distance, which will allow you to re-graph the distance data so that the ball height above the floor will be shown on the *y*-axis.

▷ TI-73

a. To enter the **max()** function, press [MATH], use [▶] to highlight the NUM menu, and press the number adjacent **max(** to paste the command to the home screen.

b. Access lists by pressing [2nd] [STAT]. Press the number next to **L6**; this enters **L6** on the home screen.

c. Press [ )] to close the maximum function.

d. Press [−].

e. Enter **L6** as you did before.

f. Press [STO▶], and enter L6 a third time to complete the expression **max(L6) − L6 → L6**. Press [ENTER] to perform the calculation.

▷ TI-83 and TI-83 Plus

a. To enter the **max(** function press [MATH], use [▶] to highlight the NUM menu, and press the number adjacent **max(** to paste the command to the home screen.

b. Press [2nd] [L6].

c. Press [ )] to close the maximum function.

d. Press [−].

e. Press [2nd] [L6].

f. Press [STO▶], and press [2nd] [L6] a third time to complete the expression **max(L6) − L6 → L6**. Press [ENTER] to perform the calculation.

2. Display a graph of ball height above the floor versus time.

   a. Press ⌜ZOOM⌝.

   b. Press ⌜▼⌝ until **ZoomStat** is highlighted; press ⌜ENTER⌝ to display a graph with the x and y ranges set to fill the screen with data.

   c. Press ⌜TRACE⌝ to determine the coordinates of a point on the graph using the cursor keys.

3. To compare the distance data to the model for bounce height, read the maximum height of each bounce from the distance versus time data. Do this by tracing across the graph using the cursor keys.

   Start with the initial release height, and call that bounce number zero. Record the consecutive maximum rebound heights for the next five bounces. Round these values to the nearest 0.001 m and record them in the Data Table on the *Data Collection and Analysis* sheet.

4. Enter the information from the Data Table into lists on the calculator.

   ▶ **TI-73**

   a. Press ⌜LIST⌝.

   b. Lists 1 and 2 are available for you to use. Press ⌜▲⌝ and ⌜◄⌝ as needed to highlight the **L1** header, and press ⌜CLEAR⌝ to clear the list.

   c. Press ⌜ENTER⌝ to move to the first element of **L1**.

   d. Enter the bounce numbers, starting from **0** and ending with **5**. Press ⌜ENTER⌝ after each entry.

   e. Use ⌜▲⌝ and ⌜►⌝ to move to the header of **L2**. Press ⌜CLEAR⌝ to clear the list.

   f. Press ⌜ENTER⌝ to move to the first element of **L2**.

   g. Enter the rebound heights, starting with the release height. You must have six elements in **L1** and in **L2** when you are done.

   ▶ **TI-83 and TI-83 Plus**

   a. Press ⌜STAT⌝ and press ⌜ENTER⌝ to see the data lists.

   b. Lists 1 and 2 are available for you to use. Press ⌜▲⌝ to highlight the **L1** header, and press ⌜CLEAR⌝ to clear the list.

   c. Press ⌜ENTER⌝ to move to the first element of **L1**.

   d. Enter the bounce numbers, starting from **0** and ending with **5**. Press ⌜ENTER⌝ after each entry.

e. Use ▲ and ► to move to the header of **L2**. Press CLEAR to clear the list.

f. Press ENTER to move to the first element of **L2**.

g. Enter the rebound heights, starting with the release height. You must have six elements in **L1** and in **L2** when you are done.

5. Now that you have the data to be plotted stored in lists in the calculator, you are ready to plot the rebound height versus bounce number.

a. Press 2nd [STAT PLOT] ([PLOT] on the TI-73) and press ENTER to select **Plot 1**.

b. Change the **Plot1** settings to match the screen shown here. Press ENTER to select any of the settings you change.

c. Press ZOOM and then select **ZoomStat** (use cursor keys to scroll to **ZoomStat**) to draw a graph with the x and y ranges set to fill the screen with data.

6. The graph you see is rebound height versus bounce number. The model is an exponential function: $y = hp^x$, where y is the rebound height and x the bounce number. h and p are two parameters that you need to determine. h represents the starting height (sometimes called the *zeroeth* bounce!), or the height before the first bounce. That is the height on the $x = 0$ line of the Data Table, which is also the y-intercept.

⇒ Answer Question 1 on the *Data Collection and Analysis* sheet.

7. To determine the parameter p, you can plot the model equation and try different values for p until one fits best. First, you need to enter the exponential model.

a. Press Y= .

b. Press CLEAR to remove any existing equation.

c. Enter the expression **H∗P^X** in the **Y1** field. (On the TI-73, access the alphabetic entry screen by pressing 2nd [TEXT].)

d. Press 2nd [QUIT] to return to the home screen.

8. Set a value for the parameters h and p, and then look at the resulting graph. To obtain a good fit, you will need to try several values for p. Use the steps below to store different values to the parameters h and p. Start with $p = 1$. Experiment until you find one that provides a good fit for the data.

   a. Enter the value for the parameter h, which is the starting height. Press `STO▸` H `ENTER` to store the value in the variable **H**.

   b. Enter a value for the parameter p. Press `STO▸` P `ENTER` to store the value in the variable **P**.

   c. Press `GRAPH` to see the data with the model graph superimposed.

   d. Press `2nd` [QUIT] to return to the home screen.

   You will not need to change the value for h further, but the best value for p will be something smaller than 1. Try a variety of values for p until you get a good fit to the experimental data.

⇒ Answer Question 2 on the *Data Collection and Analysis* sheet.

9. The exponential equation $y = hp^x$ can be made into a linear equation by taking the log of both sides:

$$y = hp^x$$
$$\ln y = \ln(hp^x)$$
$$= \ln h + \ln(p^x)$$
$$= x \ln p + \ln h$$

That is, a graph of $\ln y$ versus x is linear with a slope of $\ln p$ and y-intercept of $\ln h$. You can use the data collected so far to make this linear graph. To do this, you need to create a data list containing the natural log of the rebound heights.

▶ **TI-73**

   a. To enter the **ln(** function press `MATH`, use `▶` to highlight the LOG menu, and then press the number adjacent to **ln(** to paste the command to the home screen.

   b. Access lists by pressing `2nd` [STAT]. Press the number next to L2; this enters **L2** on the home screen.

   c. Press `)` to close the **ln(** function.

   d. Press `STO▸`, and enter **L2** to complete the expression **ln(L2) → L2**. Press `ENTER` to perform the calculation.

▶ **TI-83 and TI-83 Plus**

a. Press $\boxed{\text{LN}}$.

b. Press $\boxed{\text{2nd}}$ [L2].

c. Press $\boxed{\text{)}}$ to close the **ln(** function.

d. Press $\boxed{\text{STO▶}}$, and press $\boxed{\text{2nd}}$ [L2] to complete the expression **ln(L2) → L2**. Press $\boxed{\text{ENTER}}$ to perform the calculation.

10. Display a graph of ln(rebound height) versus bounce number.

a. Press $\boxed{\text{ZOOM}}$.

b. Press $\boxed{\text{▼}}$ until **ZoomStat** is highlighted; press $\boxed{\text{ENTER}}$ to display a graph with the x and y ranges set to fill the screen with data.

c. Press $\boxed{\text{TRACE}}$ to determine the coordinates of a point on the graph using the cursor keys.

11. Since the graph is nearly linear, have the calculator fit a line to the data.

▶ **TI-73**

a. Press $\boxed{\text{2nd}}$ [STAT] and use the cursor keys to highlight **CALC**.

b. Press the number adjacent to **LinReg(ax+b)** to copy the command to the home screen.

c. After the **LinReg(ax+b)** command, press $\boxed{\text{2nd}}$ [STAT] and select **L1** by pressing the number next to **L1**. Then press $\boxed{\text{,}}$. Repeat the procedure to select **L2**.

d. After selecting **L2**, press $\boxed{\text{,}}$ then press $\boxed{\text{2nd}}$ [VARS].

e. Use the cursor keys to select **Y-Vars** and press $\boxed{\text{ENTER}}$.

f. Press $\boxed{\text{ENTER}}$ to select **Y1** and copy it to the expression.

g. On the home screen, you will now see the entry **LinReg(ax+b) L1, L2, Y1**. This command will perform a linear regression with **L1** as the x and **L2** as the y values. The resulting regression line will be stored in equation variable **Y1**. Press $\boxed{\text{ENTER}}$ to perform the linear regression.

⇒ Answer Question 3 on the *Data Collection and Analysis* sheet.

h. Press $\boxed{\text{GRAPH}}$ to see the graph.

⇒ Answer Questions 4-7 on the *Data Collection and Analysis* sheet.

▶ **TI-83 and TI-83 Plus**

a. Press [STAT] and use the cursor keys to highlight **CALC**.

b. Press the number adjacent to **LinReg(ax+b)** to copy the command to the home screen.

c. Press [2nd] [L1] [,] [2nd] [L2] [,] to enter the lists containing the data.

d. Press [VARS] and use the cursor keys to highlight **Y-VARS**.

e. Select **Function** by pressing [ENTER].

f. Press [ENTER] to copy **Y1** to the expression.

g. On the home screen, you will now see the entry **LinReg(ax+b) L1, L2, Y1**. This command will perform a linear regression with **L1** as the x and **L2** as the y values. The resulting regression line will be stored in equation variable **Y1**. Press [ENTER] to perform the linear regression.

⇒ Answer Question 3 on the *Data Collection and Analysis* sheet.

h. Press [GRAPH] to see the graph.

⇒ Answer Questions 4-7 on the *Data Collection and Analysis* sheet.

Data Collection and Analysis

Name _____

Date _____

Activity 19: Bounce Back

Data Table

Record the consecutive maximum rebound heights for the five bounces from Step 3 of the *Analysis* section. Round to the nearest 0.001 m.

Bounce number	Maximum height (m)
0	
1	
2	
3	
4	
5	

Questions

1. Use the function $y = hp^x$ to explain why h is equal to the y-intercept.

2. Use the parameters from Step 8 to write the optimized model equation.

3. Use the parameters a and b that appear on the calculator screen to write the fitted linear equation.

4. How well does the linear regression fit the data of ln(rebound height) versus bounce number?

5. Use the values of h and p you determined by optimizing the fit of the model to find ln h and ln p. Record these values in the table below.

ln p	
ln h	

How do these values compare with the linear regression constants a and b? Do they match? Explain why they should match.
Hint: Compare the equations ln y = (ln p) x + ln h and $y = ax + b$.

6. Suppose that you repeat this activity using a ball that is not as resilient as the ball you used. For example, if you used a basketball, imagine that some air is let out of it, and then the exercise is repeated. Would the constants h and p in the equation $y = hp^x$ be affected by this? How?

7. Use either one of the models developed in this activity to determine the smallest number of bounces required by the ball for the rebound height to be less than 10% of its starting height. Remember that the number of bounces must be an integer value. Record your answer here.

Teacher Notes
Bounce Back: The Exponential Pattern of Rebound Heights

1. Foam or felt-covered balls do not reflect ultrasound very well. The data below was collected using a basketball.

2. Take care that the cord for the motion detector does not hang into the path between the detector and the ball to avoid spurious distance measurements. Keep the hands of the person releasing the ball from between the ball and the detector.

3. Data collection is most easily done with three students: One student should hold the detector, another should release the ball, and another run the calculator.

4. A TI CBR™ or Vernier Motion Detector a can be used in this activity. If a CBR is used, it must be connected through a CBL 2™ or a LabPro®, and not directly to the calculator.

5. Some motion detectors will not be automatically identified by DATAMATE. If you are using such a detector, you must manually set up DATAMATE for the detector:

   a. Select **SETUP** from the main screen.

   b. Press ⬇ until the cursor is next to DIG (CBL 2) or DIG1 (LabPro).

   c. Press ⎡ENTER⎤ to access the SELECT SENSOR menu.

   d. Select **MOTION(M)**.

   e. Select **OK** to return to the main screen.

Sample Results

Actual data will vary.

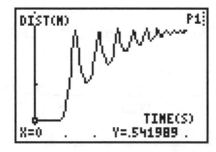

Raw distance data from DATAMATE

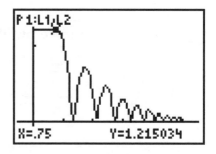

Distance data after subtraction

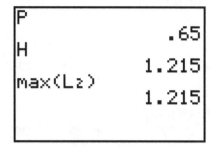

Rebound data in lists

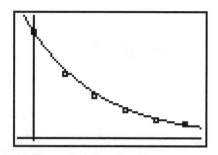

Rebound height versus bounce number

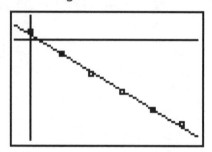

Model parameters

In (bounce height) versus bounce
number

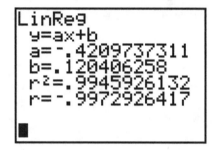

linear fit of ln(bounce height)
versus number

Data Table

Sample data; actual data may vary.

Bounce number	Maximum height (m)
0	1.215
1	0.718
2	0.467
3	0.303
4	0.204
5	0.148

Answers to Questions

1. At $x = 0$, then $y = hp^x = h$, since $p^0 = 1$ regardless of the value of p. (Well, as long as $p \neq 0$!)

2. A model equation that fits the observed exponential is $y = 1.215 * (0.65)^x$.

3. $y = {}^-0.420\ x + 0.120$.

4. The linear regression fits the log graph very well. It looks like we have a good model for the behavior of the bouncing ball.

5. From the identical position of ln$p$ and a in the model and regression equation, they must have the same value. ln$h$ and b have the same relationship. The numerical values are very similar, with ln$p = {}^-0.43$ and $a = {}^-0.42$, and ln$h = 0.19$ and $b = 0.12$.

6. If the less-resilient ball were dropped from the same starting height, the h values would be the same. However, the less-resilient ball would not bounce as high so p would be smaller.

7. Using the original model, we have the following computation. Since the number of bounces has to be an integer, it would take a total of six bounces to reach a rebound height of less than 10% of the initial value. This result will depend both on the ball and on the surface on which the ball is bouncing.

$$y = 1.215(0.65)^x$$
$$0.1 = 0.65^x$$
$$\ln(0.10) = x\ln(0.65)$$
$$x = 5.25$$

EXPLORATIONS

Activity 20

Sour Chemistry: The Exponential pH Change

Objective

♦ Record pH versus time data as an antacid tablet neutralizes the acid in lemon juice.

♦ Model the pH data with a modified exponential function.

Materials

♦ TI-83 Plus, TI-83, or TI-73

♦ CBL 2™ or LabPro® data collection device

♦ DATAMATE software

♦ pH Sensor

♦ Clean cup or beaker

♦ Distilled water

♦ Lemon juice

♦ Eyedropper

♦ Effervescent antacid tablets

Chemists quantify the acidity or alkalinity of a solution by measuring its pH on a scale ranging from 0 to 14. A neutral substance has a pH of 7. A pH lower than 7 indicates an acidic solution, while a pH higher than 7 indicates that a solution is basic.

Different pH levels must be maintained throughout the body in order for a person to remain healthy. Excessively high or low pH levels often result in discomfort or irritation. For example, common indigestion or upset stomach usually indicates the presence of excessive amounts of stomach acids. This condition can sometimes be alleviated by taking an antacid tablet, or by drinking a solution such as Alka-Seltzer® and water, designed to neutralize these acids and raise the pH level in the stomach.

In this activity, the conditions found in an acid stomach will be simulated using a solution of lemon juice and water. The effectiveness of an antacid remedy will be tested by monitoring the pH of the solution after an effervescent antacid tablet has been added to it. The resulting data will be modeled using a modified exponential function.

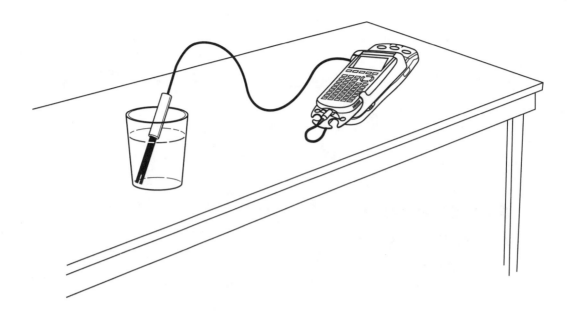

Procedure

1. Connect the pH sensor to CH 1 of the CBL 2™ or LabPro® data collection device. Use the unit-to-unit cable to connect the TI graphing calculator to the data collection device. Firmly press in the cable ends.

2. Turn on the calculator and start the DATAMATE software. Press ⌈CLEAR⌋ to reset the software.

3. Set up the calculator and data collection device for the pH Sensor.

   a. Select **SETUP** from the main screen.

   b. If the calculator displays a pH sensor in CH 1, proceed directly to Step 4. If it does not, continue with this step to set up the sensor manually.

   c. Press ⌈ENTER⌋ to select **CH 1**.

   d. Select **PH** from the SELECT SENSOR menu.

4. Set up the data-collection mode.

   a. To select **MODE**, press ⌈▲⌋ once and press ⌈ENTER⌋.

   b. Select **TIME GRAPH** from the SELECT MODE menu.

   c. Select **CHANGE TIME SETTINGS** from the TIME GRAPH SETTINGS screen.

   d. Enter **0.5** as the time between samples in seconds and press ⌈ENTER⌋.

   e. Enter **100** as the number of samples and press ⌈ENTER⌋.

   f. Select **OK** until you return to the main screen.

5. Collect pH data.

   a. Place about 125 mL of distilled water in a very clean cup. The cup must be clean to get good results.

   b. Loosen the top of the pH storage bottle, and carefully remove the bottle. Slide the top of the bottle up the shaft of the sensor so that the bottle top is out of the way. Do not remove the top from the sensor shaft.

   c. Rinse the tip of the pH sensor with distilled water.

   d. Place the pH sensor in the water, and support it so the sensor does not fall.

   e. Put 20 drops of lemon juice into the water. This will simulate an acid stomach. Stir gently with the sensor.

   f. Get ready to drop the effervescent tablet into the water.

   g. Select **START** to begin data collection. As soon as you hear the data collection device beep, drop the tablet into the water.

   h. Data collection will run for 50 seconds. After collection ends, a graph of pH versus time will be shown.

   i. The graph should show pH values that increase rapidly at first and then level off. Press [ENTER] to return to the main screen.

      If you want to repeat data collection, discard the solution, thoroughly rinse the cup and pH sensor in distilled water, and return to the beginning of Step 5.

   j. Once you are satisfied with the data, press [ENTER] to return to the main screen, and select **QUIT** to leave DATAMATE. Follow any instructions on the calculator to return to its home screen.

6. Use additional distilled water to rinse the pH sensor. Discard the solution in the cup, and rinse the cup. Replace the storage bottle on the pH sensor.

Analysis

1. To work with the data, redisplay the graph outside of the DATAMATE software.

   a. Press [ZOOM].

   b. Press [▼] until **ZoomStat** is highlighted; press [ENTER] to display a graph with the x and y ranges set to fill the screen with data.

   c. Press [TRACE] to determine the coordinates of a point on the graph using the cursor keys.

2. A modified exponential model can be used to model the data you have just collected.

$$y = A(1 - B^x) + C$$

In this expression, y represents the pH of the solution at any time x. C represents the initial pH of the solution, which is also the y-intercept. A measures the magnitude of the pH change, while B is a value between 0 and 1 which measures the rate of the change.

To fit this model to the data, first determine the y-intercept from the graph. Trace to the left edge of the graph. Round the $x = 0$ pH value to two significant digits and record it in the Data Table on the *Data Collection and Analysis* sheet.

3. At the other side of the graph the pH values should approach a constant value as the curve flattens. Trace to the right edge of the graph to estimate the value the pH curve is approaching. Record this value in the Data Table.

4. The pH approach value you just determined is related to a sum of constants in the model equation. Assume that $0 < B < 1$. If x is large, the model expression approaches the sum $A + C$.

⇒   Answer Question 1 on the *Data Collection and Analysis* sheet.

5. Use the value for the approach pH and the y-intercept to determine a value for the parameter A. Enter the result in the Data Table.

6. Enter the model expression for graphing, along with values for the parameters A and C.

    a. Press ⬚ Y= .

    b. Press ⬚ CLEAR to remove any existing equation.

    c. Enter the modified exponential model as **A∗(1–B^X) + C** in the **Y1** field. (On the TI-73, access the alphabetic entry screen by pressing ⬚ 2nd [TEXT].)

    d. Press ⬚ 2nd [QUIT] to return to the home screen.

    e. Enter the value for the parameter A. Press ⬚ STO▶ **A** ENTER to store the value in the variable **A**.

    f. Enter the value for the parameter C. Press ⬚ STO▶ **C** ENTER to store the value in the variable **C**.

7. Set a value for the parameter B and then look at the resulting graph. To obtain a good fit, you will need to try several values for B. Use the steps below to store different values to the parameter B. Start with B = 0.5.

   a. Enter a value for the parameter B. Press (STO▶) B (ENTER) to store the value in the variable B.

   b. Press (GRAPH) to see the data with the model graph superimposed.

   c. Press (2nd) [QUIT] to return to the home screen.

   Experiment until you find a value that provides a good fit for the data and record the value in the Data Table.

⇒ Answer Questions 2–5 on the *Data Collection and Analysis* sheet.

Extension

The equation used in this activity $y = A(1 - B^x) + C$ is a modified version of the exponential function $y = ab^x$. Show how $y = ab^x$ can be transformed into the model used here using reflections and shifts.

Hint: Work backwards by distributing A and regrouping.

Data Collection and Analysis

Name _____

Date _____

Activity 20: Sour Chemistry

Data Table

y-intercept C	
pH approach value	
A	
optimized B	

Questions

1. Explain why the model expression from Step 4 approaches the sum $A + C$.

2. How does the value of B affect the shape of the modeling curve?

3. How would adding more drops of lemon juice to the starting solution affect the resulting plot of pH versus time? Which of the parameters A, B and C in the model expression would change? Explain the reasoning.
    Hint: Adding more lemon juice would make the initial solution more acidic, yielding a lower pH value at the start of data collection.

4. How would adding two antacid tablets (instead of one) to the starting solution affect the resulting plot of pH versus time? Which of the parameters *A*, *B* and *C* in the model expression would change? Explain the reasoning.

5. How would you compare the effectiveness of two different brands of antacid tablets? Which of the parameters *A*, *B* and *C* in the model expression would give an indication of how well a tablet works?
   Hints: Which variable describes the speed of relief? Which variable describes the magnitude of relief?

Teacher Notes
Sour Chemistry: The Exponential pH Change

1. The antacid tablet used must contain sodium bicarbonate. Some antacids do not dissolve readily in water, making them useless for this activity. Test antacids before using them in class.

2. Distilled water, which ideally has no buffering capacity, is much better than tap water for this activity. The variable buffering capacities of tap water will affect the initial pH of the starting solution. All water should be at room temperature.

3. Note that distilled water does not necessarily have a pH of 7 due to dissolved gasses.

4. Clean glassware is critical in this activity.

5. At the completion of the activity, use distilled water to rinse the pH electrode. Tightly secure the storage solution bottle on the electrode tip. Refer to the data sheet that came with the pH sensor for detailed storage information.

Sample Results

Actual data will vary.

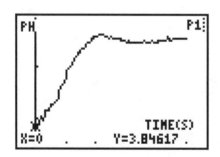
Raw data in DATAMATE

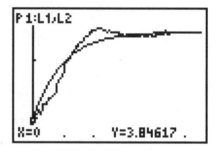
Data with model

Data Table

Sample data; actual data may vary.

y-intercept C	3.84
pH approach value	5.5
A (A = pH approach value – C)	1.66
optimized B	0.9

Answers to Questions

1. If $0 < B < 1$, then for large x, B^x approaches zero, so $y = A(1 - 0) + C = A + C$.

2. A larger value of B results in a slower rise in pH.

3. Adding more lemon juice drops would make the starting solution more acidic, and so have a lower pH. Thus C would be smaller since it represents the starting pH. A might or might not be different since the final pH could still be the same, or it could be lower.

4. Adding more antacid tablets would presumably make the pH level rise more rapidly, so B would be smaller.

5. A better antacid tablet would be fast (with a smaller B). A good tablet would also make the pH rise to an appropriate level for comfort, so A would have to be larger than some minimum value, but also smaller than some maximum value, as the stomach pH must not rise *above* the comfort level.

EXPLORATIONS

Activity 21

Stepping to the Greatest Integer: the Greatest Integer Function

Objective

- ♦ Use a motion detector to collect position data showing evenly-spaced jumps in value.

- ♦ Model the position data using the greatest integer function.

Materials

- ♦ TI-83 Plus, TI-83, or TI-73

- ♦ CBL 2™ or LabPro® data collection device

- ♦ DATAMATE software

- ♦ TI CBR™ or Vernier Motion Detector

Not all mathematical functions have smooth, continuous graphs. In fact, some of the most interesting functions contain jumps and gaps. One such function is called the *greatest integer function*, written as $y = $ int x. It is defined as the greatest integer of x equals the greatest integer less than or equal to x. For example, int 4.2 = 4 and int 4 = 4, while int 3.99999 = 3.

The graph of $y = $ int x yields a series of steps and jumps as shown here.

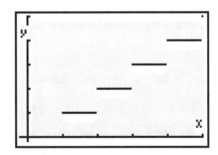

In this activity, you will create a function similar to the greatest integer function graph by having a group of students stand in a line in front of a motion detector and then step aside one by one. The equation for this graph, in the general form, is

$$y = A \text{ int } (Bx) + C$$

You can find appropriate values for the parameters A, B, and C so that the model fits the data.

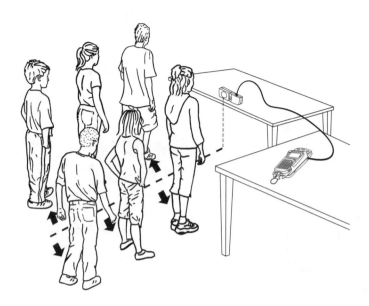

Procedure

1. Position the motion detector as shown in the drawing.

2. Connect the motion detector into the DIG/SONIC port of the CBL 2™ or DIG/SONIC 1 port of the LabPro® data collection device. Use the unit-to-unit cable to connect the TI graphing calculator to the data collection device. Firmly press in the cable ends.

3. Turn on the calculator and start the DATAMATE software. Press CLEAR to reset the software.

4. Set up DATAMATE so that data collection will run for ten seconds.

    a. Select **SETUP** from the main screen.

    b. Press ▲ to select **MODE**, and press ENTER.

    c. Select **TIME GRAPH** from the SELECT MODE menu.

    d. Select **CHANGE TIME SETTINGS** from the TIME GRAPH SETTINGS screen.

    e. Enter **0.1** as the time between samples (use **0.2** for the TI-73) and press ENTER.

    f. Enter **100** as the number of samples (use **50** for the TI-73) and press ENTER.

    g. Select **OK** twice to return to the main screen.

5. To start, line up six students in front of the motion detector as shown in the drawing. Be sure that the spacing between students is uniform (about half a meter) and that the first student in line is no closer than one meter from the detector.

6. Once you have all students standing in line and ready to move, select **START** to begin data collection. You will hear the data collection device beep. Have the first student wait for about a second before he or she moves aside. Once the detector is activated, students should step aside in evenly spaced time intervals so that the lengths of the segments appearing on the distance versus time plot are uniform.

   To help gauge the pace, you might have one student tell the others when to step aside by counting out loud every one or two seconds. Be patient; it may take several trials to obtain a plot that resembles a greatest integer function. Data collection will run for ten seconds.

7. The graph selection screen will appear; press ENTER to display the **DISTANCE** graph.

8. Examine the distance versus time graph. The distance versus time graph should show a series of increasing steps. Check with your teacher if you are not sure whether you need to repeat the data collection.

   To repeat data collection, press ENTER to return to the graph selection screen, and select **MAIN SCREEN** and repeat Step 5.

9. Once you are satisfied with the data, press ENTER, select **MAIN SCREEN**, and select **QUIT**. Follow instructions on the calculator to return to the home screen.

Analysis

1. Redisplay the graph using a scatter graph rather than the line graph shown by DATAMATE. This way the calculator will not incorrectly draw in vertical connecting lines between horizontal steps.

   a. Press 2nd [STAT PLOT] ([PLOT] on the TI-73) and press ENTER to select **Plot1**.

   b. Change the **Plot1** settings to match the screen shown here. Press ENTER to select any of the settings you change.

   c. Press ZOOM and then select **ZoomStat** (use cursor keys to scroll to **ZoomStat**) to draw a graph with the x and y ranges set to fill the screen with data.

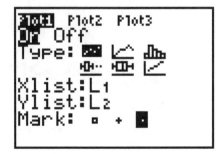

2. You can model the function with the equation $y = A \, \text{int}(Bx) + C$. Compare the graph with the graph of the greatest integer function on the first page. The graph will be different from the simple graph of $y = \text{int} \, x$ in several ways. The graph will be shifted upward by some amount C. The vertical spacing between the steps will not be one meter, but will be closer to a value A. (You can think of this parameter as creating a vertical stretch of the graph.) Finally, the graph is stretched horizontally by a parameter B.

   You can estimate values of these three parameters from the graph. Trace across the graph to the left-hand edge, at $x = 0$. This will be the vertical offset of the graph, or the parameter C. Record this value as C in the Data Table on the *Data Collection and Analysis* sheet.

3. Trace to the right across the graph. Estimate the typical magnitude of the vertical spacing between steps. Use several steps to determine the value. Record the value as A in the Data Table. You will refine this value shortly.

4. Trace back across the graph, and estimate the typical length in time of the steps. Take the inverse of the time. Record this inverse time value as B in the Data Table. You will later refine this value as well.

5. Enter the model equation $y = A \, \text{int}(Bx) + C$.

   TI-73

   a. Press [Y=].

   b. Press [CLEAR] to remove any existing equation.

   c. Enter **A∗int(B∗X) + C**. You can obtain the **int** operation by pressing [2nd] [CATALOG], and scrolling down with [▼] to **int(**. Press [ENTER] to paste it to the equation line. Access the alphabetic entry screen by pressing [2nd] [TEXT].

   d. Press [2nd] [QUIT] to return to the home screen.

   TI-83 and TI-83 Plus

   a. Press [Y=].

   b. Press [CLEAR] to remove any existing equation.

   c. Enter **A∗int(B∗X) + C**. Obtain the **int** operation by pressing [MATH] and then pressing [▶] to move to the NUM menu. Select **int(** to paste it to the equation line.

   d. Press [2nd] [QUIT] to return to the home screen.

6. Set values for the parameters A, B, and C and then look at the resulting graph. To obtain a good fit, you will need to try several values for each, but change only one value at a time. Use the steps below to store different values to the parameters. Start with values from the Data Table.

   a. Enter a value for the parameter A. Press [STO▶] A [ENTER] to store the value in the variable **A**.

   b. Repeat for parameters B and C.

   c. Press [GRAPH] to see the data with the model graph superimposed.

   d. Press [2nd] [QUIT] to return to the home screen.

   Experiment until you find ones that provide a good fit for the data. Record the optimized values for the parameters in the Data Table.

   ⇒ Answer Questions 1-7 on the *Data Collection and Analysis* sheet.

Extension

Consider the equation $y = 3$ int $(0.25x) + 5$. Discuss the significance of the numbers in this equation. Write a set of instructions describing the way a group of students would have to move in front of a motion detector to create a data set for which this equation would be an appropriate model. Collect data as before and follow the set of instructions that you developed. Enter the given equation in the **Y=** list. How well does this equation fit the data you collected?

Name other real world situations that can be modeled using the greatest integer function.

Data Collection and Analysis

Name _____

Date _____

Activity 21: Stepping to the Greatest Integer

Data Table

Parameter	From Graph	After Optimization
A		
B		
C		

Questions

1. What is the physical significance of the value of C in the model equation $y = A \text{ int}(Bx) + C$?

2. What is the physical significance of the value of A in the model equation?

3. What is the physical significance of the value of B in the model equation? **Hint**: Consider the value of $1/B$.

4. The calculator is not plotting the greatest integer function quite correctly. Study the graph and describe what the calculator is doing wrong.

5. Suppose a new group of students repeats this activity under the following conditions. The students are farther away at the start, they are spaced closer together, and they step off more quickly. State whether each constant A, B, and C would increase or decrease.

6. The greatest integer function has some interesting business applications. Suppose a phone company charges $0.25 for the first minute and $0.15 for each additional minute for a call to a certain exchange. Develop a formula, involving the greatest integer function, to describe the amount charged as a function of the amount of time spent on the phone. Remember, a customer talking for 3.01 or 3.99 minutes must be charged for 4 minutes of conversation. Give a formula with this behavior below.

7. Check to see if the formula developed in the previous question is correct if a person talks for an integer number of minutes. If not, what is wrong with the formula in this case? If necessary, modify it to make it correct in all cases. Explain your method.

Teacher Notes
Stepping to the Greatest Integer: The Greatest Integer Function

1. The biggest challenge in this activity is to get all students to do their parts at the right time and place. Space the students evenly so that the graph steps will be evenly spaced. You may want to put marks on the floor to guide the students. Space the marks by about 50 cm. At no time should anyone be closer than 1 m to the motion detector.

2. Students must step aside when it is their turn. They must move completely out of the motion detector beam.

3. Do not have the students line up next to a wall, as the wall may be detected by the motion detector.

4. You might have the students graph their trial solutions to Question 7. Since the endpoints are of interest, students might use the table function to inspect their formulas for specific values.

5. Either a TI CBR™ or a Vernier Motion Detector can be used. The CBR must be connected to a data collection device and not directly to the calculator.

6. Some motion detectors will not be automatically identified by DATAMATE. If you are using such a detector, you must manually set up DATAMATE for the detector:

   a. Select **SETUP** from the main screen.

   b. Press ⬇ until the cursor is next to DIG (CBL 2™) or DIG1 (LabPro®).

   c. Press ENTER to access the SELECT SENSOR menu.

   d. Select **MOTION(M)**.

   e. Select **OK** to return to the main screen.

Sample Results

Actual data will vary.

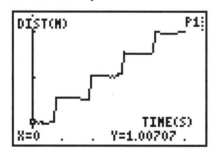

Student position data from DATAMATE

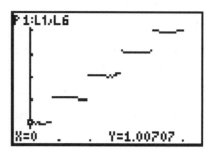

Data re-graphed as a scatter plot

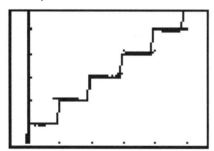

Data and optimized model

Data Table

Sample data; actual data may vary.

Parameter	From Graph	After Optimization
A	0.50 m	0.50 m
B	0.5 s^{-1}	0.45 s^{-1}
C	1.00 m	1.00 m

Answers to Questions

1. C represents the distance between the motion detector and the first student.

2. A represents the distance between students.

3. $1/B$ represents the time interval between student steps, so B is the inverse of this time. In other words, B is the rate at which students step aside, which here is about 0.5 students/s.

4. The calculator is connecting the horizontal segments of the greatest integer function with nearly vertical lines. These vertical lines should not be on the graph, since the function is defined only for the horizontal segments. Apparently, the calculator is finding function values for each pixel on the graph, and then is connecting all those points with line segments. It is this last step that is causing the incorrect plotting of this function.

5. Since the students are farther away, C will be larger. Since they are closer together, A will be smaller. Since they step aside more quickly, $1/B$ will be smaller, making B larger.

6. With y as the cost and x as the time in minutes, $y = 0.25 - 0.15$ int $(1 - x)$. Some students may answer $y = 0.25 + 0.15$ int(x), but this expression does not give the correct values for integer times.

7. The equation $y = 0.25 + 0.15$ int(x) does not work for integer x, so the endpoints of the expression need to be adjusted.

EXPLORATIONS

Activity 22

Swinging Ellipses: Plotting an Ellipse

Objective

- ♦ Record position and velocity versus time data for a swinging pendulum.

- ♦ Plot data as a velocity versus position phase plot.

- ♦ Determine an ellipse that fits the phase plot.

Materials

- ♦ TI-83 Plus, TI-83, or TI-73

- ♦ CBL 2™ or LabPro® data collection device

- ♦ DATAMATE software

- ♦ TI CBR™ or Vernier Motion Detector

- ♦ Pendulum bob

- ♦ String

- ♦ Meter stick

Any ellipse centered at the origin can be expressed in the form

$$\frac{x^2}{a^2} + \frac{y^2}{b^2} = 1$$

where $\pm a$ and $\pm b$ represent the x- and y-intercepts of the ellipse.

To graph an ellipse on a calculator, the expression above must first be solved for y to obtain

$$y = \pm b\sqrt{1 - \frac{x^2}{a^2}}$$

This equation is entered into the calculator in two parts, one expression for the positive part (upper half of the ellipse) and one for the negative part (lower half of the ellipse).

In this activity you will use the motion detector to record the position and velocity of a swinging pendulum. You will find that the plot of velocity versus position is elliptical, and that you can model it with the standard equation of an ellipse.

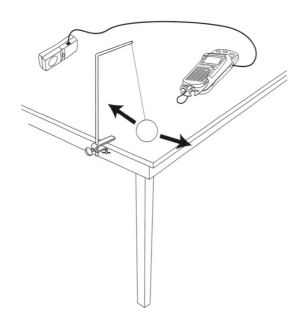

Procedure

1. Connect the pendulum bob to an 80 cm long string and suspend it from a support. Arrange the motion detector so that the bob swings back and forth in front of it and comes no closer than 50 cm.

2. Connect the motion detector into the DIG/SONIC port of the CBL 2™ or the DIG/SONIC 1 port of the LabPro® data collection device. Use the unit-to-unit cable to connect the TI graphing calculator to the data collection device. Firmly press in the cable ends.

3. Turn on the calculator and start the DATAMATE software. Press CLEAR to reset the software.

4. So that the distance data is measured from the pendulum equilibrium position, you need to zero the motion detector. Do this by allowing the bob to hang straight downward, with no motion.

    a. Select **SETUP** from the main screen.

    b. Select **ZERO** from the setup screen.

    c. Select **DIG-DISTANCE** from the SELECT CHANNEL menu.

    d. Confirm that the bob is hanging still, move your hands away from the bob, and press ENTER.

5. Practice swinging the bob by pulling it back about 15 cm and then releasing it so that the bob swings in a line directly away from the motion detector.

6. With the bob swinging properly, select **START** to begin data collection. You will hear the data collection device beep. Data collection will run for five seconds.

7. Press ENTER to display the **DISTANCE** graph.

8. Examine the distance versus time graph. The distance versus time graph should be sinusoidal and centered on zero. Check with your teacher if you are not sure whether you need to repeat the data collection.

   To repeat data collection, press (ENTER) to return to the graph selection screen, and select **MAIN SCREEN**. Select **START** to begin data collection.

9. To see a graph of velocity versus distance, you need to leave the DATAMATE software.

   a. From the distance graph, press (ENTER).

   b. Select **MAIN SCREEN** from the graph selection screen.

   c. Select **QUIT** from the main screen. Follow any instructions on the screen to return to the calculator home screen.

Analysis

1. The graph of velocity versus distance is known as a *phase plot*. The distance data is stored in **L6**, while the velocity data is in **L7**. Display the phase plot.

   ▶ **TI-73**

   a. Press (2nd) [PLOT] and press (ENTER) to select **Plot 1**.

   b. Change the **Plot1** settings to match the screen shown here. Press (ENTER) to select any of the settings you change.

   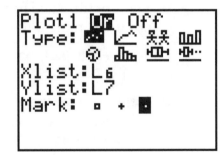

      To enter **L7**, press (2nd) [STAT] and scroll down to select **L7**.

   c. Press (ZOOM) and then select **ZoomStat** (use cursor keys to scroll to **ZoomStat**) to draw a graph with the x and y ranges set to fill the screen with data.

   d. Press (TRACE) to determine the coordinates of a point on the graph using the cursor keys.

▶ **TI-83 and TI-83 Plus**

a. Press ⟨ 2nd ⟩ [STAT PLOT] and press ⟨ENTER⟩ to select **Plot 1**.

b. Change the **Plot1** settings to match the screen shown here. Press ⟨ENTER⟩ to select any of the settings you change.

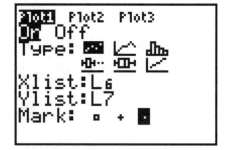

To enter **L7**, press ⟨ 2nd ⟩ [LIST] and scroll down to select **L7**.

c. Press ⟨ZOOM⟩ and then select **ZoomStat** (use cursor keys to scroll to **ZoomStat**) to draw a graph with the x and y ranges set to fill the screen with data.

d. Press ⟨TRACE⟩ to determine the coordinates of a point on the graph using the cursor keys.

2. The phase plot has multiple x- and y-intercepts. To determine the parameters for the ellipse model, you need to determine some average values of these intercepts. One way to do this is by choosing a typical intercept among those available.

   Move the cursor along the velocity versus distance plot and record a typical positive x-intercept. Then determine a typical negative x-intercept. Do the same for positive and negative y-intercepts. Round these values to 0.001 and record them in the Data Table on the *Data Collection and Analysis* sheet.

3. Find the average of the absolute values of the x-intercepts. Record this value as a in the Data Table.

   With the result of the average calculation on screen, press ⟨STO▸⟩ **A** ⟨ENTER⟩ to store the value in the variable **A**. (On the TI-73, access the alphabetic entry screen by pressing ⟨ 2nd ⟩ [TEXT].)

4. Find the average of the absolute values of the y-intercepts. Record this value as b in the Data Table.

   With the result of the average calculation on screen, press ⟨STO▸⟩ **B** ⟨ENTER⟩ to store the value in the variable **B**.

5. Enter the two halves of the ellipse equation for graphing.

   a. Press ⟨ Y= ⟩.

   b. Press ⟨CLEAR⟩ to clear the **Y1** equation.

   c. Enter the positive half of the ellipse as **B∗√(1-X²/A²)** in the **Y1** line. (On the TI-73, access the alphabetic entry screen by pressing ⟨ 2nd ⟩ [TEXT].)

   d. Press ⟨ ◂ ⟩ until the icon to the left of **Y1** is blinking. Press ⟨ENTER⟩ until a bold diagonal line is shown to display the model with a thick line.

e. Press ⟨ ▶ ⟩ ⟨ ▶ ⟩ and press ⟨ENTER⟩ to move to the next line.

f. Press ⟨CLEAR⟩ to clear the **Y2** equation.

g. Enter the negative half of the ellipse as **⁻B∗√(1–X²/A²)** in the **Y2** line.

h. Press ⟨ ◀ ⟩ until the icon to the left of **Y2** is blinking. Press ⟨ENTER⟩ until a bold diagonal line is shown to display the model with a thick line.

i. Press ⟨GRAPH⟩.

⇒ Answer Questions 1-3 on the *Data Collection and Analysis* sheet.

Extension

Show how the algebraic expression $y = \pm b \sqrt{1 - \dfrac{x^2}{a^2}}$ used in this activity can be derived from the ellipse equation $\dfrac{x^2}{a^2} + \dfrac{y^2}{b^2} = 1$.

Data Collection and Analysis

Name _____

Date _____

Activity 22: Swinging Ellipses

Data Table

First x-intercept	Second x-intercept	a

First y-intercept	Second y-intercept	b

Questions

1. How well do the curves of the model ellipses and the data points agree?

2. At what point in the pendulum's swing is its velocity the largest? Where is the velocity zero? How are these values related to the x- and y-intercepts?

3. How would the data change if the *amplitude* (the largest distance from the middle position) of the pendulum's swing were increased? Would this change affect the values of the constants a and b? If so, how?

Teacher Notes
Swinging Ellipses: Plotting an Ellipse

1. You may want to have students view the velocity versus time graph before creating the phase plot. The velocity values are positive when the bob is moving away from the detector, and negative when moving toward the detector.

2. Avoid using a soft or felt-covered ball for the pendulum bob, as the ultrasonic waves from the motion detector tend to be absorbed by these surfaces. A ball with a hole drilled through its center works well as a pendulum bob.

3. A common misconception among students is the expectation that motion plots will match the path of a moving object. You may want to ask your students why the phase plot is elliptical even though the pendulum did not follow an elliptical path.

4. In Step 2 of the analysis you ask the student to determine a typical intercept. That is, you are asking for a judgment call, similar to judging when a manually-determined parameter is optimized. If a student is uncomfortable with this step, you might have him or her average all the positive x-intercepts and use that value. Other intercepts can be determined in the same way.

5. On the TI-73/83 series, the **Y2** entry can also be –**Y1**, but we have chosen to have the student enter the entire expression rather than dig into menus for the equation variables. You may choose to have students do it differently.

6. Some motion detectors will not be automatically identified by DATAMATE. If you are using such a detector, you must manually set up DATAMATE for the detector:

    a. Select **SETUP** from the main screen.

    b. Press ⬤▼ until the cursor is next to DIG (CBL 2™) or DIG1 (LabPro®).

    c. Press ⬤ENTER to access the SELECT SENSOR menu.

    d. Select **MOTION(M)**.

    e. Select **OK** to return to the main screen.

Sample Results

Actual data will vary.

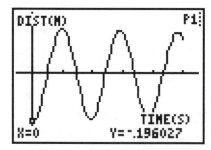

Raw distance data in DATAMATE;
motion is centered on y-axis

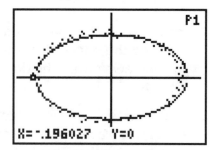

Phase plot with ellipse

Data Table

Sample data; actual data may vary.

First x-intercept	Second x-intercept	a
−0.196	0.182	0.189

First y-intercept	Second y-intercept	b
−0.552	0.574	0.563

Answers to Questions

1. The motion data and the superimposed ellipse match well, as they must since the vertices were taken from the motion data.

2. The velocity is largest in magnitude when the position value is passing through zero. These moments correspond to the y-intercepts at the top and bottom of the ellipse. The velocity is zero when the position value is at an extreme. These moments correspond to the x-intercepts at the left and right edges of the ellipse.

3. If the amplitude of the pendulum's motion were increased, both the maximum velocity and the maximum distances would increase. Those increases would directly increase both a and b, making for a larger ellipse.

Activity 23

Crawling Around: Parametric Plots

Objective

♦ Record the x- and y-coordinates of a rod moving in a figure-eight pattern.

♦ Use the recorded motion information to separately model the x- and y-motion as a function of time.

♦ Plot the experimental data in a y versus x graph.

♦ Plot the x- and y-models parametrically for comparison to the experimental data.

Materials

♦ TI-83 Plus, TI-83, or TI-73 (two if using CBL 2™, one if using LabPro®)

♦ Two CBL 2 or one LabPro data collection devices

♦ DATAMATE software

♦ Two CBR™ or Vernier Motion Detectors

♦ Dowel rod or plastic pipe, about 50 cm by 1 cm

♦ Meter stick

♦ Masking tape

Imagine you are observing a bug crawling around in a figure eight path on the floor. If we defined a Cartesian x, y plane on the floor, and you wished to completely describe the bug's movements graphically, you would need to create a graph in three dimensions. This graph would need one axis to describe the x movement of the bug, another axis for its y movement, and a third axis for the time elapsed during the motion.

It is difficult to portray a graph in three dimensions on two-dimensional paper. It is relatively simple, however, to create a two-dimensional graph.

In this activity, you will model the bug's movement by breaking the motion down into its x and y components. You can then use parametric equations to separately describe each of these components as a function of time. Finally, you will use the parametric mode in the calculator to combine these graphs and create a model that describes the motion of the bug.

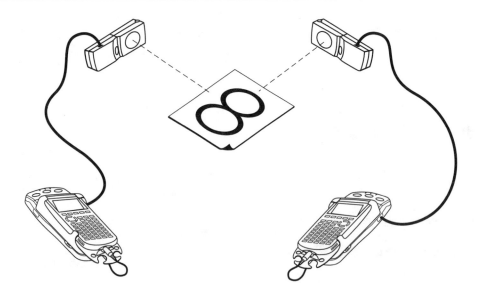

Procedure

This activity can be performed using two CBL 2™ data collection devices with two identical calculators, or one LabPro® data collection device with one calculator. The instructions address both configurations, so read carefully to find which steps to follow.

1. Use the figure-eight path sheet from the last page of this activity. Tape the sheet to the table to keep the sheet from moving.

2. Set up the motion detectors on a table or desk as shown in the figure. Use a meter stick to place each detector 50 cm from the points indicated on the figure-eight sheet. Make note of which detector will collect *x*-data and which will collect *y*-data. Each detector must have an unobstructed view of the sheet.

3. Connect the motion detectors to the DIG/SONIC port of each CBL 2 data collection device or the DIG/SONIC 1 and DIG/SONIC 2 ports of the LabPro data collection device (use Port 1 for the *x*-detector). Use the unit-to-unit cable to connect the TI graphing calculator to the data collection device. Firmly press in the cable ends.

4. Turn on the calculator(s) and start the DATAMATE software. Press CLEAR to reset the software.

5. Adjust the data collection time so you will have ten seconds to move the rod. Do this on both calculators if you are using CBL 2 data collection devices.

    a. Select **SETUP** from the main screen.

    b. Press ▲ to select mode.

    c. Press ENTER to change the data collection mode.

    d. Select **TIME GRAPH** from the SELECT MODE screen.

e. Select **CHANGE TIME SETTINGS**.

f. Enter **0.2** as the time between samples in seconds and press ENTER.

g. Enter **50** as the number of samples and press ENTER.

h. Select **OK** twice to return to the main screen.

6. Hold the rod vertically with the tip resting at the center of the figure-eight pattern. Keep your hands and arms out of the beams of the motion detectors. Practice moving the rod along the pattern, keeping the rod vertical the entire time. Trace the figure several times in ten seconds.

7. Select **START** (on both calculators simultaneously if you are using two) to begin data collection. You will hear the data collection device(s) beep and the motion detectors will begin to click. Move the rod as you practiced. You will have ten seconds to complete the motion two or more times.

8. Press ENTER to display a distance graph. (If you are using LabPro® with one calculator, to see the second graph press ENTER and use the cursor keys to select the second distance channel. Press ENTER to view the graph.)

9. Examine the distance versus time graphs. The graphs should show smooth sinusoidal functions with no large spikes. Check with your teacher if you are not sure whether you need to repeat the data collection.

    To repeat data collection, press ENTER to return to the graph selection screen, and select **MAIN SCREEN**. Select **START** to begin data collection.

    Once you are satisfied with the graph, press ENTER to return to the graph selection screen, and select **MAIN SCREEN**. Select **QUIT** to leave DATAMATE, and follow any instructions to return to the calculator home screen.

Analysis

Since there are a lot of steps to this analysis, here is an overview of what you are about to do.

• Transfer the y data to the x calculator if you used two data collection devices.

• Graph the x versus time data, and fit a sine curve to the raw data.

• Graph the y versus time data, and fit a sine curve to the raw data.

• Graph the data of the y-detector versus the data of the x-detector, which will result in a picture of the figure-eight path.

• Superimpose the two sine models on the y versus x graph, using the parametric plotting mode of the calculator.

• Evaluate the quality of the parametric sine model for the motion data.

1. Skip this step if you are using a single LabPro® with one calculator.

   To complete the analysis, you need to move the distance data from one calculator to another. In order to avoid overwriting data, first copy the data to a new location in the calculator and then send it to the receiving calculator. The following transfer instructions assume that you are moving data between two calculators of the same model. Use the y-data calculator as the sending calculator, and the x-data unit as the receiving calculator. Be sure you know which is which! Once you complete the transfer, use the receiving calculator for the remainder of this activity.

   a. Disconnect the calculators from the data collection devices, and directly connect the two calculators with a unit-to-unit cable. Firmly press in the cable ends.

   b. On the sending calculator, copy the distance data to a new list name. To do this, press [2nd] [L6] [STO▶] [2nd] [L2].

   c. The expression **L6** → **L2** is on the home screen. Press [ENTER] to copy the distance data in **L6** to **L2**.

   d. Press [2nd] [LINK].

   e. Press the number adjacent to **List** to select a data list.

   f. Press [▼] until **L2** is highlighted. Press [ENTER] to select it.

   g. Press [▶] to highlight the TRANSMIT menu.

   h. On the receiving calculator, press [2nd] [LINK].

   i. Press [▶] to highlight **RECEIVE**, and press [ENTER]. The receiving calculator will show **Waiting**.

   j. On the sending calculator, press [ENTER] to actually transmit the list.

   k. The receiving calculator may display a message screen headed **DuplicateName**. If it does, press the number adjacent to **Overwrite**. The receiving calculator will show **Done**.

2. Display just the x-component of the rod's position versus time, after which you will fit a sine curve to the data.

   a. Press [2nd] [STAT PLOT] and press [ENTER] to select **Plot 1**.

   b. Change the **Plot1** settings to match the screen shown here. Press [ENTER] to select any of the settings you change.

   c. Press [ZOOM] and then select **ZoomStat** (use cursor keys to scroll to **ZoomStat**) to draw a graph with the x and y ranges set to fill the screen with data.

3. You have already seen a graph of this data, but now you are ready to fit a sine function to the data.

   a. Press ⬚STAT⬚ and use the cursor keys to highlight **CALC**.

   b. Press ⬚▲⬚ to highlight **SinReg**; press ⬚ENTER⬚ to copy the command to the home screen.

   c. Press ⬚2nd⬚ [L1] ⬚,⬚ ⬚2nd⬚ [L6] ⬚,⬚ to enter the lists containing the data.

   d. Press ⬚VARS⬚ and use the cursor keys to highlight **Y-VARS**.

   e. Select **Function** by pressing ⬚ENTER⬚.

   f. Press ⬚ENTER⬚ to copy **Y1** to the expression.

   g. On the home screen, you will see the entry **SinReg L1**, **L6**, **Y1**. This command will perform a sine regression with **L1** as the x and **L6** as the y values. The resulting regression function will be stored in equation variable **Y1**.

      Press ⬚ENTER⬚ to perform the regression. Use the parameters a, b, c, and d that appear on the calculator screen to write a fitted equation for the x data. Round the fitted parameters to three significant digits and write them in the Data Table on the *Data Collection and Analysis* sheet.

   h. Press ⬚GRAPH⬚ to see the graph.

4. Using the same method you did for the x data, graph and fit a sine function to the y data.

   • If you used two data collection devices, the y data is in list **L2**; substitute that for any occurrence of **L6** in the instructions above.

   • If you used one LabPro® for both motion detectors, the y data is in list **L9**; substitute that for any occurrence of **L6** in the instructions above.

   Record the resulting sine model with its four parameters as the y model in the Data Table.

5. So far you have fit sine curves to both the x and y data, which gives you functions for x and y as a function of time. Now you are ready to plot the position data in a y versus x graph, which will give you a graph that looks like the actual path of the rod. You can then use a parametric graph to superimpose the separate sine curves (both functions of time) on the y versus x graph.

Display a graph of the y values versus the x values. Use the receiving calculator if you collected data using two data collection devices.

a. Press ⟨2nd⟩ [STAT PLOT] ([PLOT] on the TI-73) and press ⟨ENTER⟩ to select **Plot 1**.

b. Change the **Plot1** settings to match the screen shown here. Press ⟨ENTER⟩ to select any of the settings you change.

(If you are using LabPro® with one calculator, use **L9** for the **Y** list instead of **L2**. To enter **L9**, press ⟨2nd⟩ [LIST], scroll to **L9**, and press ⟨ENTER⟩ to paste it to the stat plot screen.)

c. Press ⟨ZOOM⟩ and then select **ZoomStat** (use cursor keys to scroll to **ZoomStat**) to draw a graph with the x and y ranges set to fill the screen with data. The graph you get is nearly, but not quite, what you want, for the proportions of the x and y scales are not the same.

d. Press ⟨ZOOM⟩ and select **ZSquare** to replot the data with equal-size x and y pixels.

6. To create a parametric plot, you must change the mode of the calculator.

a. Press ⟨MODE⟩.

b. Press ⟨▼⟩⟨▼⟩⟨▼⟩⟨▶⟩ to highlight **Par**, and press ⟨ENTER⟩ to set the parametric graphing mode.

7. Use the following steps to enter the two sine regression equations which you earlier recorded in the Data Table. Since the parametric graphing mode needs x and y as a function of t, or time, substitute t for x in the expressions.

a. Press ⟨Y=⟩.

b. Press ⟨CLEAR⟩ to remove any existing equations.

c. Enter the x model expression in the **X1T** field. Press ⟨ENTER⟩ to move to the next field.

d. Enter the y model expression in the **Y1T** field.

e. Press ⟨WINDOW⟩ to adjust the plotting window.

f. Since data collection ran for ten seconds, set **Tmin** to zero, press ⟨▼⟩ and change the **tMax** setting to **10**.

g. Press ⟨GRAPH⟩ to see the graph of y versus x data with the model superimposed.

⇒ Answer Questions 1 and 2 on the *Data Collection and Analysis* sheet.

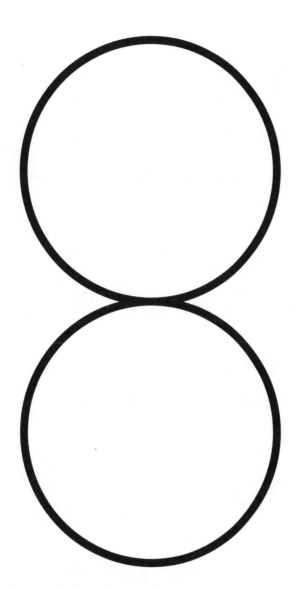

Place one motion detector (to collect *x* data) about 50 cm from this point

•

Place one motion detector (to collect *y* data) about 50 cm from this point

•

Data Collection and Analysis

Name _____

Date _____

Activity 23: Crawling Around

Data Table

x model equation	
y model equation	

Questions

1.   How does the parametric model fit the actual x and y data?

2.   In a parametric plot, how is time represented?

Teacher Notes
Crawling Around: Parametric Plots

1. A wooden dowel or a section of plastic PVC pipe works well. A very small diameter (less than 0.5 cm) may result in noisy distance data.

2. Arrange the motion detectors so that their faces are parallel to the edges of the pattern sheet.

3. The sine regression is not available on the TI-73 calculator, so the activity cannot be completed with modeling using that calculator.

4. This activity requires two motion detectors. Either TI CBR™s or Vernier Motion Detectors can be used. The TI CBR must be connected through a data collection device, and cannot be connected directly to the calculators. If the TI CBL 2™ is used, you must use two data collection devices and two calculators, and then transfer data to a single calculator for analysis. If a Vernier LabPro® data collection device is used, both detectors can be connected to a single data collection device.

   LabPros must have ROM version number 6.2 or newer. ROM versions 6.12 and older do not fully support two motion detectors. To determine ROM version, notice the numbers shown on the title screen as DATAMATE is launched. For updates to ROM (also called firmware), see www.vernier.com/calc/flash.html.

5. Note that the sine regression expressions are recorded in the Data Table as functions of x, as that is the way they are first created. When entering the sine models parametrically, you must replace x with t.

6. Some motion detectors will not be automatically identified by DATAMATE. If you are using such a detector, you must manually set up DATAMATE for the detector:

   a. Select SETUP from the main screen.

   b. Press ⟨ ▼ ⟩ until the cursor is next to DIG (CBL 2) or DIG1 (LabPro).

   c. Press ⟨ENTER⟩ to access the SELECT SENSOR menu.

   d. Select **MOTION(M)**.

   e. Select **OK** to return to the main screen.

Sample Results

Actual data will vary.

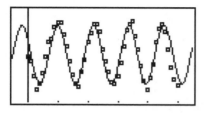

x data with sine regression

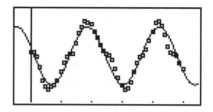

y data with sine regression

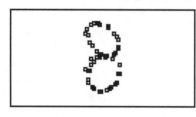

y versus *x* distance data

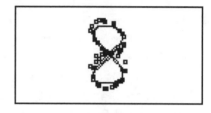

y versus *x* distance data with parametric model

Data Table

Sample data; actual data may vary.

x **model equation**	y = 0.0238*sin(x*2.650+2.53)+0.530
y **model equation**	y = 0.0538*sin(x*1.342+2.815)+0.578

Answers to Questions

1. The parametric model fits the actual data well. This makes sense because the sine curves were fit to the original data; all we have done is to plot the sine curves parametrically.

2. Each point in a parametric plot corresponds to a particular value of time.

EXPLORATIONS

Activity 24

Lights Out:
Periodic
Phenomena

Objective

♦ Record light intensity versus time data for both fast and slow variations of intensity.

♦ Describe the intensity variations using the concepts of period and frequency.

Materials

♦ TI-83 Plus, TI-83, or TI-73

♦ CBL 2™ or LabPro® data collection device

♦ DATAMATE software

♦ Light Sensor

♦ Fluorescent light

A rocking chair moving back and forth, a ringing telephone, and water dripping from a leaky faucet are all examples of *periodic* phenomena. That means that the phenomenon repeats itself every so often. The *period* is the time required to complete one cycle of the phenomenon. The number of times the cycle occurs per unit time is known as the *frequency*.

In the following activities, you will use a light sensor to collect data for two different types of periodic phenomena. You will then analyze this data with the calculator to find the period and the frequency of the observed behavior.

Procedure I – Long Period

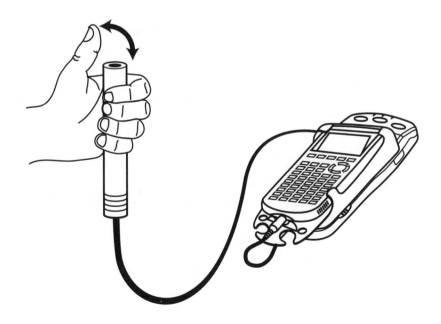

In this part you will point a light sensor towards a light source such as a window or an overhead lamp. To start, cover the end of the sensor with your thumb. When data collection starts, begin alternately lifting your thumb from the sensor and re-covering it. Light intensity readings will be displayed on the screen of the calculator after data collection is complete.

1. Attach the light sensor to CH 1 on the CBL 2™ or LabPro® data collection device. If the sensor has a range switch, set it to 6000 lux. Use the unit-to-unit cable to connect the data collection device to the TI graphing calculator. Firmly press in the cable ends.

2. Turn on the calculator and start the DATAMATE software. Press CLEAR to reset the software.

3. If CH 1 displays the light sensor and its current reading, proceed to Step 4. If it does not, set up DATAMATE for the sensor manually. To do this,

   a. Select **SETUP** from the main screen.

   b. Press ENTER to select CH 1.

   c. Choose **LIGHT** from the SELECT SENSOR list.

   d. Choose **6000 LUX** from the LIGHT list. The sensor will read in units of lux.

   e. Select **OK** to return to the main screen.

4. Once you begin data collection, you will cover and uncover the end of the light sensor using your thumb at roughly a one-covering-per-second rate. For example, you might count "one one thousand two one thousand…" and move your thumb so you cover the sensor on the start of each "thousand."

   a. Hold the sensor in your hand, with your thumb ready to cover the end of the sensor. Point the sensor toward a window or other light source.

   b. Select **START** from the main screen.

   c. After the data collection device beeps, move your thumb as described above. Data collection will run for nine seconds.

   d. The data should show intensity levels which start at a large value, and then alternate between this value and zero in a regular pattern. The time interval between cycles should be fairly uniform. If the data is not satisfactory, press ENTER and return to the start of Step 4.

5. In order to work directly with the data, leave the DATAMATE software. Press ENTER to return to the main screen, and select **QUIT** to leave the software. Follow the instructions on the screen to return to the calculator home screen.

6. Redisplay the graph outside of DATAMATE.

   a. Press [ZOOM].

   b. Press [▼] until **ZoomStat** is highlighted; press [ENTER] to display a graph with x and y ranges set to fill the screen with data.

   c. Press [TRACE] to determine the coordinates of a point on the graph using the cursor keys.

Analysis I – Long Period

⇒ Answer Question 1 – Analysis I on the *Data Collection and Analysis* sheet.

1. The function you see graphed is *periodic*. Determine the period of the cover-uncover function. To do this, use the cursor keys to trace to the first time corresponding to a transition from a plateau to zero or near zero intensity. Record this value as A in the first Data Table on the *Data Collection and Analysis* sheet.

2. Use the cursor keys to trace to another spot on the graph where the function has again gone from a plateau to a near-zero value. Count the number of cycles you traverse as you trace. Record the number of cycles in the first Data Table. (The number of cycles corresponds to the number of times you covered and uncovered the sensor during the time interval.)

   Record the time of the new location as B in the first Data Table.

3. Find the average period ΔT during the A to B time interval by dividing the time difference $B - A$ by the number of cycles during this interval. Round this value the nearest 0.05 seconds, and record it in the first Data Table.

4. While the period represents the number of seconds per cycle, the *frequency* is the number of cycles per second. Find the frequency of the cover-uncover motion by taking the reciprocal of the period you just determined. Record this value as the frequency in the first Data Table.

   Multiply the frequency you just determined by **60**, and record the value in the first Data Table.

⇒ Answer Question 2 – Analysis I on the *Data Collection and Analysis* sheet.

Extension I

What would happen to the graph if you repeated the cover/uncover cycle twice a second instead of the once a second rate you used before? Predict what would happen to the period and frequency values. Return to DATAMATE and take another run with the faster cover/uncover rate to check your prediction.

Procedure II – Short Period

In this part you will point the light sensor at a single fluorescent light and record its intensity for a very short period of time. The resulting plot of intensity versus time is interesting because it shows that fluorescent lights do not stay on continuously but rather flicker off and on very rapidly periodically. Since the human eye cannot distinguish between flashes that occur more than about 50 times a second, the light appears to be on all the time. The data you collect will be used to determine the period and frequency at which the bulb flickers.

1. Since the rate of flickering of the lights is very fast, you need to first increase the rate of data collection.

    a. Start the DATAMATE software.

    b. Select **SETUP** from the main screen.

    c. Press ⬆ to select **MODE**, and press ENTER .

    d. Select **TIME GRAPH** from the SELECT MODE screen.

    e. Select **CHANGE TIME SETTINGS** from the TIME GRAPH SETTINGS screen.

    f. Enter **0.0005** as the time between samples and press ENTER .
        (Note that the data collection device will now record light intensity at a rate of 1/0.0005 = 2000 times a second!)

    g. Enter **100** as the number of samples and press ENTER .

    h. Select **OK** twice to return to the main screen.

2. Collect data of light intensity versus time for the fluorescent light.

   a. Hold the light sensor near the fluorescent light. Since data collection will run only 1/20th of a second, you must be ready for data collection when you select **START**.

   b. Select **START** from the main screen.

   c. After the data collection device finishes beeping, data collection is done.

   d. The data should show intensity levels which alternate between a high and low value in a regular pattern. The time interval between cycles should be relatively constant. If the data is not satisfactory, press ENTER and return to the start of Step 2.

3. In order to work directly with the data, leave the DATAMATE software. Press ENTER to return to the main screen, and select **QUIT** to leave the software. Follow instructions on the screen to return to the calculator home screen.

4. Redisplay the graph outside of DATAMATE using the same method you used earlier.

Analysis II – Short Period

⇒ Answer Question 1 – Analysis II on the *Data Collection and Analysis* sheet.

1. Use the technique you used previously to determine the period and frequency of the pattern from the fluorescent light.

   Round these values to the nearest 0.0005 s and record them in the second Data Table on the *Data Collection and Analysis* sheet.

2. In North America, electric utilities use alternating current at 60 cycles per second, while in most of the world the frequency is 50 cycles per second.

⇒ Answer Question 2 – Analysis II on the *Data Collection and Analysis* sheet.

Extension II

The fluorescent light bulb intensity versus time data you collected in this activity can be modeled with an absolute value sinusoidal equation of the form:

$$y=A|\sin (B(x-C))|+D$$

Can you determine appropriate values for A, B, C, and D so that this equation properly models the data? How do the frequencies of the above equation and

$$y=A \sin (B(x-C))+D$$

compare? Be sure that the calculator is in radian mode before graphing these functions.

Data Collection and Analysis

Name _____

Date _____

Activity 24: Lights Out

Data Table – Analysis I

A (s)		frequency (s^{-1})	
B (s)		frequency * 60	
average ΔT (s)			
number of cycles			

Questions – Analysis I

1. For this intensity plot, what do the plateaus represent? What do the minimum value regions represent?

2. Multiply the frequency you just determined by **60**, and record the value in Data Table I. What does this new value represent?

Data Table – Analysis II

A (s)		frequency (s⁻¹)	
B (s)			
average ΔT (s)			
number of cycles			

Questions – Analysis II

1. What can you conclude about the flickering of a fluorescent light from the graph? What do the peaks represent? What do the valleys represent?

2. Is the frequency of the local current consistent with the measurement of the fluorescent light flicker rate? Note that alternating current flows first in one direction, then the other, so that the fluorescent light is bright *twice* per cycle.

Teacher Notes
Lights Out: Periodic Phenomena

1. The second procedure, Short Period, will work with most fluorescent lights. However, some high-efficiency lighting systems are not powered directly from the power line, and do not exhibit the standard 120 Hz intensity variation. Sometimes the rate is 400 Hz, and sometimes much higher so that the variation would not be observed when data is collected as instructed here. If you do not see the 120 Hz variation, try a cheaper light fixture. You can also see the variation when using some incandescent lamps, but the magnitude of the variation is much smaller.

2. In taking data for Procedure II, hold the sensor near a single fluorescent bulb and away from daylight. If daylight is also striking the light sensor, the flicker from the bulb may be washed out making the variations too small to observe.

3. It is possible that the light from the fluorescent fixture will saturate the light sensor. While you may have the option to change the range to the 150 000 lux setting, a simple strategy is to cover part of the sensor with your fingers until the sensor reading on the main screen is less than 1 (TI sensor) or less than 6000 lux (Vernier sensor). As long as your fingers are not moving significantly during the 1/20th second data collection, the time variation shown will be that of the light.

4. The observed 120 Hz variation in the fluorescent light corresponds to the power curve of the light.

Sample Results

Actual data will vary.

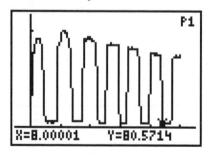

Procedure I

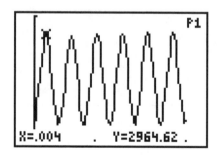

Procedure II

Data Table – Analysis I

Sample data; actual data may vary.

A (s)	1.00	frequency (s⁻¹)	0.71
B (s)	8.00	frequency * 60	42
average ∆T (s)	1.40 s		
number of cycles	5		

Answers to Questions – Analysis I

1. The plateaus represent the maximum light intensity, occurring when the sensor was uncovered. The minima represent the times when the light intensity was small, or when the sensor was covered.

2. The frequency times sixty represent the number of cycles per *minute*.

Data Table – Analysis II

Sample data; actual data may vary

A (s)	0.0040	frequency (s⁻¹)	120
B (s)	0.0455		
average ∆T (s)	0.0830		
number of cycles	5		

Answers to Questions – Analysis II

1. As before, the peaks represent times when the light intensity was high, and the valleys are times when the intensity was low. It appears that fluorescent lights are flickering!

2. The observed flicker frequency is 120 Hz, which is twice the line voltage frequency. This make sense because the fluorescent light will light regardless of the direction the current is flowing, so the light intensity would peak as the current flows first one way and then the other, or twice per cycle of the line voltage.

Activity 25

Tic, Toc:
Pendulum Motion

E X P L O R A T I O N S

Objective

♦ Record the horizontal position versus time for a swinging pendulum.

♦ Determine the period of the pendulum motion.

♦ Model the position data using a cosine function.

Materials

♦ TI-83 Plus, TI-83, or TI-73

♦ CBL 2™ or LabPro® data collection device

♦ DATAMATE software

♦ TI CBR™ or Vernier Motion Detector

♦ Pendulum bob

♦ String

♦ Meter stick

♦ Stopwatch

Pendulum motion has long fascinated people. Galileo studied pendulum motion by watching a swinging chandelier and timing it with his pulse. In 1851 Jean Foucault demonstrated that the earth rotates by using a long pendulum which swung in the same plane while the earth rotated beneath it.

As long as the swing is not too wide, the pendulum approximates simple harmonic motion and produces a sinusoidal pattern. In this activity, you will use a motion detector to plot the position versus time graph for a simple pendulum. You will time the motion to calculate the period, and use a ruler to measure the maximum displacement. You will then use the data to model the motion with the cosine function $y=A \cos (B(x-C))+D$ to mimic the position versus time graph.

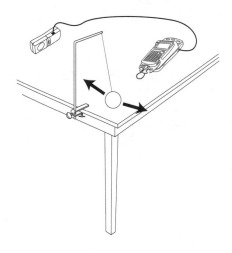

Procedure

1. Hang the pendulum bob from about 80 cm of string from a rigid support. Arrange the support so the bottom of the pendulum bob clears the table by several centimeters. Position the motion detector about 1 m away from the bob, pointing at the bob. Elevate the detector slightly so that it does not respond to the table.

2. Measure the distance from the bob to the motion detector; this distance must be at least 75 cm. Record this distance D, in meters, in the Data Table on the *Data Collection and Analysis* sheet.

3. Place the meter stick under the bob, along the line between the detector and the bob. Arrange the stick so that the zero point is under the bob when it is hanging still. Determine how far you will pull back the bob before releasing it. This distance should be less than 20 cm. Record this value, in meters, as the amplitude A in the Data Table.

4. Use the stopwatch to measure the period of the pendulum. The period is the time taken by the pendulum to complete one back and forth cycle. Use the amplitude of motion you determined in the previous step. Measure the time for *ten* complete cycles, and record this time in the Data Table.

   Take care to count carefully: One way to do this is to start the stopwatch when the bob is farthest from the motion detector, and count one cycle when it returns to that spot. Keep the stopwatch running until ten cycles are completed.

5. Connect the motion detector into the DIG/SONIC port of the CBL 2™ or the DIG/SONIC 1 port of the LabPro® data collection device. Use the unit-to-unit cable to connect the TI graphing calculator to the data collection device. Firmly press in the cable ends.

6. Turn on the calculator and start the DATAMATE software. Press (CLEAR) to reset the software.

7. Practice swinging the ball by pulling it back the distance you recorded above, and then releasing it so that the ball swings in a line directly away from the motion detector.

8. With the ball swinging properly, select **START** to begin data collection. You will hear the data collection device beep. Data collection will run for five seconds.

9. Press (ENTER) to display the distance graph.

10. Examine the distance versus time graph, which should be sinusoidal. Check with your teacher if you are not sure whether you need to repeat the data collection. To repeat data collection, press ENTER to return to the graph selection screen, and select **MAIN SCREEN**. Select **START** to begin data collection.

    Once you have a good run, press ENTER to go back to the main screen and select **QUIT**. Follow any instructions on the screen to return to the calculator home screen.

Analysis

1. Change the angle calculation mode on the calculator to radians, or confirm that it is set to radians.

2. Compare the motion detector data to the cosine model of $y = A\cos(B(x-C)) + D$. The setup measurements will allow you to determine the parameters A, B and D. To determine C, redisplay the graph of the motion detector data.

   a. Press ZOOM.

   b. Press ▼ until **ZoomStat** is highlighted; press ENTER to display a graph with the x and y ranges set to fill the screen with data.

   c. Press TRACE to determine the coordinates of a point on the graph using the cursor keys.

3. Since the cosine function starts at a maximum value when its argument is zero, you can use the location of a maximum to determine the value of C, which represents the horizontal shift of the data. Trace across the data to any maximum and read the time (x) value. Record this value as C in the Data Table.

4. Enter the model equation in the equation editor of the calculator.

   a. Press Y=.

   b. Press CLEAR to remove any existing equation.

   c. Enter the expression **A∗cos(B∗(X–C)) + D** in the **Y1** field. (On the TI-73, access the alphabetic entry screen by pressing 2nd [TEXT], and the sine function by pressing 2nd [TRIG].)

   d. To make the model equation plot with a bold line, press ◄ until the diagonal line to the left of **Y1** is highlighted. Press ENTER until the line is shown as a bold line.

   e. Press 2nd [QUIT] to return to the home screen.

5. The parameter A represents the amplitude of the motion of the bob. This distance is measured horizontally from one extreme of motion to the center position. By always starting the pendulum bob from the same position, you have the same amplitude each time. Enter the value for the parameter A in the calculator's memory. To do this, enter the value for the parameter A. Press $\boxed{\text{STO}\blacktriangleright}$ **A** $\boxed{\text{ENTER}}$ to store the value in the variable **A**.

6. You have measured the time for ten complete cycles of the pendulum. Use this value to find the period of the motion, which is the time for one complete cycle. Enter this value in the Data Table on the *Data Collection and Analysis* sheet.

7. The sinusoidal model has a parameter B that represents the number of cycles the function makes during the natural period of the sine function. Find B by taking 2π (the natural period of the cosine function) divided by the period of the pendulum (the time for one cycle). Store this value in the calculator after performing the division by pressing $\boxed{\text{STO}\blacktriangleright}$ **B** $\boxed{\text{ENTER}}$ to store the value in the variable **B**. Record the value in the Data Table.

8. Enter the value for C, the time offset, from the Data Table. Press $\boxed{\text{STO}\blacktriangleright}$ **C** $\boxed{\text{ENTER}}$ to store the value in variable **C**.

9. The parameter D represents the offset of the cosine function from the distance axis. The distance from the motion detector to the pendulum bob at rest is the value of D. Enter the value from the Data Table and store it by pressing $\boxed{\text{STO}\blacktriangleright}$ **D** $\boxed{\text{ENTER}}$ to store the value in the variable **D**.

10. You have now entered the model equation and values for the four parameters A, B, C, and D. Press $\boxed{\text{GRAPH}}$ to display a graph of the motion detector data and the model equation.

⇒ Answer Questions 1-4 on the *Data Collection and Analysis* sheet.

Calculus Extension

Once you have an equation for the position versus time graph of the pendulum motion, take the derivative of the equation. This represents the velocity of the pendulum at any time t. How does the velocity versus time graph compare with the position versus time graph? When during the pendulum motion is the velocity zero? When is the velocity a maximum?

The derivative of velocity is *acceleration*. Take the second derivative of the position equation. Describe the position and velocity when the acceleration is a maximum. Do the same when the acceleration is zero.

Give a general description of the pendulum's position, velocity, and acceleration when the bob is passing through the at-rest position and when it is farthest from the detector.

Data Collection and Analysis

Name _____

Date _____

Activity 25: Tic, Toc

Data Table

A (m)	
B	
C (s)	
D (m)	
Time for ten cycles (s)	
Period (s)	

Questions

1. How well does the model equation fit the data? If the fit is acceptable, write the model equation below, and suggest explanations for any discrepancies. If the fit of the model is not acceptable, deduce which of the parameters is producing the problem. Make changes as necessary to the parameters, and discuss why the changes were necessary. Write out the equation that produced a good fit.

2. How would the parameters A, B, C, and D change if you were to use the sine function $y=A \sin (B(x-C))+D$ instead of the cosine function? Predict the values below and explain your reasoning for each.

3. Test your predictions by storing any changed values in the four parameters using the same method you used above. Also using the same method as above, change the model equation to a sine function. Redisplay the graph to compare the data and sine model. How well does the sine model fit the data? Explain any discrepancies.

4. Give a physical interpretation of each of the parameters A, B, C, and D from the model $y = A \cos (B(x-C)) + D$ in terms of the pendulum.

Teacher Notes
Tic, Toc: Pendulum Motion

1. This activity has the student measure the amplitude, period, and offset distance for a pendulum using a meter stick and a stopwatch. Although these values could be obtained from the motion detector graph, independent measurements show the student that the motion detector is using the same distance and time standards as conventional instruments.

2. Avoid using a soft or felt-covered ball for the pendulum bob, as the ultrasonic waves from the motion detector tend to be absorbed by these surfaces. A ball with a hole drilled through its center works well as a pendulum bob.

3. A TI CBR™ or a Vernier Motion Detector can be used in this activity. If a CBR is used, it must be connected through a CBL 2™ or a LabPro®, and not directly to the calculator.

4. Some motion detectors will not be automatically identified by DATAMATE. If you are using such a detector, you must manually set up DATAMATE for the detector:

   a. Select **SETUP** from the main screen.

   b. Press ⟨ ▼ ⟩ until the cursor is next to DIG (CBL 2) or DIG1 (LabPro).

   c. Press ⟨ENTER⟩ to access the SELECT SENSOR menu.

   d. Select **MOTION(M)**.

   e. Select **OK** to return to the main screen.

Sample Results

Actual data will vary.

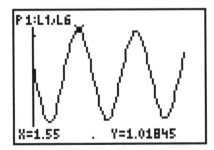

Raw data graphed outside of DATAMATE

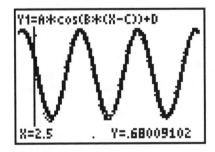

Model superimposed on data

Data Table

Sample data; actual data may vary.

A (m)	0.17
B	3.27
C (s)	1.53
D (m)	0.85
Time for ten cycles (s)	19.2
Period (s)	1.92

Answers to Questions

1. The model fits the experimental data well. $y = 0.17 * \sin(3.27 * (x - 1.53)) + 0.85$.

2. The values of A, B, and D would not change. The value of C would change because the horizontal shifts needed to fit a sine and cosine curve are different. Students may use a trial and error method to find the new value of C. Some students may reason that the sine curve is the cosine curve shifted right by one-fourth of the period. They may calculate one-fourth of the period and subtract it from the current value of C to find the new value of C. In this case, $1.53 - (1.53/4) = 1.91$. This would be a good method to share in a post-activity discussion for those students who do not discover it.

3. The new sine model fits as well as the cosine model, as long as the appropriate adjustment is made in the C parameter.

4. A is the distance that the pendulum swings to either side of the stationary point. B is the number of cycles in the natural period of the function. C is the amount of time that passed between the start of the software and the time the pendulum was a maximum distance from the detector. D is the stationary point of the pendulum or the position of the pendulum when it is at rest.

EXPLORATIONS

Activity 26

Stay Tuned: Sound Waveform Models

If you throw a rock into a calm pond, the water around the point of entry begins to move up and down, causing ripples to travel outward. If these ripples come across a small floating object such as a leaf, they will cause the leaf to move up and down on the water. Much like waves in water, sound in air is produced by the vibration of an object. These vibrations produce pressure oscillations in the surrounding air which travel outward like the ripples on the pond. When the pressure waves reach the eardrum, they cause it to vibrate. These vibrations are then translated into nerve impulses and interpreted by your brain as sounds.

These pressure waves are what we usually call *sound waves*. Most waves are very complex, but the sound from a tuning fork is a single tone that can be described mathematically using a cosine function $y = A\cos(B(x - C))$. In this activity you will analyze the tone from a tuning fork by collecting data with a microphone.

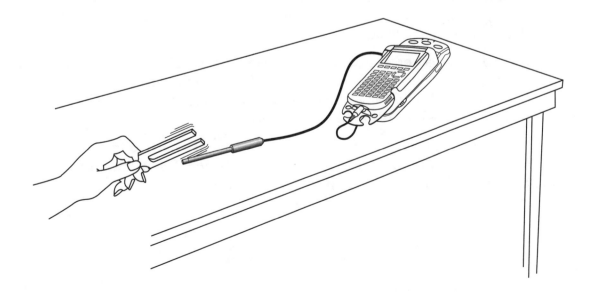

Procedure

1. Turn on the calculator. If the calculator is in degree mode, change it to radian mode.

2. Connect a Vernier microphone to the CH 1 input of the CBL 2™ or LabPro® data collection device. Use the unit-to-unit cable to connect the data collection device to the TI graphing calculator. Firmly press in the cable ends.

3. Start the DATAMATE software. Press `CLEAR` to reset the software.

4. Set up DATAMATE for the microphone.

   a. Select **SETUP** from the main screen. If CH 1 displays the microphone, proceed directly to Step 5.

   b. Press `ENTER` to select CH1.

   c. Choose **MICROPHONE** from the SELECT SENSOR list.

   d. Select **CBL, ULI**, or **MPLI**, according to the type of microphone you are using.

5. To center the waveform on zero, zero the microphone channel. To do this:

   a. Select **ZERO** from the setup screen.

   b. Select **ALL CHANNELS** from the select channel screen.

   c. With the room quiet, press `ENTER` to zero the channel.

6. If you are using a keyboard, set it to a flute sound. Use Middle C as the note. If you are using a tuning fork, strike it against a soft object such as a rubber mallet or the rubber sole of a shoe.

   Caution: Striking the tuning fork against a hard object can damage it. If you strike it too hard or too softly, the waveform may be rough.

   Produce a sound with a tuning fork or keyboard, hold it close to the microphone, and select **START** to collect data. Data collection begins after the data collection device beeps.

7. After data collection ends, a graph appears. The waveform should resemble a sine function. Check with your instructor if you are not sure if you need to repeat data collection. If you need to repeat data collection, press `ENTER` to return to the main screen; then do Step 6 again.

8. Once you are satisfied with the data, press `ENTER` to return to the main screen. Select **QUIT** to leave the DATAMATE software. Follow any instructions on the calculator to return to its home screen.

Analysis

1. Redisplay the graph.

    a. Press [ZOOM].

    b. Press [▼] until **ZoomStat** is highlighted. Press [ENTER] to display a graph with the x and y ranges set to fill the screen with data.

    c. Press [TRACE] to determine the coordinates of a point on the graph using the cursor keys.

2. Use the cursor keys to trace across the graph. Record the times for the first and last peaks of the waveform. Record the number of complete cycles that occur between the first measured time and the last. Divide the difference, Δt, by the number of cycles to determine the period of the waveform.

    Record the period, to three significant figures, in the Data Table on the *Data Collection and Analysis* sheet. For example, 0.00230 has three significant figures.

3. Trace across the graph again and note the maximum and minimum y values for an adjacent peak and trough. Calculate the amplitude of the wave by taking half of the absolute value of the difference between the maximum and minimum y values.

    Record the amplitude A, to two significant figures, in the Data Table on the *Data Collection and Analysis* sheet.

4. Since the cosine function starts at a maximum value when its argument is zero, you can use the location of a maximum to determine the value of C, which represents the horizontal shift of the data. Trace across the data to any maximum and read the time (x) value. Record this value as C in the Data Table on the *Data Collection and Analysis* sheet.

5. To compare the model to the data, enter the model equation into the calculator.

    a. Press [Y=].

    b. Press [CLEAR] to remove any existing equation.

    c. Enter the expression **A∗cos(B∗(X–C))** in the **Y1** field. (On the TI-73, access the alphabetic entry screen by pressing [2nd] [TEXT], and the cosine function by pressing [2nd] [TRIG].)

    d. To make the model equation plot with a bold line, press [◄] until the diagonal line to the left of **Y1** is highlighted. Press [ENTER] until the line is shown as a bold line.

    e. Press [2nd] [QUIT] to return to the home screen.

6. The parameter A represents the amplitude of the waveform. Enter your value for the parameter A in the calculator's memory. To do this, enter the value for the amplitude from the Data Table. Press $\boxed{\text{STO}\blacktriangleright}$ **A** $\boxed{\text{ENTER}}$ to store the value in the variable **A**.

7. The sinusoidal model has a parameter, B, that represents the number of cycles the sinusoidal function makes during the natural period of the sine function. Find B by taking 2π (the natural period of the sine function) divided by the period of the waveform (the time for one cycle). Store this value in the calculator after performing the division by pressing $\boxed{\text{STO}\blacktriangleright}$ **B** $\boxed{\text{ENTER}}$ to store the value in the variable **B**.

8. Enter the value for C from the Data Table and press $\boxed{\text{STO}\blacktriangleright}$ **C** $\boxed{\text{ENTER}}$ to store the value in variable **C**.

9. You have now entered the model equation and values for the three parameters A, B, and C. Press $\boxed{\text{GRAPH}}$ to display a graph of the microphone data with the model equation.

⇒ Answer Questions 1 and 2 on the *Data Collection and Analysis* sheet.

10. Most tuning forks are marked with the frequency. Check the tuning fork you used and record its frequency in the Data Table. If you used a keyboard, note that middle C is approximately 263 Hz.

⇒ Answer Questions 3-7 on the *Data Collection and Analysis* sheet.

Extension

The calculator can automatically fit a sine function to the waveform data. The format of the calculator's fit is a little different than the one you used: $y = A\sin(Bx+C)$. You can work out the translation for the new usage of the parameter C.

Use the calculator to fit a sine curve to the waveform data. How do the fit parameters compare to those of your model?

The TI-73 cannot perform this regression.

TI-83 and TI-83 Plus

1. Press [STAT] and use the cursor keys to highlight **CALC**.

2. Press [▲] to highlight **SinReg**; press [ENTER] to copy the command to the home screen.

3. Press [2nd] [L1] [,] [2nd] [L2] [,] to enter the lists containing the data.

4. Press [VARS] and use the cursor keys to highlight **Y-VARS**.

5. Select **Function** by pressing [ENTER].

6. Press [ENTER] to copy **Y1** to the expression.

7. On the home screen, you will now see the entry **SinReg L1**, **L2**, **Y1**. This command will perform a sine regression with **L1** as the x and **L2** as the y values. The resulting regression line will be stored in equation variable **Y1**. Press [ENTER] to perform the regression. Use the parameters a, b, c, and d that appear on the calculator screen to write down the fitted equation. Write the fitted parameters to three significant digits.

8. Press [GRAPH] to see the graph.

Data Collection and Analysis

Name _____

Date _____

Activity 26: Stay Tuned

Data Table

Period (s)	
Amplitude A	
Time offset C	
Frequency (measured)	
Frequency (marked)	

Questions

1. How well does your model equation fit the data?

   If your fit is acceptable, write the model equation below, and suggest explanations for any discrepancies. If the fit of the model is not acceptable, deduce which of the parameters is producing the problem. Make changes as necessary to the parameters, and discuss why the changes were necessary. Write out the equation that produced a good fit.

2. The frequency of a sound wave is the number of cycles-per-second. The period is the number of seconds-per-cycle. Explain the relationship between frequency and period.

   The unit Hertz, or Hz, is equivalent to cycles-per-second. Calculate the frequency of the tuning fork in Hz, and record it in the Data Table above.

3. The amplitude of a sound wave increases with the loudness of the sound. Explain how you could alter the value of A if you repeated this investigation.

4. *Pitch* is associated with the frequency of the tuning fork. A higher pitched tone would have a higher frequency. Explain how your graph would change if you used a tuning fork of higher frequency.

    How would the value of the period change if the frequency were higher? Explain your reasoning clearly.

5. How many different values of C are possible in order to match this graph? Explain your reasoning.

    Find another value of C that will work and record it below. Check this in the equation, and discuss your reasoning.

6. How would the parameters A, B, and C change if you were to use the sine function $y = A\sin(B(x-C))$ instead of the cosine function? Predict the values below and explain your reasoning for each.

7. Test your predictions by storing any changed values in the three parameters, A, B, and C, using the same method you used earlier. Also change the model equation to a sine function using the method used earlier. Redisplay the graph to compare your data and sine model. How well does your sine model fit the data? Explain any discrepancies.

Teacher Notes
Stay Tuned: Sound Waveform Models

1. A tuning fork of relatively low frequency works best. Use tuning forks with frequencies between 256 and 300 Hz for best results.

2. You may want to introduce the term *sinusoidal curve* to your students as a curve which has an equation of the form $y = A\cos(B(x - C))$. Many books use the form $y = A\cos(Bx + C)$. Written the latter way, the parameter C is an angular offset, while in the first form C is a time offset. The time offset is easily determined from the graph, so the first form is used in the activity. The latter form is more difficult for most students to understand, but could be used if you prefer it.

3. Data collection is very brief; the fork or keyboard must be sounding when the **START** command is given.

4. Use a rubber mallet (or the sole of a rubber shoe) to strike the tuning fork to obtain a clean sinusoidal curve. If the fork is struck on a hard surface, there will be overtones, which will yield a rough waveform. Note that the fork must be loud enough to hear. If you can't hear the fork over the room noise, neither can the microphone.

5. An inexpensive electronic keyboard is an excellent substitute for the tuning fork. The flute setting will give a sine waveform. Turn off any vibrato to obtain clear frequency measurements. It is easier to obtain consistently good waveforms with a keyboard than a tuning fork. Middle C will produce a frequency of about 263 Hz, appropriate for this exercise.

Sample Results

Actual data will vary.

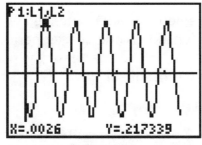

Raw data

Model equation

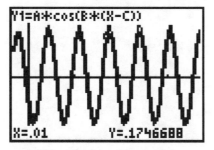

Waveform with model

Data Table

Sample data; actual data may vary.

Period (s)	0.00390
Amplitude A	0.22
Time offset C	0.026
Frequency (measured)	256 Hz
Frequency (marked)	256 Hz

Answers to Questions

1. The model fits the sound waveform data quite well. The model equation is $y = 0.22 \cos(1607(x - 0.026))$.

2. Frequency and period are inversely related.

3. The waveform would be taller, if plotted on the same scale, if the sound produced were louder. This can be accomplished by making the fork sound louder or moving the microphone closer to the fork.

4. A higher frequency would create a shorter period, so there would be more cycles displayed on the screen if the axis settings were the same.

5. Multiple values of C could create a good fit of the model. Since the graph repeats every time the period of time passes, additional values of C could be obtained from $C = C_0 + K$ (*Period*), where K is any integer and C_0 the original value. Using this formula and the example data, a C of $0.010 + 0.0039 \cong 0.014$ would produce a plot looking just like the one shown above.

6. The amplitude, A, and the frequency parameter, B, are unchanged by the sine function substitution. Since the sine function is one quarter period behind the cosine function, we need to subtract one quarter of the period from the original C to adjust C for the sine function, or

   $$0.010 - 0.0039 / 4 \cong 0.009.$$

7. Graphing the sine function with the reduced value for C shows the discussion in Question 6 to be correct. The fit is excellent and indistinguishable from the cosine fit.

EXPLORATIONS

Activity 27

Up and Down: Damped Harmonic Motion

Objective

♦ Record the motion data for a plate bouncing at the end of a light spring.

♦ Analyze the motion data to determine frequency, period and amplitude information.

♦ Model the oscillatory part of the data using trigonometric functions.

♦ Model the damping using an exponential function.

♦ Create a composite model of damping and oscillation.

♦ Compare the composite model to experimental data.

Materials

♦ TI-83 Plus, TI-83, or TI-73

♦ CBL 2™ or LabPro® data collection device

♦ DATAMATE software

♦ TI CBR™ or Vernier Motion Detector

♦ Ring stand

♦ Slinky™ or light spring

♦ Paper plate

♦ Standard slotted mass hanger

An object hanging from a spring can bounce up and down in a simple way. The vertical position of the object can be described mathematically in terms of a simple sinusoidal equation. In the real world, however, resistive forces such as friction are always present and cause the object to slow down. This effect is called *damping*.

Most oscillating objects experience damping and move in a modified periodic manner so that the amplitude gets smaller and smaller with each cycle. Common examples of damped oscillators include an empty rocking chair as it comes to rest after being pushed and a vibrating diving board after a swimmer leaves it. At first, the problem of modeling this type of motion with a mathematical equation may seem extraordinarily complex. Surprisingly, it can be analyzed rather thoroughly using basic math concepts with which you are already familiar.

In this activity, you will collect motion data as a paper plate attached to a light spring oscillates up and down above a motion detector. Then, you will find an appropriate mathematical model for the resulting data set.

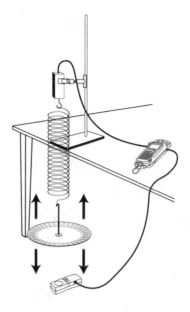

Procedure

1. Position the motion detector on the floor so that the disc is pointing straight upward.

2. Plug the motion detector into the DIG/SONIC port of the CBL 2™ or DIG/SONIC 1 port of the LabPro® data collection device. Use the unit-to-unit cable to connect the TI graphing calculator to the data collection device. Firmly press in the cable ends.

3. Suspend the spring and its plate over the motion detector from a ring stand or other fixed support. Be sure that no table edge or other barrier is near the path between the plate and the motion detector. Wait until the plate and spring stop moving. The distance to the motion detector should be at least 70 cm. This position is called the *equilibrium* position.

4. Turn on the calculator, and set the angle mode to radian. Start the DATAMATE software. Press CLEAR to reset the software.

5. The plate and spring system typically takes about ten seconds for the amplitude of motion to decay significantly. To collect data for ten seconds, you need to adjust the data collection parameters.

    a. Select **SETUP** from the main screen.

    b. Press ▲ to select **MODE**, and press ENTER.

    c. Select **TIME GRAPH** from the SELECT MODE menu.

    d. Select **CHANGE TIME SETTINGS** from the TIME GRAPH SETTINGS menu.

    e. Enter **0.1** as the time between samples and press ENTER. (Use **0.2** for the TI-73.)

    f. Enter **100** as the number of samples and press ENTER. (Use **50** for the TI-73.)

    g. Select **OK** from the TIME GRAPH SETTINGS menu.

6. So that the zero reference position will be the equilibrium position of the plate, zero the motion detector.

   a. Select **ZERO** from the setup screen.

   b. Select **DIG-DISTANCE** from the SELECT CHANNEL menu.

   c. Confirm that the plate is still stationary. Press ⌈ENTER⌉ to zero the motion detector.

7. Pull the plate downward about 10 cm, and allow it to oscillate up and down. Select **START** to begin data collection. You will hear the data collection device beep. Data collection will run for ten seconds.

8. Press ⌈ENTER⌉ to display the **DISTANCE** graph.

9. Examine the distance versus time graph. The graph should contain a sine curve of diminishing amplitude. Check with your instructor if you are not sure whether you need to repeat the data collection.

   To repeat data collection, press ⌈ENTER⌉ to return to the graph selection screen, and select **MAIN SCREEN**. Return to Step 7.

10. Once you are satisfied with your data, press ⌈ENTER⌉, select **MAIN SCREEN**, and select **QUIT** to leave the DATAMATE software. Follow any instructions on the calculator to return to the home screen.

Analysis

1. Redisplay the graph outside of DATAMATE.

   a. Press ⌈ZOOM⌉.

   b. Press ⌈▼⌉ until **ZoomStat** is highlighted; press ⌈ENTER⌉ to display a graph with the x and y ranges set to fill the screen with data.

   c. Press ⌈TRACE⌉ to determine the coordinates of a point on the graph using the cursor keys.

2. The graph shows several features, each of which you will model with an appropriate mathematical function.

   First, notice the envelope of the back-and-forth, or *oscillatory*, motion. The amplitude of the motion decreases in time in a regular way. You will model the time variation of the amplitude with one function. This oscillatory part of the motion can be modeled with a cosine function $y = A\cos(B(x - C))$, where

   • x is time, in seconds,

   • y is distance, in meters, and

   • A is the amplitude of the motion, or the largest distance above the center position.

To estimate the amplitude parameter, A, trace across the graph using the [▶] key to the first positive maximum. Record the y value as A in the Data Table on the *Data Collection and Analysis* sheet. Record this, and all distance values, to three significant figures.

3. The shortest time it takes for a repetitive motion to repeat itself is called the *period*. One way to find the period of the plate is to find the time between two successive maximum or minimum points. Continue to trace across the graph to determine the x values for two adjacent maximum or minimum peaks. Record these two values as t_1 and t_2. Calculate the difference, which is the period T, and record it in the Data Table.

4. The parameter C represents the horizontal shift of the cosine function. Since the cosine function has a maximum value when its argument is zero, the time when the data first reaches a maximum will serve as an estimate for C. Trace to the first maximum and note the time (x) value. Record this value as C in the Data Table.

5. To compare the model to the data, enter the model equation into the calculator.

    a. Press [Y=].

    b. Press [CLEAR] to remove any existing equation.

    c. Enter the expression **A*cos(B*(X–C))** in the **Y1** field. (On the TI-73, access the alphabetic entry screen by pressing [2nd] [TEXT], and the cosine function by pressing [2nd] [TRIG].)

    d. To make the model equation plot with a bold line, press [◀] until the diagonal line to the left of **Y1** is highlighted. Press [ENTER] until the line is shown as a bold line.

    e. Press [2nd] [QUIT] to return to the home screen.

6. The parameter A represents the amplitude of the waveform. Enter your value for the parameter A in the calculator's memory. To do this, enter the value for the amplitude from the Data Table. Press [STO ▶] **A** [ENTER] to store the value in the variable **A**.

7. The sinusoidal model has a parameter, B, that represents the number of cycles the sinusoidal function makes during the natural period of the cosine function.

    Find B by taking 2π (the natural period of the cosine function) divided by the period T of the waveform (the time for one cycle). Store this value in the calculator after performing the division by pressing [STO ▶] **B** [ENTER] to store the value in the variable **B**. Also record the value in the Data Table.

8. Enter the value of C from the Data Table, and press [STO ▶] **C** [ENTER] to store the value in variable **C**.

9. You have now entered the model equation and values for the three parameters A, B, and C. Press GRAPH to display a graph of the motion data with the cosine model equation.

⇒ Answer Question 1 on the *Data Collection and Analysis* sheet.

10. Now that you have modeled the oscillatory part of the motion, turn off the plotting of the cosine model.

    a. Press Y=.

    b. Press ◄ so that the = sign is highlighted. Press ENTER to turn off plotting of the equation.

    c. Press 2nd [QUIT] to return to the home screen.

11. To model the time variation of the amplitude, you need to record the maximum values and their times in a temporary table of your own design.

    a. Press GRAPH.

    b. Press TRACE to determine the coordinates of a point on the graph using the cursor keys.

    c. Record the x and y values of each maximum peak to three significant digits. Continue tracing and recording values until you have reached the end of the graph or until you reach six points.

12. To plot the points you just recorded, you need to enter them into new lists in the calculator.

    TI-73

    a. Press LIST.

    b. Lists 2 and 3 are available for you to use. Use the cursor keys to highlight the **L2** header, and press CLEAR to clear the list.

    c. Press ENTER to move to the first element of **L2**.

    d. Enter all of the time values, ending each entry with ENTER.

    e. Use ▲ and ► to move to the header of **L3**. Press CLEAR to clear the list.

    f. Press ENTER to move to the first element of **L3**.

    g. Enter the maximum distance data values, ending each entry with ENTER. You must have the same number of elements in **L2** as in **L3** when you are done. If not, check the entries for errors and correct them.

▶ **TI-83 and TI-83 Plus**

a. Press [STAT] and press [ENTER] to see the data lists.

b. Lists 2 and 3 are available for you to use. Use the cursor keys to highlight the **L2** header, and press [CLEAR] to clear the list.

c. Press [ENTER] to move to the first element of **L2**.

d. Enter all of the time values, ending each entry with [ENTER].

e. Use [▲] and [►] to move to the header of **L3**. Press [CLEAR] to clear the list.

f. Press [ENTER] to move to the first element of **L3**.

g. Enter the maximum distance data values, ending each entry with [ENTER]. You must have the same number of elements in **L2** as in **L3** when you are done. If not, check the entries for errors and correct them.

13. Now that you have the data to be plotted stored in lists in the calculator, you are ready to plot just the peak values of the distance and time data.

a. Press [2nd] [STAT PLOT] ([PLOT] on the TI-73) and press [ENTER] to select **Plot1**.

b. Change the **Plot1** settings to match the screen shown here. Press [ENTER] to select any of the settings you change.

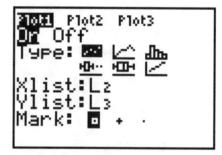

c. Press [ZOOM] and then select **ZoomStat** (use cursor keys to scroll to **ZoomStat**) to draw a graph with the *x* and *y* ranges set to fill the screen with data.

14. The graph should show a gradual decay in the amplitude of the oscillations of the plate. To incorporate the decay into a model for the data, fit an exponential function to the amplitude curve.

▶ **TI-73**

a. Press [2nd] [STAT], and use the cursor keys to highlight **CALC**.

b. Press the number adjacent to **ExpReg** to copy the command to the home screen.

c. After the **ExpReg** command, press [2nd] [STAT] and select **L2** by pressing the number next to **L2**. Then press [,]. Repeat the procedure to select **L3**.

d. After selecting **L3**, press [,] then press [2nd] [VARS].

e. Use the cursor keys to select **Y-Vars** and press ENTER .

f. Press ▼ and ENTER to select **Y2** and copy it to the expression.

g. On the home screen, you will see the entry **ExpReg L2**, **L3**, **Y2**. This command will perform an exponential regression with **L2** as the x and **L3** as the y values. The resulting regression equation will be stored in equation variable **Y2**. Press ENTER to perform the regression.

h. Press GRAPH to see the graph.

TI-83 and TI-83 Plus

a. Press STAT and use the cursor keys to highlight **CALC**.

b. Press the number adjacent to **ExpReg** to copy the command to the home screen.

c. Press 2nd [L2] , 2nd [L3] , to enter the lists containing the data.

d. Press VARS and use the cursor keys to highlight **Y-VARS**.

e. Select **Function** by pressing ENTER .

f. Press ▼ and ENTER to copy **Y2** to the expression.

g. On the home screen, you will see the entry **ExpReg L2**, **L3**, **Y2**. This command will perform an exponential regression with **L2** as the x and **L3** as the y values. The resulting regression equation will be stored in equation variable **Y2**. Press ENTER to perform the regression.

h. Press GRAPH to see the graph.

15. The new graph shows the maximum amplitude points and the fitted exponential function. To combine the exponential decay (often known as the *envelope* of the oscillations) with the oscillatory cosine model, you can define a new function that is the product of the cosine model and the exponential function. The cosine model includes the parameter A to represent the amplitude; the **Y2** exponential function can replace the amplitude parameter to improve the model function.

TI-73

a. Press Y= .

b. The cursor will be flashing on the A parameter in **Y1**. Press 2nd [VARS] and select **Y-VARS**.

c. Select **Y2** to paste the **Y2** function to the equation screen, replacing the A variable.

d. Press ⬛▾ until you highlight the **Y2** function. Since you no longer need this part plotted, press ⬛◄ until the = sign is flashing, and press ⬛ENTER to disable plotting of **Y2**.

e. Record the composite model equation in the Data Table on the *Data Collection and Analysis* sheet, including both the exponential and oscillating parts.

▶ TI-83 and TI-83 Plus

a. Press ⬛Y=.

b. The cursor will be flashing on the *A* variable in **Y1**. Press ⬛VARS and press ⬛▶ to highlight the **Y-VARS** menu.

c. Press ⬛ENTER to display the function menu.

d. Select **Y2** to paste the **Y2** function to the equation screen, replacing the *A* variable.

e. Press ⬛▾ until you highlight the **Y2** function. Since you no longer need this part plotted, press ⬛◄ until the = sign is flashing, and press ⬛ENTER to disable plotting of **Y2**.

f. Record the composite model equation in the Data Table on the *Data Collection and Analysis* sheet, including both the exponential and oscillating parts.

16. Now you can view a graph of the final model plotted with the complete experimental data.

a. Press ⬛2nd [stat plot] ([PLOT] on the TI-73) and press ⬛ENTER to select **Plot 1**.

b. Change the **Plot1** settings to match the screen shown here. Press ⬛ENTER to select any of the settings you change.

c. Press ⬛ZOOM and then select **ZoomStat** (use cursor keys to scroll to **ZoomStat**) to draw a graph with the *x* and *y* ranges set to fill the screen with data.

⇒ Answer Questions 2-4 on the *Data Collection and Analysis* sheet.

Extensions

1. What would a plot of velocity versus time look like for the damped oscillations you studied in this activity? Create a scatter plot of velocity versus time.

2. Use the numerical computation tools of the calculator to find a mathematical equation that models velocity as a function of time. How well does the modeling curve fit the data?

3. What would a plot of velocity versus position look like for a damped oscillator? Make a sketch of your prediction, and then create a scatter plot of velocity versus position. How can the mathematical models you created for position and velocity, as functions of time be used to model the velocity-position data plot?
    Hint: You will need to set the calculator to *parametric* mode.

Data Collection and Analysis

Name _____

Date _____

Activity 27: Up and Down

Data Table

A		
t_1, t_2		
T		
B		
C		
Composite Model		

Questions

1. How well does your model equation fit the data? What aspect of the model fits the data? What aspect of the model does not fit the data?

2. How well does the final model fit the experimental data? Is it a good model? Describe the model equation in words, without specifying any numeric values.

3. (Optional) Modify either of the B or C parameters to improve the fit. Which variable improved the fit? What did you do to the variable to improve the fit?

4. List some physical characteristics of the oscillating mass that you think might affect the nature of the functions you used to model the data set.

Teacher Notes
Up and Down: Damped Harmonic Motion

1. If the spring or Slinky™ is particularly stretchy, you may want to omit the mass hanger. The sample data were collected with a miniature Slinky taped to a paper plate.

2. Be sure the plate is suspended directly over the motion detector. Do not allow the plate to come closer than 50 cm to the detector.

3. If you have students hold the Slinky instead of using fixed supports, remind the students to hold their hands motionless. It is easy to pump the system up and down, or move the hand from the position used for zeroing the motion detector. For this reason a fixed support will give better quality data, but a hand-held spring can be used.

4. Either a TI CBR™ or a Vernier Motion Detector can be used. The CBR must be connected to a data collection device and not directly to the calculator.

5. Some motion detectors will not be automatically identified by DATAMATE. If you are using such a detector, you must manually set up DATAMATE for the detector:

   a. Select **SETUP** from the main screen.

   b. Press ⬇ until the cursor is next to DIG (CBL 2) or DIG1 (LabPro).

   c. Press ENTER to access the SELECT SENSOR menu.

   d. Select **MOTION(M)**.

   e. Select **OK** to return to the main screen.

Sample Results

Actual data will vary.

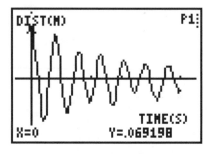

Raw data in DATAMATE

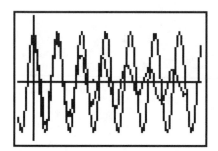

Distance data and cosine model

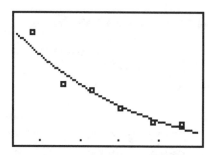

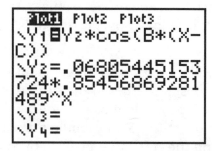

Peak amplitude data entered in lists

Peak amplitude data with exponential fit

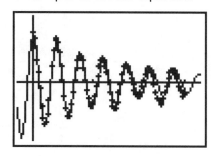

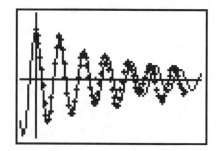

Composite model equation

Composite model and data

Optimized composite model

Data Table

Sample data; actual data may vary.

A	0.0692 m	
t_1, t_2	1.6 s	3.2 s
T	1.6 s	
B	$2\pi/1.6 \cong 3.9$	
C	1.6 s	
Composite Model	$y = 0.068*(0.85)^x* \cos(3.9(x-1.6))$	

Answers to Questions

1. The model equation fits the oscillating part of the data, but the amplitude is only approximately correct for early times. At later times, the amplitude is quite wrong.

2. The composite model fits well, reflecting both the oscillatory part and the decaying amplitude part of the experimental data. The period could fit better, however.

3. Increasing the size of B makes for a better fit of the model to the data. It looks like my period measurement was a little low, possibly due to 0.1 s time resolution of the graph.

4. Starting the plate going with a larger displacement from the equilibrium position would make the multiplicative constant larger in the exponential function. Using a smaller plate (less damping) would make the decay constant in the exponential smaller. Using a stiffer Slinky would make the period smaller, making B larger. Changing the starting time of data collection could change C.

EXPLORATIONS

Activity 28

How Tall? Describing Data with Statistical Plots

Objective

♦ Measure the heights of your classmates using a motion detector.

♦ Describe the height data using statistical concepts.

♦ Describe the height data using a box plot.

Materials

♦ TI-83 Plus, TI-83, or TI-73

♦ CBL 2™ or LabPro® data collection device

♦ DATAMATE software

♦ TI CBR™ or Vernier Motion Detector

How tall are students in your class? Is there anyone especially tall? Or short? What is the average height of your classmates? One way to answer these questions is to measure the height of everyone in the class and then analyze the data statistically.

An easy way to measure everyone's height rapidly is to use the motion detector. You can fasten the detector above the floor, and students can stand under it to quickly record their heights. Once you have a set of heights for your classmates, you will plot the results using a special statistical plot called a *box plot*.

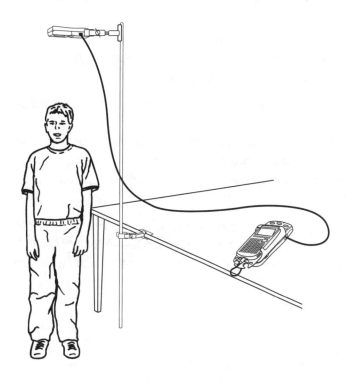

Procedure

1. Position the motion detector about 2.5 m from the floor, so that the disc is pointing straight downward. There must be no obstructions beneath the detector.

2. Plug the motion detector into the DIG/SONIC port of the CBL 2™ or DIG/SONIC 1 port of the LabPro® data collection device. Use the unit-to-unit cable to connect the TI graphing calculator to the data collection device. Firmly press in the cable ends.

3. Turn on the calculator and start the DATAMATE software. Press (CLEAR) to reset the software.

4. The main screen will show the distance to the floor in meters. Record this value in the Data Table on the *Data Collection and Analysis* sheet. Check to see that the value makes sense.

5. To have the motion detector record the distance to the head of each student and *not* record the distance to the floor in between student measurements, set up DATAMATE to record only selected events.

    a. Select **SETUP** from the main screen.

    b. Press (▲) to move to the mode selection.

    c. Press (ENTER) to move to the SELECT MODE menu.

    d. Select **SELECTED EVENTS** from the SELECT MODE menu.

    e. Select **OK** to return to the main screen.

    f. Select **START**.

6. Have the first student stand directly under the motion detector. Press (ENTER) to make a measurement. Repeat for all students. After the last student is measured, press (STO▸) to end data collection.

7. Press (ENTER) to see a plot of distance readings. You should see a scatter of points, corresponding to the distance from the motion detector to the head of each student. In a moment, you will convert these readings to heights. Scroll across the graph to the right-hand point using the cursor keys, and make a note of the number of measurements, n, you made. Record the value in the Data Table.

8. Press (ENTER) to return to the graph selection screen. Select **MAIN SCREEN** to return to the main screen. Select **QUIT** to leave DATAMATE. Follow instructions on the calculator screen to return to the calculator home screen.

Analysis

1. Remember that the motion detector points downward toward the floor, and measured distance to the top of each student. To convert these readings into heights, you need to subtract the readings from the distance to the floor, leaving the heights.

    ### TI-73

    a. Enter the distance to the floor in meters.

    b. Press ⌐ − ⌐ ⌐ 2nd ⌐ [STAT].

    c. Select the list **L6** by pressing the digit next to **L6** (usually 6).

    d. Press ⌐ STO ▶ ⌐ ⌐ 2nd ⌐ [STAT].

    e. Again, select the list **L6** by pressing the digit next to **L6** to complete an expression like **2.5 − L6 → L6**.

        Note: The distance to the floor may be different from 2.5 m.

    f. Press ⌐ ENTER ⌐ to complete the operation.

    ### TI-83 and TI-83 Plus

    a. Enter the distance to the floor in meters.

    b. Press ⌐ − ⌐ ⌐ 2nd ⌐ [L6] ⌐ STO ▶ ⌐ ⌐ 2nd ⌐ [L6] to enter an expression like **2.5 − L6 → L6**.

    Note: The distance to the floor may be different from 2.5 m.

    c. Press ⌐ ENTER ⌐ to complete the operation.

2. You now have a list of the heights of your classmates. One way to determine the minimum and the maximum values is to sort the data and see what values are first and last. You can also determine the median value, which is the middle value of an ordered list. (If there is an even number of students in the data set, then the median is the average of the middle two values.)

    To find these three values (the minimum, median, and maximum) you first need to sort the data.

    ### TI-73

    a. To sort the values in **L6**, the height data, press ⌐ 2nd ⌐ [STAT].

    b. Press ⌐ ▶ ⌐ to reveal the **OPS** menu. Press ⌐ ENTER ⌐ to paste **SortA(** to the home screen.

    c. Press ⌐ 2nd ⌐ [STAT] again, and highlight **L6** in the list. Press ⌐ ENTER ⌐ to paste it to the home screen.

d. Press ⬤ to close the **SortA** function, and press (ENTER) to sort the data in ascending order. The calculator will sort the values in ascending order and then show **Done**.

e. Press (LIST) and use the cursor keys to scroll to **L6**.

f. Record the first element in the list, which is the minimum height, in the Data Table on the *Data Collection and Analysis* sheet.

g. Scroll down to the middle element in the list (or the middle two, if you have an even number of elements, and average the two values). Record the median height in the Data Table.

h. Use the cursor keys to scroll down to the last value, and record the maximum height in the Data Table.

i. Select (2nd) [QUIT] to leave the list editor.

TI-83 and TI-83 Plus

a. To sort the values in **L6**, the height data, press (2nd) [LIST].

b. Press (►) to reveal the **OPS** menu. Press (ENTER) to paste **SortA(** to the home screen.

c. Press (2nd) [L6].

d. Press ⬤ to close the **SortA** function, and press (ENTER). The calculator will sort the values in ascending order and then show **Done**.

e. Press (STAT) (ENTER) and use the cursor key to scroll to **L6**.

f. Record the first element in the list, which is the minimum height, in the Data Table on the *Data Collection and Analysis* sheet.

g. Scroll down to the middle element in the list (or the middle two, if you have an even number of elements, and average the two values). Record the median height in the Data Table.

h. Use the cursor keys to scroll down to the last value, and record the maximum height in the Data Table.

i. Select (2nd) [QUIT] to leave the list editor.

3. You have found the maximum, median and minimum values in a very direct way—by scrolling through the sorted list elements. The calculator can perform these and other, more detailed, calculations. The following steps will have the calculator find a set of descriptive statistics, including the mean, median, minimum, and maximum values of the height data.

▷ **TI-73**

a. To enter the **1-Var Stats** function, press [2nd] [STAT] and press [▶] three times to open the **CALC** menu. Press [ENTER] to paste the **1-Var Stats** function to the home screen.

b. Access lists by pressing [2nd] [STAT]. Press the number next to **L6**; this enters **L6** on the home screen.

c. Press [ENTER] to complete the calculation.

d. The **1-Variable Statistics** command calculates a number of statistics all at once. Use the [▼] key to scroll down to reveal values of the mean (shown as $\bar{x}$), **minX**, **Med**, and **maxX**.

e. Record the mean, minimum, median, and maximum heights in the Data Table on the *Data Collection and Analysis* sheet.

f. Press [2nd] [QUIT] to return to the calculator's home screen.

▷ **TI-83 and TI-83 Plus**

a. To enter the **1-Var Stats** function, press [STAT] and press [▶] to open the **CALC** menu. Press [ENTER] to paste the **1-Var Stats** function to the home screen.

b. Press [2nd] [L6].

c. Press [ENTER] to complete the calculation.

d. The **1-Variable Statistics** command calculates a number of statistics all at once. Use the [▼] key to scroll down to reveal values of the mean (shown as $\bar{x}$), **minX**, **Med**, and **maxX**.

e. Record the mean, minimum, median, and maximum heights in the Data Table on the *Data Collection and Analysis* sheet.

f. Press [CLEAR] to return to the calculator's home screen.

⇒ Answer Question 1 on the *Data Collection and Analysis* sheet.

4. Two other important values listed in the statistical summary are the *lower quartile* (denoted Q1 or Qrtl1) and the *upper quartile* (denoted Q3 or Qrtl3). These numbers represent the medians of the lower and upper halves of the data respectively. Record these values in the Data Table on the *Data Collection and Analysis* sheet.

5. A special type of graph, called a *box-and-whiskers* plot or *box plot* for short, can be used to provide a statistical picture of a data set. It gives a graphical representation of the minimum, lower quartile, median, upper quartile, and maximum by displaying a view of the data distribution. Draw a box plot with the calculator.

a. Press ⬚2nd⬚ [STAT PLOT] ([PLOT] on the TI-73) and press ⬚ENTER⬚ to select **Plot 1**.

b. Change the **Plot1** settings to match the screen shown here. Press ⬚ENTER⬚ to select any of the settings you change.

c. Press ⬚ZOOM⬚ and then select **ZoomStat** (use cursor keys to scroll to **ZoomStat**) to draw a graph with the x and y ranges set to fill the screen with data.

d. Press ⬚TRACE⬚ to read values from the graph.

⇒ Answer Questions 2-7 on the *Data Collection and Analysis* sheet.

Extension

1. Another way to analyze the data you collected in this activity is to create a *histogram*. A histogram is simply a graphical representation of the number of times each height or range of heights occurs in the data set. Redraw the data in histogram form.

a. Press ⬚2nd⬚ [STAT PLOT] ([PLOT] on the TI-73) and press ⬚ENTER⬚ to select **Plot 1**.

b. Change the **Plot1** settings to match the screen shown here. Press ⬚ENTER⬚ to select any of the settings you change.

c. Press ⬚ZOOM⬚ and then select **ZoomStat** (use cursor keys to scroll to **ZoomStat**) to draw a graph with the x and y ranges set to fill the screen with data.

2. Describe the data features summarized in this graph. Are the statistical features depicted in the histogram consistent with those shown in the box plot you created earlier? Discuss the similarities and differences between these two plots. What are some advantages and disadvantages to using each type of plot to describe a set of data? Is the box plot or histogram more sensitive to distortion from outliers?

Data Collection and Analysis

Name _____

Date _____

Activity 28: How Tall?

Data Table

Distance to floor		

n =	From Data List	Descriptive Statistics
Minimum		
Median		
Mean		
Maximum		
Q1		
Q3		

Questions

1. How do the mean and median values determined by the calculator compare with the ones you read directly from the lists?

2. Notice that the *box* part of the plot represents the middle portion of the data, while the *whiskers* stretch to the lowest and highest numbers in the data set. The size and location of the box tells you about the distribution of values in the data set. A large box indicates that the data is spread out, while a smaller box means the data is clustered closely. Discuss the size and location of the box part of the plot; describe how it relates to the heights of the members of the class.

3. Is the median located near the center of the box? What does the location of the median line in the box tell you about the distribution of heights for the middle half of the data?

4. The length of the whiskers on the box plot gives a hint as to the distribution of the data. If one whisker is significantly longer than the other, we say the data is *skewed* in the direction of the shorter whisker. This usually means that the values are bunched together near the shorter whisker. Describe the whiskers on the plot. What do the whisker lengths tell you about the heights for the class?

5. The presence of an outlier might cause you to think that the data is skewed in one direction or another when it really is not. Use the method you learned earlier to scroll through the data. Pay close attention to the numbers at the very beginning and very end of the list. Can you identify any outliers in the data set? If so, how does this change your answer to Question 4, if at all?

6. Describe how the box plot would be affected if one of the members of your class was exceptionally tall at 2.3 m.

7. Suppose that the values for the tallest and shortest members of the class were removed from the data set. How would the median, lower quartile and upper quartile values change, if at all?

Teacher Notes
How Tall? Describing Data with Statistical Plots

1. The cable must not be allowed to dangle below the motion detector, or the height measurements will be unreliable.

2. General features and trends are sometimes hard to detect for small data samples. For best results, use at least 25 students in the class sample. You may wish to combine data sets from several classes for this activity.

3. It is convenient to fasten the motion detector to a horizontal ladder or pipe on the ceiling. Many classrooms have projections on the ceiling that can be used with the clamp supplied with the motion detector. A balcony might also be used.

4. Either a TI CBR™ or a Vernier Motion Detector can be used. The CBR must be connected to a data collection device and not directly to the calculator.

5. Some motion detectors will not be automatically identified by DATAMATE. If you are using such a detector, you must manually set up DATAMATE for the detector. To do this:

   a. Select **SETUP** from the main screen.

   b. Press ⌐▼⌐ until the cursor is next to DIG (CBL2™) or DIG1 (LabPro®).

   c. Press (ENTER) to access the SELECT SENSOR menu.

   d. Select **MOTION(M)**.

   e. Select **OK** to return to the main screen.

Sample Results

Actual data will vary.

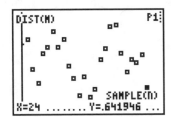

Raw data in DATAMATE

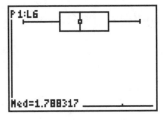

Box plot

Data Table

Sample data; actual data may vary.

n = 29	From Data List	Descriptive Statistics
Minimum	1.50 m	1.50 m
Median	1.78 m	1.78 m
Mean		1.79 m
Maximum	2.09 m	2.09 m
Q1		1.68 m
Q3		1.93 m

Answers to Questions

1. The maximum, minimum, and median values are the same by direct table inspection as by the calculator's statistics summary, as they should be.

2. The box is somewhat small compared to the range of the whiskers, implying that the class heights are somewhat bunched to the middle values.

3. The median is 1.78 m.

4. The whisker location tells us that the shortest person is about as much shorter than average as the tallest person is taller than average.

5. There are no clear outliers, so the answer to the previous question does not change.

6. The right-hand whisker would extend considerably, the Q3 value would increase slightly, but the other values would remain the same.

7. The median value would not change, while the Q1 value would increase slightly. The Q3 value would decrease slightly.

EXPLORATIONS

Activity 29

And Now, the Weather: Describing Data with Statistics

♦ Record temperature data over a day-long period.

♦ Describe the temperature data using statistical concepts.

♦ TI-83 Plus, TI-83, or TI-73

♦ CBL 2™ or LabPro® data collection device

♦ DATAMATE software

♦ Temperature probe

♦ Fresh batteries or AC adapter

Meteorologists use mathematics to interpret weather patterns and make predictions. Part of the job involves collecting and analyzing temperature data. Once meteorologists have collected a large number of measurements, they have a problem: How do they make sense of a long list of numbers? What is needed is a way of describing the set of data with just a few numbers. We call those numbers *descriptive statistics*. One important need is to be able to represent the set of measurements with a single number. There are several ways to do this:

♦ The *mean* temperature is what we usually think of when we hear the word "average." It is the sum of the temperature values in the data set divided by the number of elements in the set.

♦ The *median* temperature represents the center data point of the set after all the elements have been placed in order from lowest to highest.

Almost any weather report includes a summary of the day's high temperature, called the *maximum* value, and the day's low temperature, called the *minimum* value. The difference between these two statistics, called the *range*, shows the variability or *spread* of the data.

In this activity you will collect outdoor temperature readings over a 24-hour period using a temperature probe. After this data has been transferred to the calculator, you will use its statistical analysis tools to create your own temperature report.

Procedure

1. In order to collect weather data for a 24-hour period, you need to change the data collection rate and time. DATAMATE only uses seconds as a time unit. How many seconds are there in a 24-hour period? Determine this number and record it on the *Data Collection and Analysis* sheet.

    If you want to record the temperature every 600 seconds (1200 if you are using a TI-73), how many points do you want recorded? Subtract one from the value you get to be sure the run is done tomorrow at the start of the class, and to have an odd number of measurements. Record this value on the *Data Collection and Analysis* sheet. You will need it during set-up.

2. Connect a temperature probe to CH 1 on the CBL 2™ or LabPro® data collection device. Use the unit-to-unit cable to connect the data collection device to the TI graphing calculator. Firmly press in the cable ends.

3. Turn on the calculator and start the DATAMATE software. Press CLEAR to reset the software.

4. Set up DATAMATE for a temperature probe.

    a. Select **SETUP** from the main screen.

    b. If CH 1 shows a temperature probe reading in units of (C), then skip to Step 5.

    c. Press ENTER to select **CH1**.

    d. Select **TEMPERATURE** from the SELECT SENSOR list.

    e. Select the type of temperature probe you are using, with units of (C).

5. Set up DATAMATE for remote data collection.

    a. Press ⬛▲⬛ to select mode and press (ENTER).

    b. Select **TIME GRAPH** from the mode screen.

    c. Select **CHANGE TIME SETTINGS** from TIME GRAPH SETTINGS.

    d. Enter **600** as the time between samples in seconds (use **1200** if you are using a TI-73) and press (ENTER). In other words, the data collection device will record the temperature every 10 minutes (20 minutes for TI–73 users).

    e. Enter the number of samples you want to take and press (ENTER). (This is the number you determined in Step 1.)

    f. In order to collect data with the data collection device and probe alone, you need to set up DATAMATE for remote data collection. Select **ADVANCED** from the TIME GRAPH SETTINGS screen.

    g. Select **CHANGE TRIGGERING** from the ADV. TIME GRAPH SETTINGS screen.

    h. Select **MANUAL TRIGGER** from SELECT TRIGGERING.

    i. Select **OK** until you return to the main screen.

    j. Select **START** from the main screen. Note that on the data collection device a yellow light comes on. Data collection will not begin immediately, but will start later when you press the **START/STOP** key on the data collection device.

    k. Press (ENTER) to dismiss the confirmation screen, and select **QUIT** from the main screen. Follow any instructions on the calculator to return to the home screen.

    l. Disconnect the data collection device from the calculator, taking care not to press the **START/STOP** button on the data collection device. The yellow light on the data collection device must remain on.

6. Place the temperature probe outside a window with the cable running through the window to the data collection device inside. Take care that the cable is not pinched tightly in the window.

    Press the **START/STOP** key on the data collection device. The data collection device will beep, and the yellow light will go off. Leave the data collection device in place for 24 hours. Make a note of the time you started data collection and write it on the *Data Collection and Analysis* sheet.

7. The next day, retrieve the data stored in the data collection device.

    a. Reconnect the calculator to the data collection device, and start DATAMATE.

    b. DATAMATE will display a screen confirming that data collection is complete. Press (ENTER) to move to the main screen.

    c. Select **TOOLS** from the main screen.

d. Select **RETRIEVE DATA** from the TOOLS menu.

e. After the data is transferred to the calculator, DATAMATE will display a graph of temperature versus time.

f. Look at the temperature versus time plot that appears on the screen.

g. Press (ENTER) to return to the main screen, and select **QUIT**. Follow any instructions on the screen to return to the calculator's home screen.

Analysis

1. (Optional) Since the DATAMATE software uses only time units of seconds, convert the times to hours to make interpreting the graph a little easier. To do this, determine a scale factor by which you will divide the times in seconds to convert to hours, as in (time in seconds) / scale factor → (time in hours).

   Your time values are in **L1**. To do the conversion you just planned, perform these steps.

   ▶ **TI-73**
   _____

   a. Access lists by pressing (2nd) [STAT]. Press the number next to **L1**; this enters **L1** on the home screen.

   b. Press (÷).

   c. Enter the numerical scale factor you determined.

   d. Press (STO▸), and enter **L1** a second time to complete the expression **L1 / 12345** → **L1**. Press (ENTER) to perform the calculation. (Your scale factor should be different.)

   ▶ **TI-83 and TI-83 Plus**
   _____

   a. Press (2nd) [L1].

   b. Press (÷).

   c. Enter the numerical scale factor you determined.

   d. Press (STO▸), and enter **L1** a second time to complete the expression, **L1 / 12345** → **L1**. Press (ENTER) to perform the calculation. (Your scale factor should be different.)

2. Redisplay the graph.

   a. Press (ZOOM).

   b. Press (▼) until **ZoomStat** is highlighted; press (ENTER) to display a graph with the x and y ranges set to fill the screen with data.

   c. Press (TRACE) to determine the coordinates of a point on the graph using the cursor keys.

3. Use the cursor keys to move along the temperature plot. The *x*-values that appear at the bottom of the screen represent the time since data collection began. Identify at least two time intervals during the 24-hour collection period where there was a significant change in the temperature, and record this information in the Data Table on the *Data Collection and Analysis* sheet.

4. Can you relate these times to specific weather events that occurred during the day such as rain showers, periods of cloudiness, sunrise or sunset? Record your answers in the Data Table.

5. The mean temperature is the sum of all the readings divided by the number of readings. For example, the mean of {23, 25, 30} is (23 + 25 + 30)/3 = 26. During data collection, you obtained a series of temperature measurements. To calculate the mean temperature, add the values in the list of temperature measurements and divide by the number of measurements, which you set earlier.

TI-73

a. To enter the **sum(** function, press [2nd] [STAT] and press [▶] twice to open the MATH menu. Select **7:sum(** to paste it to the home screen.

b. Access lists by pressing [2nd] [STAT]. Press the number next to **L2**. This enters **L2** on the home screen.

c. Press [ )] to close the **sum** function.

d. Press [÷] and enter the number of temperature measurements in the list.

e. Press [ENTER] to complete the calculation.

f. Round and record the mean temperature in the second column of the Data Table on the *Data Collection and Analysis* sheet. Use three significant digits for this and all following entries.

TI-83 and TI-83 Plus

a. To enter the **sum(** function press [2nd] [LIST] and press [▶] twice to open the MATH menu. Select **5:sum(** to paste it to the home screen.

b. Press [2nd] [L2].

c. Press [ )] to close the **sum** function.

d. Press [÷] and enter the number of temperature measurements in the list.

e. Press [ENTER] to complete the calculation.

f. Round and record the mean temperature in the second column of the Data Table on the *Data Collection and Analysis* sheet. Use three significant digits for this and all following entries.

6. The median temperature is the data value exactly in the middle of the ordered list; for example, it would be the 50th out of 99 elements. To find the median temperature, you need to sort the temperatures so they are in ascending order, and then find the middle reading.

▶ **TI-73**

a. To sort the values in **L2**, the temperature values, press [2nd] [STAT].

b. Press [▶] to reveal the OPS menu. Press [ENTER] to paste **SortA(** to the home screen.

c. Press [2nd] [STAT] again, and press the number adjacent to **L2** in the list.

d. Press [)] to close the **SortA** function, and press [ENTER]. The calculator will sort the values in ascending order and then show **Done**.

e. To show the middle data value, press [2nd] [STAT] again, and paste **L2** to the home screen. Press [(], and enter the place of the middle element in the list. For example, enter **50** if you have 99 elements.

f. Press [)] to close the argument as **L2(50)**, and press [ENTER].

g. Record the median temperature in the second column of the Data Table.

▶ **TI-83 and TI-83 Plus**

a. To sort the values in **L2**, the temperature values, press [2nd] [LIST].

b. Press [▶] to reveal the OPS menu. Press [ENTER] to paste **SortA(** to the home screen.

c. Press [2nd] [L2].

d. Press [)] to close the **SortA** function, and press [ENTER]. The calculator will sort the values in ascending order and then show **Done**.

e. To show the middle data value, press [2nd] [L2]. Press [(], and enter the place of the middle element in the list. For example, enter **50** if you have 99 elements.

f. Press [)] to close the argument as **L2(50)**, and press [ENTER].

g. Record the median temperature in the second column of the Data Table.

7. You have calculated the mean and the median temperatures in a very direct way—by finding the sum of the elements, or by sorting the list elements and looking for the middle one. The calculator can perform the same kind of calculations, and more.

The following steps will have the calculator find a set of descriptive statistics, including the mean, median, minimum, and maximum values of the temperature measurements.

TI-73

a. To enter the **1-Var Stats** function, press [2nd] [STAT] and press [▶] three times to open the CALC menu. Press [ENTER] to paste the **1-Var Stats** function to the home screen.

b. Access lists by pressing [2nd] [STAT]. Press the number next to **L2**; this enters **L2** on the home screen.

c. Press [ENTER] to complete the calculation.

d. The **1-Variable Statistics** command calculates a number of statistics all at once. Use the [▼] key to scroll down to reveal values of the **mean** (shown as $\bar{x}$), **minX**, **Med**, and **maxX**.

Record the mean, minimum, median, and maximum temperatures in the third column of the Data Table on the *Data Collection and Analysis* sheet.

e. Press [2nd] [**QUIT**] to return to the calculator's home screen.

⇒ Answer Questions 1-4 on the *Data Collection and Analysis* sheet.

TI-83 and TI-83 Plus

a. To enter the **1-Var Stats** function, press [STAT] and press [▶] to open the CALC menu. Press [ENTER] to paste the **1-Var Stats** function to the home screen.

b. Press [2nd] [L2].

c. Press [ENTER] to complete the calculation.

d. The **1-Variable Statistics** command calculates a number of statistics all at once. Use the [▼] key to scroll down to reveal values of the **mean** (shown as $\bar{x}$), **minX**, **Med**, and **maxX**.

Record the mean, minimum, median, and maximum temperatures in the third column of the Data Table on the *Data Collection and Analysis* sheet.

e. Press [2nd] [**QUIT**] [CLEAR] to return to the calculator's home screen.

⇒ Answer Questions 1-4 on the *Data Collection and Analysis* sheet.

Extensions

1. What differences would you expect if this activity were repeated three months from today? Indicate how each statistic you found would change, if at all. Make a rough graph of temperature versus time corresponding to these projections. Be sure to include scale markings and axis labels on the graph.

2. Suppose you are designing a travel brochure for your city. Assume that the mean and median temperatures for the tourist season matched the values you found during the 24-hour collection period for this activity. Which of these statistics would you advertise as the average temperature for your city and why? Explain how your choice might depend on regional tourist attractions.

3. Write a weather report for your local newspaper summarizing the 24-hour period during which you collected data for this activity. Use your own words, together with the statistical information you gathered during this activity to write the report.

Data Collection and Analysis

Name _____

Date _____

Activity 29: And Now, the Weather

Data Tables

Seconds in a day	
Number of data collection points	
Time data collection started	

Time Interval of Rise/Fall	Corresponding Weather Event
to	
to	
to	
to	

	By Direct Calculation	From Calculator Stats
Mean		
Median		
Maximum		
Minimum		

Questions

1. How do the mean and median values determined by the calculator compare with the ones you found earlier?

2. Compare the maximum and minimum temperature values with high and low temperature results printed in the local newspaper or quoted on the local weather report. Are the results in close agreement with the local meteorologist's reported values? Justify any discrepancies.

3. Determine the *range* (high temperature minus low temperature) and record it below:

    Range = _____

4. People often listen to a local weather forecast before choosing what they will wear for the day. Would knowing the predicted temperature range for a given day provide enough information for this decision? What other statistic(s) would you need to know?

Teacher Notes
And Now, the Weather: Describing Data with Statistics

1. Since data collection will run for almost 24 hours, use fresh batteries or use an AC adapter to power the data collection device.

2. A 24-hour data collection time allows you to set up on one day, and then to have the data collection done during class the following day. You may choose to adjust the data collection time, but be sure that the total number of samples is less than about 180 (90 if you are using a TI-73).

3. Keep the sensor tip out of direct sunlight, or the correlation with weather reports will be poor.

4. If it is necessary to end data collection early, press the **START/STOP** button on the data collection device. In this case, the number of samples will be smaller than chosen during set-up. See the next point to determine the number of samples.

5. If a student does not record the number of samples chosen during set-up on the first day, the number of elements in the list can be determined using the **dim(** command. One place to find this on any calculator is on the CATALOG screen.

6. You may need to review unit conversions with students if the only weather report available is in °F.

Sample Results

Actual data will vary.

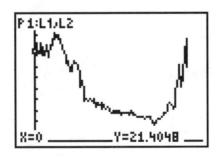

Data Table

Sample data; actual data may vary.

Answers in the first two tables will depend upon data collected.

	By Direct Calculation	From Calculator Stats
Mean	17.8 °C	17.8 °C
Median	16.7 °C	16.7 °C
Maximum		23.1 °C
Minimum		14.6 °C

Answers to Questions

1. The mean and median values calculated directly from the lists and by using the built-in calculator functions are the same.

2. The max and min temperatures recorded at school are similar to, but a few degrees different from, the weather report. The difference is probably due to the weather station values being measured at a different location.

3. Answers will vary.

4. The range alone is not enough. You would need the minimum or maximum temperature in addition to the range to dress for a 15 °C range, since the 15 °C could start at ⁻20 °C or at + 25 °C.

Activity 30

Meet You at the Intersection: Solving a System of Linear Equations

Objective

♦ Record motion data for two walkers.

♦ Graph both motions on a common axis and find their intersection.

♦ Find linear equations to model the motions.

♦ Solve the system of two linear equations to determine the intersection.

♦ Compare the algebraic solution to the graphical solution.

Materials

♦ TI-83 Plus, TI-83, or TI-73 (two if using CBL 2™, one if using LabPro®)

♦ Two CBL 2 or one LabPro data collection devices

♦ DATAMATE software

♦ Two TI CBR™ or Vernier Motion Detectors

♦ Meter stick

♦ Stopwatch

Many times, the solution to a real-life problem involves solving more than one mathematical equation at the same time. The simplest situation of this type involves a pair of equations with two unknown quantities called a *linear system*. Graphically, the solution to this kind of system represents the point where the graphs of these two lines intersect.

For example, imagine that a person is running to catch up to his friend who is walking ahead of him. These motions can be modeled graphically by plotting distance versus time. The motion graphs are linear if each person is moving at a constant speed. If the plots are made on the same set of axes, the point where the two lines cross represents the physical location where the two friends pass each other.

It is possible to model situations of this type in the classroom using two motion detectors. In this activity you will collect and analyze motion data in order to determine the solution to a linear system of equations.

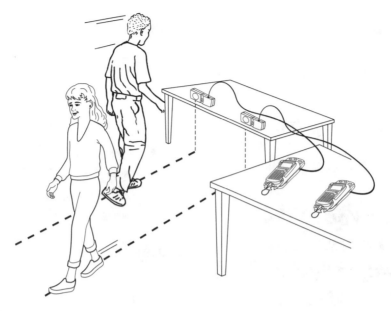

Procedure

This activity can be performed using two CBL 2™ data collection devices with two calculators, or one LabPro® data collection device with one calculator. The instructions address both configurations, so read carefully to find which steps to follow.

1. Set up the motion detectors on a table or desk. The detectors should be about two meters apart, parallel to one another, and about 1.2 m above the floor.

2. Connect the motion detectors to the DIG/SONIC port of each the CBL 2 data collection devices or DIG/SONIC 1 and DIG/SONIC 2 ports of the LabPro data collection device. Use the unit-to-unit cable(s) to connect the TI graphing calculator(s) to the data collection device(s). Firmly press in the cable ends.

3. Turn on the calculator(s) and start the DATAMATE software. Press CLEAR to reset the software.

4. Adjust the data collection time so you will have ten seconds to walk. Do this on both calculators if you are using CBL 2 data collection devices.

    a. Select **SETUP** from the main screen.

    b. Press ⬛ ▲ to select mode.

    c. Press ENTER to change the data collection mode.

    d. Select **TIME GRAPH** from the SELECT MODE screen.

    e. Select **CHANGE TIME SETTINGS**.

    f. Enter **0.2** as the time between samples in seconds and press ENTER. (Use **0.4** for the TI-73.)

    g. Enter **50** as the number of samples and press ENTER. (Use **25** for the TI-73.)

    h. Select **OK** twice to return to the main screen.

5. You will need two people to walk, a third (the Timer) to operate the stopwatch, and a fourth (the Marker) to mark the place where the two walkers pass each other.

   Practice walking in the following manner:

   ♦ Walker One stands about two meters from the first detector, and prepares to walk directly toward that detector.

   ♦ Walker Two stands just over half a meter from the second detector, and prepares to walk directly away from that detector.

   ♦ Once data collection starts (the data collection devices will beep) the Timer must start timing.

   ♦ At the moment the two walkers pass one another, the Marker must note the position on the floor, while the Timer stops the stopwatch. The walkers then continue to walk at a slow but uniform pace until data collection ends. Walker One must never get closer than 0.5 m to the motion detector.

   Practice the procedure several times before collecting data.

6. Select **START** (on both calculators simultaneously if you are using two) to begin data collection. You will hear the data collection device beep and the motion detectors will begin to click. Walk as you practiced. Data collection occurs for 10 seconds.

7. Press ⌑ENTER⌑ to display the **DISTANCE** graph. (If you are using LabPro® with one calculator, to see the second graph press ⌑ENTER⌑ and use the cursor keys to select the second distance channel. Press ⌑ENTER⌑ to view the graph.)

8. Examine the distance versus time graphs. Walker One's graph should be a nearly linear and uniformly decreasing function. Walker Two's graph should be a nearly linear and uniformly increasing function. If the final few seconds of data are not useful, do not be concerned.

   Check with the teacher if you are not sure whether you need to repeat the data collection step. To repeat data collection, press ⌑ENTER⌑ to return to the graph selection screen, and select **MAIN SCREEN**. Select **START** to begin data collection.

   Once you are satisfied with the graph, press ⌑ENTER⌑ to return to the graph selection screen, and select **MAIN SCREEN**. Select **QUIT** to leave DATAMATE, and follow any instructions to return to the calculator home screen.

9. After a good data collection run, have the Marker use the meter stick to measure the distance from the point where the two walkers passed one another to the midpoint of the line between the two motion detectors.

   Record this directly measured distance in the Data Table on the *Data Collection and Analysis* sheet. (Round this and all other data to three significant figures.) Record the directly measured time interval determined by the Timer in the Data Table.

Analysis

1. (Skip this step if you are using LabPro® with one calculator.)

   To complete the analysis, you need to move the distance data from one calculator to another. In order to avoid overwriting data, first copy the data to a new location in the calculator and then send it to the receiving calculator. The following transfer instructions assume that you are moving data between two calculators of the same model. Use Walker One's calculator as the sending calculator, and Walker Two's as the receiving calculator. Be sure you know which is which!

   ▶ **TI-73**

   a. Disconnect the calculators from the data collection devices, and directly connect the two calculators with a unit-to-unit cable. Firmly press in the cable ends.

   b. On the sending calculator, copy the distance data to a new list name. To do this, press [2nd] [STAT] and press the number adjacent to **L6**.

   c. Press [STO▶].

   d. Press [2nd] [STAT] and press the number adjacent to **L2**. You will now have the expression **L6 → L2** on the home screen. Press [ENTER] to copy the distance data in **L6** to **L2**.

   e. Press [APPS] and press the number adjacent to **Link**.

   f. Press the number adjacent to **List** to select a data list.

   g. Press [▼] until **L2** is highlighted. Press [ENTER] to select it.

   h. Press [▶] to highlight **TRANSMIT**.

   i. On the receiving calculator, press [APPS] and press the number adjacent to **Link**.

   j. Press [▶] to highlight **RECEIVE**, and press [ENTER]. The receiving calculator will show **Waiting**.

   k. On the sending calculator, press [ENTER] to actually transmit the list.

   l. The receiving calculator may display a message screen headed **DuplicateName**. If it does, press the number adjacent to **Overwrite**. The receiving calculator will show **Done**.

> **TI-83 and TI-83 Plus**

a. Disconnect the calculators from the data collection devices, and directly connect the two calculators with a unit-to-unit cable. Firmly press in the cable ends.

b. On the sending calculator, copy the distance data to a new list name. To do this, press ⌐2nd⌐ [L6] ⌐STO▶⌐ ⌐2nd⌐ [L2].

c. You will now have the expression **L6** → **L2** on the home screen. Press ⌐ENTER⌐ to copy the distance data in **L6** to **L2**.

d. Press ⌐2nd⌐ [LINK].

e. Press the number adjacent to **List** to select a data list.

f. Press ⌐▼⌐ until **L2** is highlighted. Press ⌐ENTER⌐ to select it.

g. Press ⌐▶⌐ to highlight **TRANSMIT**.

h. On the receiving calculator, press ⌐2nd⌐ [LINK].

i. Press ⌐▶⌐ to highlight **RECEIVE**, and press ⌐ENTER⌐. The receiving calculator will show **Waiting**.

j. On the sending calculator, press ⌐ENTER⌐ to actually transmit the list.

k. The receiving calculator may display a message screen headed **DuplicateName**. If it does, press the number adjacent to **Overwrite**. The receiving calculator will show **Done**.

2. Display the two distance graphs together. Use the receiving calculator if you collected data using two data collection devices.

   a. Press ⌐2nd⌐ [STAT PLOT] ([PLOT] on the TI-73) and press ⌐ENTER⌐ to select **Plot 1**.

   b. Change the **Plot1** settings to match the screen shown here. Press ⌐ENTER⌐ to select any of the settings you change.

      (On the TI-73, enter list names by pressing ⌐2nd⌐ [STAT] and selecting the desired list.)

   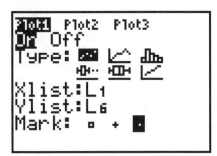

   c. Press ⌐2nd⌐ [STAT PLOT] ([PLOT] on the TI-73) and press ⌐▼⌐ ⌐ENTER⌐ to select **Plot 2**.

d. Change the **Plot2** settings to match the screen shown here. Press (ENTER) to select any of the settings you change.

(If you are using LabPro with one calculator, use **L9** instead of **L2**. To enter **L9**, press (2nd) [LIST], scroll to **L9**, and press (ENTER) to paste it to the stat plot screen.)

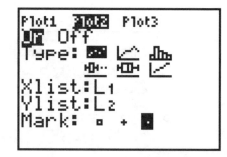

e. Press (ZOOM) and then select **ZoomStat** (use cursor keys to scroll to **ZoomStat**) to draw a graph with the x and y ranges set to fill the screen with data.

f. Press (TRACE) to determine the coordinates of a point on the graph using the cursor keys.

⇒ Answer Question 1 on the *Data Collection and Analysis* sheet.

3. Trace across either line to the place where the two lines cross. Record the coordinates as the graphical trace result in the Data Table on the *Data Collection and Analysis* sheet.

4. To create two linear models for the data, you need to record two points from each line. Ignore any short horizontal sections at the beginning or end of the lines. Press (▼) to move from one line to the other. Trace across the graphs and record the coordinates of two well-separated points from each line. Record these values in the Data Table.

5. Find the slope of each line using the standard slope formula, and enter the slopes in the Data Table.

$$m = \frac{y_2 - y_1}{x_2 - x_1}$$

6. The point-slope form of the line equation, or $y - y_1 = m(x - x_1)$, will let you determine the y-intercept from the two points you have already recorded. Here y and x are variables, m is the slope, and x_1 and y_1 are the values of a point on the line. Use this relation to determine the y-intercept of the line fitting each walker's record from the traditional $y = mx + b$ form, and record the intercepts in the Data Table.

7. To graph the two lines, you must enter the equations in the calculator's equation editor.

a. Press (Y=).

b. Press (CLEAR) to remove any existing equation.

c. Enter the equation for the first line you determined in the **Y1** field. For example, if the expression is $y = 4x + 3$, enter **4∗x+3**.

d. Press (ENTER) to move to the **Y2** field. Press (CLEAR) to remove any existing equation.

e. Enter the equation for the second line in the **Y2** field.

f. Press (GRAPH) to see the data with the model graph superimposed.

⇒ Answer Question 2 on the *Data Collection and Analysis* sheet.

8. The calculator can determine the point of intersection of the two lines.

a. Press (2nd) [CALC].

b. Press the number adjacent to **intersect** to start the intersection search.

c. You will see the graphs again, with the prompt **First curve?** The flashing cursor will be on the **Y1** function. Press (ENTER) to select the line.

d. The cursor will jump to the **Y2** function. Press (ENTER) to select that function.

e. The calculator will prompt **Guess?** to ask for your best guess of an intersection. Since there is only one intersection, the calculator will have no problem finding it. Press (ENTER) to have the calculator locate the intersection point.

f. Record the coordinates of the intersection point as the calculator intercept search in the Data Table.

9. Finally, you can find the intersection of the two lines algebraically. Using the slope and intercept of the Walker One and Walker Two lines, write down two linear equations in the form $y = mx + b$. That is, you will have one equation for each line, each in terms of its own intercept and slope.

What you have is a *system of equations*. There are two equations, each with two unknowns, x and y. Usually (but not always!), when you have two equations and two unknowns, you can solve the system to find specific values for x and y that satisfy both equations simultaneously. In this case, that solution will yield the time and location that both walkers had in common— that is, the time and location when they passed each other.

Solve the system of equations, and write the solution as the solve equation system answer in the Data Table.

⇒ Answer Questions 3 – 5 on the *Data Collection and Analysis* sheet.

Extension

Repeat the activity, but have the walkers move by starting slowly and then speeding up. The distance versus time plots will be non-linear, so that you can no longer use a linear model. What type of function might be used to model the motion?

Data Collection and Analysis

Name _____

Date _____

Activity 30: Meet You at the Intersection

Data Tables

	Direct Measure	Graphical Trace	Calculator Intercept Search	Solve Equation System
Intersection Time				
Intersection Position				

	x_1, y_1	x_2, y_2	Slope	Intercept
Walker One				
Walker Two				

Questions

1. How can you identify which trace is Walker One and which is Walker Two? Identify the trace of each walker for future reference.

2. How do the model lines fit the walker data?

3. Compare the values you obtained for the intersection time by all four methods: (1) direct measurement by stopwatch and meter stick, (2) graphical intersection by tracing, (3) the calculator's intersection search, and (4) by solving the system of equations. Are the values consistent?

4. Is it possible for the walkers to move in front of the motion detectors so that the resulting plots would not intersect? If so, give an example; if not, explain why.

5. Could the walkers move so that their plots intersect more than once? If so, how?

Teacher Notes
Meet You at the Intersection: Solving a System of Linear Equations

1. This activity requires two motion detectors. Either TI CBR™s or Vernier Motion Detectors can be used. The TI CBR must be connected through a data collection device and cannot be connected directly to the calculators. If the CBL 2™ is used, you must use two data collection devices and two calculators, then transfer data to a single calculator for analysis. If a LabPro® is used, both detectors can be connected to a single data collection device.

    LabPros must have ROM version number 6.2 or newer. ROM versions 6.12 and older do not fully support two motion detectors. To determine ROM version, notice the numbers shown on the title screen as DATAMATE is launched. For updates to ROM (also called firmware), see www.vernier.com/calc/flash.html.

2. Place the motion detectors at waist-high level for each walker. The walkers should never be closer than 0.5 meter to the detectors. Clear the area of other materials such as desks or chairs.

3. The walkers must maintain a constant and slow rate while walking directly toward or away from the motion detectors.

4. The point-slope form of the line is used in this activity in case the walkers were not moving at the time data collection started. By using two points along the uniform motion portion of the graphs, the model lines will not be influenced by poor-quality data at the $t = 0$ point.

5. If the students have not solved a system of equations before (Step 9), you may need to provide the following hint:

    > One easy way to solve this system of equations is to set the x sides equal to each other. After all, both are equal to y. You will have an equation for x; solve for x and find the value. Once you have the value for x, you can insert it in either equation to find the matching y.

    This step of finding the solution to the system of equations is important for students to perform so that the calculator-provided solutions are verified. The activity has students find the intersection time and place by direct measurement, by graphical means, by the calculator intersection function, and by solving the system of equations.

6. Some motion detectors will not be automatically identified by DATAMATE. If you are using such a detector, you must manually set up DATAMATE for the detector:

   a. Select **SETUP** from the main screen.

   b. Press ⟨ ▼ ⟩ until the cursor is next to DIG (CBL 2™) or DIG1 (LabPro®).

   c. Press ⟨ENTER⟩ to access the SELECT SENSOR menu.

   d. Select **MOTION(M)**.

   e. Select **OK** to return to the main screen.

Sample Results

Actual data will vary.

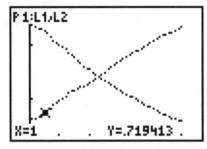

Data from both walkers

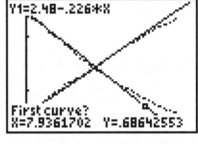

Model lines with walker data, also first step of intersection search

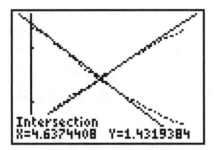

Intersection search result

Data Tables

Sample data; actual data may vary.

	Direct Measure	Graphical Trace	Calculator Intercept Search	Solve Equation System
Intersection Time	4.5 s	4.60 s	4.63 s	4.63 s
Intersection Position	1.4 m	1.40 m	1.43 m	1.43 m

	x_1, y_1	x_2, y_2	Slope	Intercept
Walker One	1.0, 2.26	6.0, 1.13	-0.226 m/s	2.48 m
Walker Two	1.0, 0.719	6.0, 1.70	+0.196 m/s	0.523 m

Answers to Questions

1. Walker One walks toward the detector, so the slope of that graph has decreasing values, or the negative slope graph.

2. Each model line fits the graph well, except at the end of data collection. It looks like the walkers did not maintain quite a constant speed as instructed.

3. The intersection values are all consistent with one another although they are not identical. The calculator search intersection and the intersection from the solution to the system of equations are identical.

4. Yes, the walkers could both move away at the same speed from the detectors, starting at slightly different positions. Then the graphs would be parallel.

5. If one walker stood still, and the other moved out past the first and then back, again past the first walker, there will be two intersections. The key is that the velocities of at least one walker must not be constant.

EXPLORATIONS

Activity 31

Titration Curves:
An Application of
the Logistic
Function

Objective

♦ Record pH versus base volume data for an acid-base titration.

♦ Manually model the titration curve using a logistic function.

♦ Describe the role of each parameter in the logistic function.

Materials

♦ TI-83 Plus, TI-83, or TI-73

♦ CBL 2™ or LabPro® data collection device

♦ DATAMATE software

♦ pH Sensor

♦ Safety goggles

♦ 50 mL or 100 mL graduated cylinder, cup, or beaker

♦ Distilled water in wash bottle

♦ 25 mL household vinegar

♦ 50 mL household ammonia

Think about how cold germs spread through a school. One person comes to class with a cold and infects other students. At first, the disease spreads slowly, but as more students catch cold and spread it to other classmates, the disease spreads more rapidly. The rate of infection slows down again when most students are infected and there is no one left at school to infect. The maximum number of students in the school who can contract the disease is the number of students in the school.

A logistic function is often used to model this type of situation. The logistic function is an exponential function, but it contains a ratio and offset which make its behavior interesting. The formula for a logistic function is:

$$y = \frac{A}{1 + B^{x-c}} + D$$

You can use this logistic function to model an acid-base titration activity. Chemists combine acid and base solutions while monitoring the pH of the mixture to determine the concentrations of one of the reactants in a process called *titration*. Concentrations are usually made in very small numbers such as 0.000001 or 1×10^{-6}. Instead of working with these small numbers, chemists use a logarithmic scale. pH is the $-\log[H+]$ where $[H+]$ is the positive hydrogen ion concentration of a solution. For example, the pH of a solution with a hydrogen ion concentration of 1×10^{-6} is 6. The pH scale runs from 0 to 14. Solutions with a pH of less than 7 are called acids, and solutions with a pH greater than 7 are called bases. Solutions with a pH of 7 are considered neutral.

The change of pH during the titration of an acid with a base produces a titration curve. This curve is not quite a true logistic, but it does have some of the same features as a logistic function. During the first part of the titration, the pH does not change very much because there is enough acid to react with the added base. At the equivalence point, the acid has completely reacted with the base solution. As more base solution is added to the mixture, the pH increases rapidly. Once the solution becomes basic, the pH levels off and approaches the pH of the base being added.

The point at which the most rapid change occurs is called the *equivalence point*. At this point, knowing the volume and concentration of the acid and the volume of the base added allows the chemist to calculate the concentration of the base using a simple proportion.

In this activity, you will add base to an acid and use a logistic function to model the data and locate the equivalence point.

Procedure

1. Obtain and wear goggles.

2. Prepare the pH sensor for data collection.

   a. Plug the pH sensor into CH 1 of the CBL 2™ or LabPro® data collection device. Use the unit-to-unit cable to connect the TI graphing calculator to the data collection device. Firmly press in the cable ends.

   b. Loosen the top of the pH storage bottle, and carefully remove the bottle. Slide the top of the bottle up the shaft of the sensor so that the bottle top is out of the way. Do not remove the top from the sensor shaft.

   c. Rinse the tip of the pH sensor with distilled water.

   d. Place the pH sensor in a clean beaker or cup, and support it so that the beaker or cup does not fall.

   e. Add 25 mL of vinegar to the beaker or cup. The vinegar should cover the tip of the sensor.

3. Turn on the calculator and start the DATAMATE software. Press CLEAR to reset the software.

4. Set up the calculator and data collection device for a pH sensor.

   a. Select **SETUP** from the main screen.

   b. If the calculator displays a pH sensor in CH 1, proceed directly to Step 5. If it does not, continue with this step to set up the sensor manually.

   c. Press ENTER to select **CH 1**.

   d. Select **PH** from the SELECT SENSOR menu.

5. Set up the data collection mode.

   a. Press ⌐▲⌐ once and press [ENTER] to select **MODE**.

   b. Select **EVENTS WITH ENTRY** from the SELECT MODE menu.

   c. Select **OK** to return to the main screen.

6. You are now ready to collect data. The data points you will collect are the pH of the mixture and the volume of base added to the mixture. In this experiment, the acid used is vinegar and the base is ammonia. It is best if one person adds ammonia while a second person operates the calculator.

   a. Select **START** to begin data collection.

   b. Press [ENTER] to record the pH of the vinegar before any ammonia is added.

   c. The calculator will prompt for a value. Since you have added no ammonia, enter **0** and press [ENTER].

   d. Add 5 mL ammonia to the beaker or cup, and gently stir.

   e. Press [ENTER] to measure the new pH.

   f. Enter **5** for the total amount of ammonia you have added and press [ENTER].

   g. Repeat Steps d-f until you have added a total of 40 mL of ammonia. Remember that the volume of ammonia in the mixture is cumulative, so the volume data point entered increases each time you record the pH and volume. For example, the second ammonia volume data point is 10, the third is 15, and so forth until you reach 40 mL.

   h. Press [STO▶] to end data collection.

   i. The graph of pH versus volume of ammonia will be displayed.

7. Examine the data pairs on the displayed graph. As you move the cursor right or left, the volume (x) and pH (y) values of each data point are displayed below the graph. If you want to collect more data using a fresh sample of vinegar, press [ENTER], select **MAIN SCREEN**, and return to Step 6.

8. If you are satisfied with this data, press [ENTER] and select **MAIN SCREEN**, then select **QUIT** to leave DATAMATE. Follow any instructions to return to the calculator's home screen.

9. When data collection is completed, use additional distilled water to rinse the pH sensor. Replace the storage bottle on the pH sensor.

Analysis

1. Redisplay the graph outside of DATAMATE, and prepare to read values off of the graphs using the TRACE function.

    a. Press ZOOM.

    b. Press ▼ until **ZoomStat** is highlighted. Press ENTER to display a graph with the x and y ranges set to fill the screen with data.

    c. Press TRACE to determine the coordinates of a point on the graph using the cursor keys.

2. Before analyzing the collected data and the behavior of the logistic function, you need a better understanding of how the parameters (A, B, C, and D) relate to one another.

$$y = \frac{A}{1 + B^{x-c}} + D$$

In this activity, the value of parameter B is between zero and one, and the other parameters have values between 4 and 10. If x is very small so that the exponential B^{x-C} is large (remember that B is less than one), then the first term is very small. The value of y is then approximately equal to D.

On the calculator, trace to the extreme left side of the pH versus volume graph, and find the pH at the smallest x value. Record this value as D in the Data Table on the *Data Collection and Analysis* sheet. Record all values to two significant figures.

3. For a large x, or more added ammonia, then the exponential B^{x-C} becomes small, and the first term is approximately A. Then y is approximately $A + D$. Trace to the extreme right side of the graph, and note the pH value at this point. This is the sum $A + D$. Use this pH value to calculate the value for A, and record it in the Data Table.

4. A special situation exists when $x = C$. This makes $B^0 = 1$, and the first term is ½ A. You can use this special situation to determine a value for C by finding the x, or the volume of added ammonia, that gives a pH with an approximate value of $D + ½ A$.

    Trace across the graph to determine this value, and record it as C in the Data Table on the *Data Collection and Analysis* sheet.

5. Enter the logistic equation for the model plotted against the data.

    a. Press Y=.

    b. Press CLEAR to remove any existing equation.

    c. Enter the logistic equation A/(1+B^(X–C)) + D in the **Y1** field. (On the TI-73, access the alphabetic entry screen by pressing 2nd [TEXT].)

    d. Press 2nd [QUIT] to return to the home screen.

6. Enter values for the three parameters for which you have values: A, C, and D. For example, to store the value for A, enter a value for the parameter A. Press (STO▶) A (ENTER) to store the value in the variable **A**. Repeat for the other parameters.

7. The Data Table has one parameter, B, with no value. You need to set a value for this parameter. To obtain a good fit (this is called optimizing the value), you will need to try several values for B. Start with B = 0.5, and experiment with different values until you find one that provides a good fit for the data.

   To store a value for B in the calculator:

   a. Enter a value for the parameter B. Press (STO▶) B (ENTER) to store the value in the variable **B**.

   b. Press (GRAPH) to see the data with the model graph superimposed.

   c. Press (2nd) [QUIT] to return to the home screen.

   Record this optimized value for B in the Data Table.

8. Display the graph with the model one more time.

⇒ Answer Question 1 on the *Data Collection and Analysis* sheet.

Extension

▷ **TI-73**

The TI-73 cannot perform the following analysis.

▷ **TI-83 and TI-83 Plus**

The calculator can perform an automatic logistic regression, although the form of the calculator's logistic expression is slightly different from the one used in the model earlier. The calculator uses the form:

$$y = \frac{c}{1 + ae^{-bx}}$$

The key difference between this and the form used earlier is that there is no additive term + D. The other difference between this and the form used earlier is that the exponential function is based on *e*, rather than a direct exponential on a parameter. Because of the additive term, you will have to subtract a constant value from the data in order to use the calculator's form. Do that first. Afterward, you can perform the calculator fit and compare it to the model.

1. The data in the pH column must be positive, but for this analysis, we need it to start near zero. Press (GRAPH) to see the collected data, and press (TRACE) to

read values from the graph. Find the smallest pH value of the data (*not* the model) and make a note of that value.

2. Press [2nd] [QUIT] to return to the home screen. Subtract a number just smaller than the minimum value from the actual pH values:

   a. The pH values are stored in **L2**. Press [2nd] [L2]. Press [−], and enter a value just smaller than the minimum pH.

   b. Press [STO▶] [2nd] [L2] [ENTER] to store the altered values back in **L2**.

3. Have the calculator fit its logistic equation to the data.

   a. Press [STAT] and use the cursor keys to highlight **CALC**.

   b. Press [▼] until **Logistic** is highlighted. Press [ENTER] to copy the command to the home screen.

   c. Press [2nd] [L1] [,] [2nd] [L2] [,] to enter the lists containing the data.

   d. Press [VARS] and use the cursor keys to highlight **Y-VARS**.

   e. Select **Function** by pressing [ENTER].

   f. Press [ENTER] to copy **Y1** to the expression.

   g. On the home screen, the entry **Logistic L1, L2, Y1** is shown. This command will perform a logistic regression with **L1** as the x and **L2** as the y values. The resulting regression line will be stored in equation variable **Y1**.

   Press [ENTER] to perform the linear regression. Write the values for the parameters a, b, and c in the second column of the Extension Data Table on the *Data Collection and Analysis* sheet.

⇒ Answer Extension Question 1 on the *Data Collection and Analysis* sheet.

   h. Press [ZOOM]. Press [▼] until **ZoomStat** is highlighted. Press [ENTER] to display a graph with the x and y ranges set to fill the screen with data.

⇒ Answer Extension Questions 2-4 on the *Data Collection and Analysis* sheet.

Data Collection and Analysis

Name _____

Date _____

Activity 31: Titration Curves

Data Table

A	B	C	D

Question

1. Is the logistic equation a good model for the titration data?

Extension Data Table

	Algebraic Expression	Parameters from calculator	Parameters as calculated from model
a (in terms of B and C)			
b (in terms of B)			
c (in terms of A)			

Extension Questions

1. Use the three parameters a, b and c to write down the calculator's fit equation.

2. From the graph appearance, how does the calculator's fit compare to yours?

3.   How do the calculator's parameters compare to those you determined?

To answer this question, you need to determine the correlation of A, B, and C to a, b, and c. By comparing corresponding locations in the expressions, fill in the Extension Data Table. You will need to use properties of exponential expressions to find the correspondences. After you find these expressions, insert the values of A, B and C from the model to calculate comparison values to those of the calculator.

4.   How do the model parameters, when expressed in terms of the calculator's parameters, compare? Should they be similar?

Teacher Notes
Titration Curves: An Application of the Logistic Function

1. Before using the pH sensor, rinse the sensor tip in distilled water.

2. At the completion of the activity, use distilled water to rinse the pH electrode. Tightly secure the storage solution bottle on the electrode tip. Refer to the data sheet that came with the pH sensor for detailed storage information.

3. Students must wear safety goggles while handling chemicals.

4. Use real ammonia, not a cleaning solution that includes ammonia, in the activity.

5. Rinse all containers well at the end of the activity, flushing the waste with lots of water.

6. The ß parameter is not well determined by the activity, so that a 10 or 15% change in ß will produce a barely visible change in the graph. Do not expect consistent values for this parameter, even if students are working with the same data set. For the same reason, the parameter related to ß will likely be quite different in the calculator curve fit, perhaps even by a factor of five.

7. The logistic function is not an optimum model for a titration curve; chemists use a much more complex model for titration. However, the pH data roughly follows the logistic function, so we use the logistic function as a simplified model.

Sample Results

Actual data will vary.

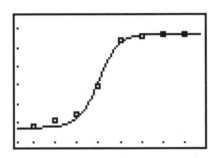

Titration data with model equation

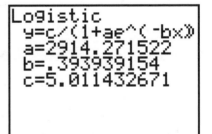

Logistic fit (extension)

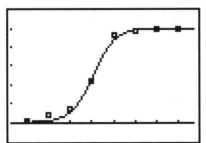

Calculator regression and adjusted data

Data Table

Sample data; actual data may vary.

A	B	C	D
5.0	0.65	20	5.7

Answer to Analysis Question

1. The logistic model fits the titration data very well.

Extension Data Table

Sample data; actual data may vary.

	Algebraic Expression	Parameters from calculator	Parameters as calculated from model
a **(in terms of** B **and** C**)**	$a = B - C$	2100	5500
b **(in terms of** B**)**	$b = -\ln B$	0.39	0.43
c **(in terms of** A**)**	$c = A$	5.01	5.00

Answers to Extension Questions

1. Answers will vary.

2. The calculator fit looks to be about the same as my model.

3. The data table is completed as shown above.

4. The parameters from the calculator and the model are similar but not exactly the same. From my experience in adjusting the B parameter in the original model, noting that a significant change in B made for a small change in the observed fit, I am not surprised to see that the term depending on both B and C (which is B raised to a large power) is not very close to the calculator fit.

Appendix A

Sensors for Real-World Math

You can purchase the sensors used in this book from Vernier Software & Technology at **www.vernier.com** or from a distributor for Texas Instruments and Vernier products. The TI CBR™ is also available directly from Texas Instruments at **education.ti.com** or 1-800-TI-CARES.

Item	Activity	Vernier Order Code
Vernier Motion Detector or TI CBR™	1, 6, 8-14, 19, 21-23, 25, 27, 28, 30	MD-BTD CBR
Microphone	26	MCA-BTA
Dual-Range Force Sensor	2, 4, 8, 9	DFS-BTA
Vernier Light Sensor or TI Light Sensor (packaged with the CBL 2 or the original CBL System)	16, 24	LS-BTA
Gas Pressure Sensor	3, 5, 15	GPS-DTA
pH Sensor	20, 31	PH-BTA
Voltage Probe (packaged with the CBL 2 and LabPro)	18	VP-BTA
Vernier Stainless Steel Temperature Probe or TI Stainless Steel Temperature Probe (packaged with the CBL 2)	7, 17, 29	TMP-BTA

Motion Detector

The Motion Detector functions like an automatic range finder on a Polaroid camera. This sonar device emits ultrasonic pulses at a rate adjustable between 10 and 50 times per second. The time it takes for the reflected pulses to return is used to calculate distance, velocity, and acceleration. The range is 0.5 to 6 meters.

Microphone

The new Vernier microphone is housed in a wand, with an electret microphone on one end. Use it to display and study the waveform of sounds from voices, musical instruments, or tuning forks.

Dual-Range Force Sensor

This affordable force sensor has two ranges: − 10 to +10 N and −50 to +50 N. It can be easily mounted on a ring stand or dynamics cart, or used as a replacement for a spring scale. Use it to study friction, simple harmonic motion, impact in collisions, or centripetal force.

Light Sensor

The Vernier Light Sensor approximates the human eye in spectral response and can be used over three different illumination ranges, selected with a switch. It can be used for inverse square law experiments or for studying solar energy.

Gas Pressure Sensor

The Gas Pressure Sensor has a range of 0 to 210 kPa, or about 2.1 atmospheres. It includes an accessory kit consisting of a syringe for Boyle's law experiments, tubing, connectors, and rubber stoppers.

pH Sensor

The pH sensor is a Ag-AgCl combination electrode sensor with a range of 0 to 14 pH units.

Voltage Probe

The Voltage Probe is included with the LabPro and CBL 2 interfaces, and is used to measure electrical potential between −10 and 10 V.

Stainless Steel Temperature

The Stainless Steel Temperature Probe is an accurate, durable, and inexpensive sensor for measuring temperature. Range: −25°C to +125°C

Other Sensors

In addition to these suggested sensors, other sensors can be used in these activities. Most will require the use of a DIN-BTA adapter.

- The ULI or MPLI Microphones can be used in place of the MCA-BTA Microphone.

♦ The Biology Gas Pressure sensor or the Pressure Sensor can be used in place of the Gas Pressure Sensor.

♦ The Direct Connect Temperature Probe or the Standard Temperature Probe can be used in place of the Stainless Steel Temperature Probe.

Appendix B

Equipment and Supplies

A list of equipment and supplies for all experiments is given below. The amounts listed are for a class of up to 30 students working in groups of two, three, or four students in a classroom equipped with eight computers. The materials have been divided into **nonconsumables**, and **consumables**. Most consumables will need to be replaced each year. Most nonconsumable materials may be used many years without replacement. Some substitutions can be made.

All of these items are very common in a physics or chemistry stockroom. Most math teachers can obtain these items by borrowing them from their science colleagues.

Nonconsumables

Item	Amount	Experiment
ball, rubber (5-20 cm)	8	11, 19
battery, 9V	8	18
beaker, 250 mL (or cup)	8	20
bottle, soda, 1 L	8	5
bucket, small	8	4
capacitor, 220 µF	8	18
cart, small	8	10
clamp, utility	8	8
cup, Styrofoam™	16	7
DC point light source (such as a Maglite®)	8	16
dowel, wooden (1 x 50 cm)	8	14, 23
eyedropper	8	20

funnel	8	4
goggles, safety	30	5, 20, 31
graduated cylinder, 25 mL	8	31
mass hanger, slotted	8	8, 27
measuring cup, graduated	8	7
meter stick	8	3, 6, 14, 16, 21, 25, 30
paper clip	8	3
pendulum bob	8	22, 25
pipe, clear with cap (1.2 m)	8	3
ramp, board or track (1.2 m)	8	10
resistor, 100 kΩ	8	18
ring stand	8	8
rubber band, large	8	9
spring (small spring) or a Slinky ®	8	8, 27
stopper, rubber, single-hole (#1)	8	5
stopwatch	8	25, 30
string	10 m	4, 6, 21, 25
tubing, clear, aquarium	12 m	3
tuning fork, 256 Hz	8	26
wash bottle	8	20, 31
weight, small	8	3

Consumables

Item	Amount	Experiment
ammonia, household	500 mL	31
antacid tablets, effervescent	24	5, 20
juice, lemon	40 mL	20
plate, paper	8	27
tape, masking	1 roll	14
vinegar, household	500 mL	31
water, distilled	4 L	20, 31

Appendix C

DATAMATE
Reference

In this book, you use the CBL 2™ or LabPro® data collection device with TI graphing calculators to collect, examine, analyze, and graph data in the activities. DATAMATE is the data collection software used by the CBL 2 and LabPro. DATAMATE is a group of programs that runs collectively as a single program or application. On the TI-83 Plus, DATAMATE is a single application (or APP). On the other calculators, DATAMATE is a series of programs and you access it using the PRGM key. On these calculators, you will see a list all of the sub-programs, but you will always choose the main program, DATAMATE. DATAMATE will automatically access the other sub-programs as needed.

Loading DATAMATE

The DATAMATE software comes already loaded on your CBL 2. Before you use the CBL 2 for the first time, you must transfer the DATAMATE software to the calculator.

To transfer DATAMATE to the calculator, follow these steps:

1. Connect the calculator to the CBL 2 with the unit-to-unit link cable.

2. Put the calculator in RECEIVE mode. (On the TI-73, press APPS, select **1:Link**, **Receive**, and press ENTER. On the TI-83 or TI-83 Plus, press 2nd [[LINK], select **RECEIVE**, and press ENTER.)

3. On the CBL 2, press **TRANSFER**. The program or APP is transferred and appears in the calculator's program list or application list.

4. When the transfer is complete, press 2nd [[QUIT] on the calculator.

Starting DATAMATE

Use the unit-to-unit link cable to connect the CBL 2™ or LabPro® to the TI Graphing Calculator. Firmly press in the cable ends, and then turn on the calculator. Follow the steps below to start DATAMATE.

TI-73 or TI-83 Calculators

Press [PRGM], and then press the calculator key for the *number* that precedes DATAMATE. Press [ENTER] and wait for the main screen to load.

TI-83 Plus Calculators

Press [APPS], and then press the calculator key for the *number* that precedes DATAMATE in the list. Wait for the main screen to load.

The following description of DATAMATE highlights major features. Additional detail about calibration is given. For full details see the Guidebook packaged with the CBL 2 or LabPro, or see the DATAMATE Guidebook, available at **www.vernier.com/calc/** or one of the CBL 2 guidebooks at **education.ti.com/guides**.

DATAMATE Main Screen

The DATAMATE main screen is shown at the right. The top half of the screen shows the current sensor setup and data collection mode. The portion below the double bar displays the menu options.

```
CH 1:TEMP(C)        21.82



MODE:TIME GRAPH-100
─────────────────────────
1:SETUP       4:ANALYZE
2:START       5:TOOLS
3:GRAPH       6:QUIT
```

CBL 2 and LabPro will automatically identify auto-ID sensors, display the channel each is connected to, and display the current reading. Only active channels will be displayed. The screen will update as auto-ID sensors are added from the device. Some sensors do not have auto-ID and must be manually configured in DATAMATE.

The main screen supports a meter mode displaying readings for active probes every few seconds. The meter option can be toggled on and off by pressing [+] on the calculator.

SETUP

To change the current setup, select **1: SETUP** from the main screen. On the SETUP screen, you can change sensors, change the data-collection mode, load or save an experiment, and calibrate or zero a sensor. (**SAVE/LOAD** is not available on the TI-73 and TI-83 due to memory constraints.)

Note: The screen at the right appears on the CBL 2. When using LabPro, four channels display and two DIGs display.

```
▶ CH 1:STAINLESS TEMP(C)
  CH 2:
  CH 3:
  DIG :
  MODE:TIME GRAPH-100


1:OK          3:ZERO
2:CALIBRATE 4:SAVE/LOAD
```

Changing Sensors

To change a sensor or add a sensor that is not automatically identified, use the ▼ key to position the cursor opposite the desired channel. Press (ENTER) and a list of sensors will be displayed.

```
▶CH 1:STAINLESS TEMP(C)
 CH 2:
 CH 3:
 CH 4:
 DIG1:
 DIG2:
 MODE:TIME GRAPH-100
1:OK          3:ZERO
2:CALIBRATE 4:SAVE/LOAD
```

Select the appropriate sensor or choose MORE to see the next list of sensors.

```
      SELECT SENSOR
1:TEMPERATURE
2:PH
3:CONDUCTIVITY
4:PRESSURE
5:FORCE
6:HEART RATE
7:MORE
8:RETURN TO SETUP SCREEN
```

Changing Data-Collection Modes

To change modes from the SETUP screen, use the ▼ and ▲ keys to move the ▶ cursor to **MODE** and press (ENTER).

```
▶CH 1:STAINLESS TEMP(C)
 CH 2:
 CH 3:
 CH 4:
 DIG1:
 DIG2:
 MODE:TIME GRAPH-100
1:OK          3:ZERO
2:CALIBRATE 4:SAVE/LOAD
```

The SELECT MODE screen (shown at the right) appears.

```
       SELECT MODE
1:LOG DATA
2:TIME GRAPH
3:EVENTS WITH ENTRY
4:SINGLE POINT
5:SELECTED EVENTS
6:RETURN TO SETUP SCREEN
```

TIME GRAPH is the default data-collection mode. The sensor you are using in Channel 1 will set its own sample interval and length of run. For example, if you select a Temperature Probe, DATAMATE will automatically set the CBL 2™ or LabPro® to collect one sample per second for 180 seconds. (These settings may be different on the TI-73.) These settings can be changed by choosing CHANGE TIME SETTINGS from the TIME GRAPH SETTINGS screen.

```
    TIME GRAPH SETTINGS
TIME INTERVAL:      1
NUMBER OF SAMPLES:  180
EXPERIMENT LENGTH: 180

1:OK          3:ADVANCED
2:CHANGE TIME SETTINGS
```

A TIME GRAPH will be displayed live unless you are sampling at a rate faster than 10 samples per second or slower than one sample every 270 seconds. If you are using multiple sensors and they are identical, all of the data will be displayed live on one graph. If they are not identical, only one channel can be displayed live.

LOG DATA: Lets you collect data using the CBL 2 or LabPro without being attached to the calculator. DATAMATE can then retrieve the data from the data collection device.

EVENTS WITH ENTRY: Data is collected one point at a time and only when you press ENTER on the calculator. The calculator will then prompt you to enter the corresponding value, such as distance or trial. This mode is used for Activity 15 (Under Pressure) and Activity 16 (Light at a Distance).

SINGLE POINT: The data collection device collects data for 10 seconds and reports a single, averaged value on the calculator screen.

SELECTED EVENTS: Data is collected one point at a time and only when you press ENTER on the calculator.

Calibrating a Sensor

When a sensor is selected, DATAMATE automatically loads the appropriate default calibration information. The default calibration is useful for nearly all experiments.

If you choose to calibrate a sensor, choose 2: CALIBRATE from the SETUP screen.

```
▶ CH 1:STAINLESS TEMP(C)
  CH 2:
  CH 3:
  CH 4:
  DIG1:
  DIG2:
  MODE:TIME GRAPH-100
─────────────────────────
1:OK           3:ZERO
2:CALIBRATE 4:SAVE/LOAD
```

The screen at the right is displayed.

Note: For complete instructions for calibration, refer to the information provided with the sensor. The paragraphs below provide a brief overview.

```
        CALIBRATION
PH
CALIBRATION:LINEAR
SLOPE          INT
-3.838         13.72
─────────────────────────
1:OK
2:CALIBRATE NOW
3:MANUAL ENTRY
```

There are two ways to calibrate a sensor. The first is a two-point calibration using two known reference values; the second is to manually enter calibration information. The examples shown on the next page are for the Dual-Range Force Sensor, although the process is similar for all analog sensors.

To calibrate a Force Sensor using the two-point method, you must apply two known forces. You can do this using a 500-gram mass. No mass suspended from the sensor will represent zero force, and hanging the 500-g mass from the sensor represents 4.9 Newtons applied force. The following steps will complete a two-point calibration.

a. On the Setup screen, press ⬛▾⬛ as needed to move the ▶ cursor to the sensor to be calibrated.

b. Select **CALIBRATE**.

Note: Not all sensors can be calibrated. If you select a sensor that cannot be calibrated, DATAMATE does not respond when you select CALIBRATE.

c. The current calibration information will be displayed. Select **CALIBRATE NOW**.

d. For the first point, position the Force Sensor so the empty hook hangs straight down. In other words, there is zero applied force. Wait until the voltage number on the screen stabilizes and then press ⬛ENTER⬛.

e. Enter **0**.

f. For the second point, position the Force Sensor so the empty hook hangs straight down. Hang the 500-g mass from the hook. The mass has a weight of 4.9 N; this is the applied force. Wait until the voltage number on the screen stabilizes and then press ⬛ENTER⬛.

g. Enter **4.9**.

h. The calculator displays slope and intercept information. You may want to record this information for use later in manual entry calibration.

i. Select **OK** to return to the SETUP screen.

You can also calibrate a sensor by entering known slope and intercept values manually. These values are usually determined from a prior two-point calibration.

```
         CALIBRATION
PH
CALIBRATION:LINEAR
SLOPE          INT
-3.838         13.72

1:OK
2:CALIBRATE NOW
3:MANUAL ENTRY
```

a. On the SETUP screen, press ⬛▾⬛ as needed to move the cursor to the sensor to be calibrated

b. Select **CALIBRATE**.

c. Select **MANUAL ENTRY**.

d. Enter the slope and press ⬛ENTER⬛.

e. Enter the intercept and press ⬛ENTER⬛. The CALIBRATION screen is displayed with the new values.

f. Select **OK** to return to the SETUP screen

Zeroing a Sensor

From the SETUP screen you can also zero one or more sensors. After you choose **ZERO**, a screen appears with a list of channels. Select one of the sensors you want to zero or **ALL CHANNELS** to zero all sensors. Another screen displaying the current reading or readings appears. Press (ENTER) to zero the sensor or sensors.

Saving and Loading Experiment Data

For the TI-83 Plus and TI-83 Plus Silver Editions, DATAMATE allows you to save experiments in the flash memory of the CBL 2™ or LabPro®, recall them later, and delete them when you no longer need them. You can save all program setups, sensor selections, calibrations, graph settings, and so forth, as well as any data you have collected.

The SAVE/LOAD function lets you save setups with or without data. When you have entered the settings for an experiment but have not yet taken data, the settings only are saved. Saved experiments without data are useful if you need to rapidly return DATAMATE to a prior configuration. If you have entered the settings and taken data, both are saved. It is possible to store data from many runs using the SAVE EXPERIMENT feature. Follow these steps to save an experiment:

a. From the main screen, select **SETUP**.

b. From the SETUP screen, select **4: SAVE/LOAD**.

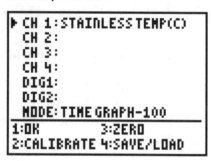

c. From the EXPERIMENT menu, select **SAVE EXPERIMENT**.

d. Enter a name and press (ENTER). The experiment is saved to the CBL 2 or LabPro and the EXPERIMENT menu reappears.

To retrieve a previously saved experiment:

a. From the main screen, select **SETUP**.

b. From the SETUP screen, select **SAVE/LOAD**.

c. From the EXPERIMENT menu, select **LOAD EXPERIMENT**.

d. Select the desired experiment from the list.

The experiment and any data present are loaded to the calculator from the CBL 2™ or LabPro®. DATAMATE returns to the Main Screen.

Other Options on the Main Screen

START

The START option begins data collection using the current mode. If at any time you wish to stop the data collection prematurely in a TIME GRAPH, press the [STO▶] key.

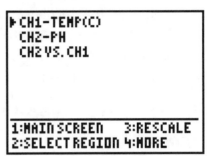

GRAPH

The GRAPH option lets you manipulate your graph. Press [ENTER] to see the screen at the right. In this example, a Temperature Probe is in Channel 1 and a pH Sensor is in Channel 2. When this option is chosen and only one sensor is connected, the graph will be redrawn.

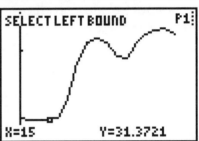

SELECT REGION: Allows the selection of a region of the graph for further analysis. This will delete the portion of data that was not selected.

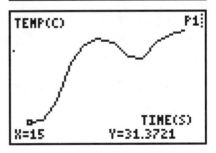

RESCALE: Lets you change the *x*- or *y*-axis scale or autoscale your graph.

ANALYZE

The ANALYZE option produces the list of analysis features shown at the right.

```
     ANALYZE OPTIONS
1:RETURN TO MAIN SCREEN
2:CURVE FIT
3:ADD MODEL
4:STATISTICS
5:INTEGRAL
```

CURVE FIT: Displays a list of curve fit options including linear, power, quadratic, and exponential fits.

ADD MODEL: Allows manipulation of the coefficients of a function entered in the Y = Editor on the calculator(outside of DATAMATE). This feature is not available on the TI-73 due to memory constraints.

STATISTICS: Displays the mean, min, max, standard deviation, and number of data points of a selected region.

INTEGRAL: Integrates a selected region of the graph.

TOOLS

The TOOLS option produces the list of options shown at the right.

```
          TOOLS
1:STORE LATEST RUN
2:RETRIEVE DATA
3:CHECK BATTERY
4:RETURN TO MAIN SCREEN
```

STORE LATEST RUN: Temporarily stores the latest run by moving it to list three (L3). Only one sensor can be used and only two runs can be stored. (This will not work with motion data.)

RETRIEVE DATA: Retrieves data stored on the CBL 2™ or LabPro® from remote data collection.

CHECK BATTERY: Displays the battery level of the CBL 2 or LabPro.

Using the Sample Data Files

The CD inside the back cover of this book includes sample data files for each calculator for each activity. The sample data lets you evaluate the activity without setting up and performing the activity procedures. To use the sample data:

To use the sample data on a PC using TI-Connect™:

1. Connect a TI-GRAPH LINK™ cable between your computer and calculator. You can use the USB, gray, or black TI-GRAPH LINK™ cable.

   Note: If you have the gray TI-GRAPH LINK cable, you may need to use the 25-pin to 9-pin adapter to connect to the computer. The black cable, which works with Windows® 95 or higher, has a built-in 9-pin adapter.

2. Turn the calculator on and make sure it is on the home screen.

3. Start TI Connect™ software on the computer.

4. Click **Device Explorer**. TI Connect will automatically identify what type of cable and TI calculator you are using.

5. Open Windows Explorer and navigate to the sample data file.

6. Drag the file into the TI Connect Device Explorer window and drop it on the name of the TI device (for example, TI-83 Plus).

   The sample data has now been stored in the calculator lists (**L1**, **L2**, etc.)

7. Go to the **Analysis** section of the activity and follow the instructions for working with the data.

To use the sample data on a Macintosh using TI-GRAPH LINK™ 2:

1. Connect a gray TI-GRAPH LINK cable between your computer and calculator.

2. Turn the calculator on and make sure it is on the home screen.

3. Start TI-GRAPH LINK and open a calculator connection by selecting **Connection** and then selecting your calculator model. Select the port to which TI-GRAPH LINK is connected and select **Connect**.

4. Find the sample data file on your computer and select it.

5. Drag the selected file(s) to the calculator window.

When you run the program on the calculator, it will install the sample data in the List Editor.

Appendix D

Firmware Updates for CBL 2 and LabPro

Three of the activities in this book require two motion detectors. While the activities can be completed using two data collection devices (either CBL 2™ or LabPro®, or one of each), it is convenient to use a single Vernier LabPro, since it has two digital input ports.

Some LabPro units must be updated to a newer version of the internal software (called firmware or ROM) to work properly with two motion detectors. You can determine if an update is needed from the ROM version numbers shown on the title screen as DataMate is launched. LabPros must have ROM version number 6.13 or newer. ROM versions x.12 and older do not fully support two Motion Detectors.

Updating the firmware on a CBL 2 or LabPro requires a TI-GRAPH LINK™ cable (either gray, black or USB type) and a computer connected to the Internet.

For instructions and downloadable software for updating the CBL 2, go to **education.ti.com**, click on **Products**, **CBL 2**, and then **Apps**.

For complete instructions for updating the LabPro, customized to your particular combination of equipment, and for software downloads, go to **www.vernier.com/calc/flash.html**.